BE
THE HERO
you've been waiting for

Yvonne & Rich Dutra St. John, MA MFT

CHALLENGE associates

Published by
Challenge Associates Press
Po Box 2208, Martinez, CA 94553 USA
www.bethehero.us

Copyright © 2009 by Yvonne and Rich Dutra-St. John

Printed in the United States of America by McNaughton & Gunn
Editing: Tess Clark; Steve Ryals
Book design: Steve Ryals - Rock Creek Press
Cover design: Paintbox Productions
Typesetting: Steve Ryals - Rock Creek Press
All photos © Challenge Day
Printed with soy-based ink
Paper: 60# Enviro 100 acid-free, 100% post-consumer recycled paper

FSC
Recycled
Supporting responsible
use of forest resources
Cert no. SW-COC-002283
www.fsc.org
© 1996 Forest Stewardship Council

Publisher's Cataloging-in-Publication
(Provided by Quality Books, Inc.)

St. John-Dutra, Yvonne.
    Be the hero you've been waiting for / by Yvonne St.
John-Dutra and Rich Dutra-St. John. -- 1st ed.
    p. cm.
    Includes index.
    ISBN-13: 978-1-935253-00-6
    ISBN-10: 1-935253-00-X

    1. Success--Psychological aspects.
    2. Self-actualization (Psychology) 3. Interpersonal
relations. 4. St. John-Dutra, Yvonne. 5. Dutra-St.
John, Rich. I. Dutra-St. John, Rich. II. Title.

BF637.S8S685 2009   158.1
                      QBI09-200002

10 9 8 7 6 5 4 3 2

Dedication

We dedicate this book to all of the young people who have demonstrated that love and connection are indeed possible in our schools and communities.

A portion of the proceeds from *Be the Hero* will support the continuing work of Challenge Day and the Be the Change Movement.

Be the Hero Contents

Acknowledgements

It takes a thousand voices to tell a single story.

~ Native American Saying

Of all the pieces we've written for this book, this is perhaps the most challenging of all. Where do we start? How do we begin to adequately acknowledge a lifetime filled with family, friends, and colleagues who have joined us in our crazy dream?

This book began as a vision several years ago. Since that time, we have had planning sessions, created outlines, and even re-started three different times. Our list of thanks could be endless, however, there are several people who have not only been involved with its completion but without their help, this book, and much of the work we have done in Challenge Day and the Be the Change Movement, would literally not have been possible.

First, we'd like to thank our parents, brothers, sisters, and grandparents for providing a lifetime filled with love and growth opportunities, and for being the right and perfect families for our spiritual and emotional development. We give thanks to Tom, Jamie, Tami, and Doug, our kids' other parents who have continually loved and co-parented our girls over the years. We'd especially like to thank our children, godchildren, grandbaby, and our other special young ones who have served, and continue to serve, as the inspiration for the work we do. Aimee, Andraya, Loren, Corinne, Jesi, Shayna, Rocklyn,

Kavi, Jeremy, Rachael, and Crystal, we thank you for the hope and inspiration you continually bring our hearts.

We give thanks for every time we received the gift of unconditional love and patience from our adored family and friends who, over the years, have missed out on time and connection while we were out doing our part to change the world.

We honor our mentors and teachers, Harrison Simms, Hugh Vasquez, Jean Gibbs, Beverly Jacobs, Jeff Idelson, John Dwyer, the Dale Family, and Randy Snowden for the many lessons and opportunities they brought us in our early years.

We are grateful to our friend Justin Hilton and all the visionary Challenge Day coordinators across the U.S., including Diane Cariss, Anne Fowler, Sue Schilling, Judy Greenman, Yvonne Pappas, Jim Kooler, Marge Pearson, Marylis Tognetti, David Nye, Carolyn Kelly, Amy Clark, Joan Zappettini, Teena Ellison, Sherry Cramer, Debbie McGuire, April Wolfe, and the other passionate visionaries who paved the way for the expansion of Challenge Day well before it was in vogue.

We thank the members of the Challenge Associates transition team who envisioned the possibility of a Challenge Day organization long before we knew it was possible – Mike Assum, Ben Schick, Rob Lewis, Peter Sandhill, Vicki Abadesco, Desire Storch, Gary Nicolassi, and Phillip Garrison.

We give thanks to all the media groups and individuals who have been touched and inspired enough to support us in sharing our message with the world. To Virginia Saenz-McCarthy and her production team for being the first to capture the Challenge Day program on film. To Arnold Shapiro and his production team for so brilliantly capturing the power and impact of our work in his *Teen Files: Surviving High School* documentary series. We are grateful for his friendship and continued support. To Jill Croteau and the people at Global News Canada for featuring our work in *The Bully Solution* documentary. To Kimberly Kirberger for including us in two different versions of the book series, *Chicken Soup for the Teenage Soul.* Deep gratitude to Oprah Winfrey and her team at Harpo Productions for sharing our work with her incredible community across the world. To Discovery Communications for granting us the right to offer a 15-minute portion of the *Teen Files: Surviving High School* documentary along with this book.

We celebrate the courageous young people who knowingly exposed the depths of their souls for national and international audiences in the filming of *Teen Files: Surviving High School, The Bully Solution, Oprah's High School Challenge,* and the most recent Oprah program on the "hunger" behind teen obesity. Their courage and vulnerability opened the door to healing, and shined the light of possibility into the lives of countless teens and adults worldwide.

We celebrate the staff, board members, and Challenge Day leaders who have walked the talk over the years, and committed their lives to living and teaching the tools and principles of Challenge Day and the Be the Change Movement. We give thanks to the partners and kids of Challenge Days leaders who have so selflessly shared their love, and their mommies and daddies, with the young people of the world.

We honor Steve Bucherati and Renae Murphy from the Global Diversity Group at the Coca-Cola® Corporation, for having the wisdom and foresight to risk bringing Challenge Day into the corporate environment.

We thank Carol Levow and Lisa de Mondesir for their efforts to introduce Challenge Day to the International School community.

We celebrate Marianne Williamson, Wendy Greene, Mike Robbins, Dot Maver, Matthew Albracht, and the other leaders of the Peace Alliance for advancing the cause of peace on the planet, and for showcasing Challenge Day and the Be the Change Movement as one of their primary initiatives.

We honor the members of Challenge Day's Global Leadership Council who have offered their names and support to Challenge Day and the Be the Change Movement: Richard and Kris Carlson, Peter Yarrow, Lisa Ling, Marshall Rosenberg, Marianne Williamson, Debbie Ford, Alanis Morissette, Brenda Blasingame, Ocean Robbins, John Robbins, Lynne Twist, Van Jones, Arnold Shapiro, Leeza Gibbons, Kokomon Clottey, Aeeshah Ababio-Clottey, Stephan Rechtschaffen, Jim Kooler, Greg Jamison, Shannon Durig, Patch Adams, and Dan Millman.

To all those who have heard the call and showed up at exactly the right and perfect time with the right and perfect gifts needed to support us in realizing our vision – we give thanks for your love, friendship, and support, and for acting on the call from deep inside of you.

We honor the countless young people and adults who have participated in Challenge Day, who have proven over and over again that love and connection are indeed possible in our schools and communities, and in the world.

We thank the Be the Change Team members, and Circle Leaders and members, who keep the fire of inspiration burning on a daily basis by helping to create undeniable miracles and breakthroughs of hope and healing in their schools, communities, homes, and places of worship.

For the many people over the years who have had conversations, made suggestions, or otherwise influenced the content of this book – Sela Gaglia, John Robbins, Debbie Ford, Ted Graves, Mike Assum, Garvin DeShazer, Ana Ballonoff, Wendy Greene, Jennie Mish, Donna Stevens, Larry Boxer, Rob Lewis, Judy, Kelley, Katie and Suzie Greenman, Amber Starfire of Starfire Photography, Pam Dunn, Chris Prima, Susan Lang, Randy Zucker, Mark Chimsky, DJ Colbert, Anna

Acknowledgements

Torres, Jon Gordon, Nola Boyd, Sonika Tinker, Dinyah Rein, Debbie Armstrong and Cherine Badawi.

We offer our deepest appreciation to our dear friends and mentors Richard and Kris Carlson, and their daughters Jazzy and Kenna, for believing in our message and challenging us to get it out in book form.

We give thanks to all those who had a direct hand in inspiring, editing, or birthing this book. To Vicki Abadesco for helping us formulate the vision and outline while pushing us to step into action. To Barb Carpenter for helping formulate our words and stories. To Natalie Tucker for helping us with a greater window into the writing world, and for providing a glimpse of what was possible. To Susan Davis for her artistic talents and design of our book cover and website. To Paul Plamondon for his website development skills. To Rodrigo Torres for all his technical support and love. To Bruce Robertson for sharing the wisdom and brilliance of a wise professor and teacher, without which we might still be living in doubt. This book would literally not exist without his support and guidance. To JoDee Robertson for the beautiful and gentle way she holds us in this and every other endeavor in our lives.

Immense gratitude to Betsy Leighton and Sue Schilling for setting the bar for what this book could be, and ultimately for having the courage to challenge us to not settle.

To our dear friends Sarah and Peter Sandhill, Kris Carlson, Bobbi "Quana" Ryals, Matthew Marzel, Jeff Gabrielson, Jaime Polson, Penny Sands, Tamara Goldsmith, Shereef Bishay, Neil Reeder, Natalie Puljiz, Dan Guida, and our daughters Aimee, Andraya, Loren and Corinne for taking the time to review, dive into and edit the many different facets of this book in love and truth.

We express deep gratitude to Galaxy Gayle Hasley for generously stepping up as project manager and cheerleader, and seeing this project to fruition. Special thanks to our beloved friend, coach, graphic designer and editor Steve Ryals of Rock Creek Press for holding our hand and guiding us through our fears and into the process of putting our hearts into our words.

Finally to Tess Clark for masterfully pulling from us the very last and best vestiges of what it is we were meant to say, for helping us put the final touches on our longtime dream of writing this book, and for sharing the gift of her brilliance and editing while bringing this book to completion.

We give heartfelt thanks as well to every person on this planet who has heard the call and been willing to Be the Hero in their own lives.

Forward

YOU are a one-of-a-kind miracle of creation. On the day you were born, a precious and unique set of possibilities came into existence.

Regardless of your family or the circumstances you were born into, you came into the world filled with divine light and loaded with special gifts. You were born with a purpose, a destiny that only you can fill. And what if you have been endowed with a unique set of "super powers" in order to do it?

Maybe you remember a time as a child when you "knew" you could save the world. A time when you had fantasies of being Superman, Wonder Woman, Batman, Amazing Man, Jet, Samurai, or some other Super Hero. A time when you knew you had infinite power, that you were important and that your life would make a difference.

What if you were right? What if you are predisposed to greatness? What if the hero in your story is YOU?

That's exactly what we want you to realize as we share with you some of our own personal journeys toward becoming the heroes we've been waiting for. We see *Be the Hero* not only as the title of our book, but also as a collective challenge, a call to action.

Because one day it dawned on us…

When we were in school, we learned how to read, write, and do math – we even learned how to drive a car – but no one ever taught us how to be ourselves. No one taught us how to deal with the thoughts and feelings we carried inside us every day. No one taught us how to discover our personal truths, how to express our love, how to connect in a deep and honest way with other human beings, how to communicate with our siblings or our parents, and certainly no one taught us how to grow into the parents we wanted to be to our future children.

Today, as adults, we pose the question: if we never learn these things – truth, love, connection, communication – then does learning anything else *really* matter?

This book is our gift to young people everywhere and to the young person who still lives within each and every one of us.

Be the Hero is our attempt to pass on some of the lessons we most needed to learn but never received in school. This book is filled with what we call our "aha" moments, or epiphanies – the times in our lives when the light suddenly came on and we could see answers that had once been hidden. These epiphanies include many of the lessons we teach in schools all over the country through our organization called Challenge Day, as well as our Next Step to Being the Change workshops and other programs.

We do not expect you to take anything we share in this book as the "right" way to do things. Our goal is simply to share some of our experiences, and along the way to challenge you to consider the lessons and possibilities of your own.

Our hope is that *Be the Hero* will become a road map for your own self-discovery. Whether you choose to read this book alone, in a group, a Circle of Change, a Be the Change team, a classroom, or with a partner, family member or friend, we challenge you to dream big. We want you to risk doing things differently. And most of all, we encourage you to be the hero you've been waiting for.

A Note to Our Readers

If you have never attended a Challenge Day program, we suggest you watch the attached video before you read this book. The video is a 15-minute excerpt from the Emmy Award-winning documentary, *Teen Files: Surviving High School*, which highlights a typical Challenge Day.

Additional videos and information on both Challenge Day and the Be the Change Movement can be found at www.challengeday.org.

Openings

There can be no keener revelation of a society's soul than the way it treats its children.

~ Nelson Mandela

Nothing is more powerful than sharing our truth. We've known that for a long time but as we stood in the wings of the Grand Ballroom's stage at the Westin St. Francis hotel in San Francisco, we felt its power again. With our arms wrapped around each other's waists, we eyed the crowd of more than a thousand people who had joined us for our annual Challenge Day fundraising brunch.

It was a gorgeous Saturday morning and they could have been anywhere, but they were here, in rapt attention, listening as Juan, a student who had recently attended Challenge Day, courageously told his story. In another setting, Juan probably would have appeared to many as a gangster. With his shaved head and dark, baggy clothes, he certainly didn't fit most people's image of someone commanding center stage at a gala event. On this day, however, they were spellbound as Juan shared hardships and challenges that no one, much less a 16-year-old boy, should ever have to endure.

Undaunted by the standing-room-only crowd, Juan spoke through a stream of his tender tears. Only two years earlier, he had felt trapped in a web of drugs, alcohol, and gang violence. In the storage container that his family called home, he had regularly helped his mother shoot drugs.

The crowd sat in stunned horror, their jaws gaping, and not a dry eye in the house. Then Juan spoke about how his participation in Challenge Day had helped him to find the courage and support he needed to turn his life around. He realized he no longer had to live as a victim of his circumstances. When he finished speaking, the room exploded into a thunderous, sustained, standing ovation.

Nothing is more powerful than sharing our truth.

We were standing off to the side, laughing through our tears and thinking, *That's it! We made a difference. Even if we never touch another life, our part in Juan's healing was worth a lifetime of hard work and commitment.*

Yes! We are ecstatic to have played our part in Juan's life…

But that's not it. We want more. Much, much more.

We are Yvonne and Rich Dutra-St. John, co-founders of Challenge Day and the Be the Change Movement. And we are exceedingly proud to know that the hearts and lives of close to a million young people and adults in our schools and communities have been touched by the transformational power of Challenge Day.

Challenge Day is a day-long program that brings students, parents, teachers, and community members together to discover what's possible when they have the courage to open their hearts and unlearn the lies that cause separation. The program, originally created for schools, has since expanded into communities, workplaces, churches, camps, and other places where people gather. It is a life-changing experience utilizing a combination of games, icebreakers, vulnerable shares, heart-opening group discussions, and activities designed to break down the walls of separation, prejudice, fear, and mistrust. Participants open their eyes, see one another in a way they may never have before, and realize that respect, connection, love, and forgiveness are possible for us all.

People often ask us, "What was your inspiration for creating Challenge Day?" The answer is simple: we are parents. When we first developed the program, our kids were ages one, two, three, and four. And we desperately didn't want them to go through the same pain and humiliation that we had experienced when we were in school.

Our dream is to create a world where every child feels safe, loved, and celebrated.

We don't just want this for every young person, but also for the child who lives inside each of our hearts.

Many people believe that the biggest challenges facing young people today are issues such as alcohol or other drug abuse, eating disorders, violence, truancy, low test scores, poverty, depression and suicide. These issues, although very real, are actually *symptoms* of a bigger problem.

We believe that the core issues in our schools and in our communities are *separation, isolation* and *loneliness*. This may seem ridiculous because our schools are packed with hundreds, and sometimes even thousands of kids. It's clear then that if our kids are feeling lonely, it is not because there is a lack of people; it is because there is a lack of love and connection between them.

When we met, we were both already living our passion to make a difference with young people. The intense flame of our connection ignited a new, shared dream. Our vision was to bring together young people who represented every clique, group, and culture on campus. We were determined to unite youth of different shapes, sizes, skin colors, and genders, as well as different religious beliefs and sexual orientations. We imagined connecting youth who didn't know or perhaps even hated each other. Our outrageously ambitious goal was to bring them together in *love*, not just in tolerance.

Although society values teaching tolerance, we believe that if we settle for tolerance, we have failed. If our kids don't experience love and connection in their schools, how will they ever believe that peace on *earth* is possible?

You are the Hero You've Been Waiting For

Courage is resistance to fear, mastery of fear – not absence of fear.

~ Mark Twain

Our world is more ready than ever for heroes to emerge. Even though most of us grew up with images of heroes with magical powers, complete with capes, wands, and armor, real life heroes can appear in many forms. Heroes can be political, spiritual, or community leaders standing in integrity on behalf of the earth and its people. They can also be youth speaking out boldly, reminding us of what is most important. They can be any one of us who has the courage to face our biggest fears – just like *you*.

It is time to be like alchemists who transform metal into gold. We must have the audacity to allow ourselves to change from the inside out in order to prepare ourselves to complete what we were born to do. What if there is no accident that each one of us is alive on the planet right now? Like a butterfly morphing from its past life as a caterpillar and now ready to spread its wings, it is time to become the heroes we've been waiting for.

Yvonne

If you really knew me, you would know that shortly after high school, one of the most pivotal transfromations of my life happened in a psychiatric hospital.

I woke to the sound of someone screaming. It was a young woman, but it wasn't my sister. I wasn't even in my bedroom. I sat up confused. I watched two men in white coats wrestle the girl in the bed next to me into a strait jacket as though caging a wild animal. Only then did I remember the nightmare that had started long before I fell asleep.

I glanced at the sterile, white bandages that hid the cuts on my arms and hands. Not so long ago, I had been the high school homecoming queen and class vice president – a person people looked up to, someone my parents were proud of. Now, locked in a psychiatric hospital, I had become my parents' worst nightmare.

If you really knew me, you would know a part of me wanted to die…but I didn't really want to be dead.

I lay in bed for hours barely breathing, staring at the chipped paint on the barren, white walls. At some point, I heard someone enter the room. I rolled over lifelessly and saw a nurse coming toward me. With a compassionate, genuine smile, she invited me to come with her. I felt nervous as I followed her down a long corridor to a musty-smelling room where several other patients sat in a circle. One of them, a man with dark, stringy hair was clenching his head between his knees, wracked with sobs that shook his entire body.

I was the last person to arrive. I timidly perched myself on the edge of a cold metal chair and I watched the sobbing man, my heart pounding with fear. I desperately wanted to escape this waking nightmare. It seemed as though my entire world had caved in around me.

I stared at the group leader, surprised that he seemed so calm. A few minutes later, he turned and looked straight at me as if to say, "It's your turn." Though his gentle presence was inviting, I sat frozen in my seat. My mind was racing a hundred miles an hour, but I couldn't say a word. *How can I let these strangers know how I'm feeling? They will think I'm crazy.* The funny thing was that a part of me was feeling crazy. My biggest fear was that if I let my feelings out, they would pull me down to a place of no return. So I did my best to barricade them inside. I kept swallowing hard and blinking back tears. I could hardly breathe.

Then, like a balloon filled beyond capacity, I burst. Tears began to pour down my cheeks. I kept telling myself, *Be strong! Stop crying!* But I couldn't stop. I felt as though I was sinking in emotional quicksand and, terrified, I had no choice but to let go. I searched for the group leader's soft eyes, and for the first time in my life I felt like I was being encouraged to cry and let it out, so that is exactly what I did. I erupted.

I buried my face in a pillow and I screamed with the force of a raging river crashing through the dam. I yelled and sobbed and seethed and boiled over for what seemed like an eternity. When the fury had finally ended, my eyes were swollen, I was dripping with sweat, and I thought nothing remained. Then suddenly a new wave of emotion flooded into the emptiness. I cried my mother's tears, my father's tears, my sister's and my brother's. It was as though I was releasing the silent screams of everyone who had come before me – everyone who had ever suppressed a lifetime of pain, anger, fear, and rage. I had no idea where their heartache ended and mine began. I was simply an earthquake of emotions, shaking, trembling, my body moving to its own rhythm.

I wanted something to fix me – a pill, a doctor, a magic wand – *anything* that would stop my suffering. Lost and out of control, I spun my way to a corner of the room and crouched into a ball hoping to hide. Finally exhausted and depleted, it all just stopped. It was as if a delicate emotional thread had gently led me to my center, my core. And once I had truly entered myself, I was met with a quiet river of peace that seemed to be waiting to cleanse me. There I was, raw, vulnerable, and oddly serene.

For the first time in years, I was finally able to take a deep, full breath. In my head, none of it made sense. In my soul, though, something started to feel very "right." It dawned on me that I had made it to the other side. I did it! I had found myself. My inner spark, my light, vaguely familiar from my childhood, dim as it may have been, was still *my* light. I felt alive. I felt hope. I felt me.

For years, I had been waiting for someone to save me, but in that moment I realized no one was going to ride in on a horse or fly in with a cape. No pill, no doctor, no magic wand could ever take away the pain. The way out of the pain was to dive into the feelings, move all the way through them, and come out the other side. Ironically, the way *out* was *in*! Like Dorothy in *The Wizard of Oz*, I suddenly realized that I always had the power to go home.

My biggest lesson came in my darkest moment. It was me. I was the hero I had been waiting for.

So many of us live our lives unconscious, completely encased in petrified layers of unexpressed passion, hurt, and fear. These layers include passed-on wounds from family members or even ancestors from generations past. They often seem to keep us immobilized, depressed, apathetic, and isolated.

Looking back almost 30 years, I don't consider my time in the psychiatric hospital as a tragedy. Although horrifying, I now believe that there are no accidents and that I was merely on course with my "hero" training. The unexpected gift of completely hitting bottom silenced my ego long enough for something greater to take over. Not only did the experience serve to reveal my soul, it intuitively gave me an opportunity to become a student of the work I was born to teach. Sinking into quicksand and coming out the other side was, in reality, my Ph.D. birthing course for life. Transforming my depression into passion woke me up to the realization that my life mattered and I could make a difference.

I invite you to join me. The world needs us. *All* of us. The question we must ask ourselves is not, "*Can* I make a difference?" but rather, "*How* will I make a difference?"

One of our personal heroes, Mahatma Gandhi, summarized what is necessary for creating a better world.

We must Be the Change we wish to see in the world.

2 About Us

I am only one; but still I am one.
I cannot do everything, but still I can do something.
I will not refuse to do something I can do.

~ Helen Keller

Rich

As I was growing up, school was like an unpredictable rollercoaster ride. In elementary school, I was popular and well liked; I felt safe and loved, but all that changed the very first day of junior high. All at once, school went from being my refuge to my personal hell.

I was a "late bloomer" so I was smaller and shorter than most of the other guys, and suddenly I didn't belong in my new environment. I became the target of relentless bullying and harassment. It was as though there was a new rulebook for how I was supposed to look and act, and no one would share it with me. I responded the only way I knew how – I pretended. On the outside I acted as if I was fine. On the inside I felt scared, depressed, and completely alone. The feelings, the humiliation, and the fear went on for the entire two years of my junior high experience.

Things radically changed again the summer before high school. I worked out, took protein powder to build my muscles, and started puberty simultaneously. Since I was bigger now, and I'd become a good athlete, I had a new start in another new school. I immediately immersed myself in sports – football, wrestling, and baseball – and I became a member of the "jock" group on campus. To most people, I appeared to be part of the in-crowd.

It was as if I finally had it all. I was the tall, dark and handsome scholar-athlete many parents wanted their daughters to bring home. I was the picture of success. However, if you really knew me, you would know that below the surface I lived with an unrelenting sense of brokenness. I felt constantly afraid that I was a fraud. I lived in a world of desperation and "trying" – trying to please, trying to impress, trying to get love, and most of all, trying to make my father proud of me. But it seemed as though, in his eyes, I could never do anything right. As hard as I tried, it wasn't enough. *I* wasn't enough. And although I never tried to kill myself, there were many times in my life that I felt like I wanted to die.

My dad was raised in a violent home. He was also part of a gang called "the Pachucos" which roamed the streets of Oakland, California. Although he accomplished a great deal in his life, I don't remember him being truly happy. He wasn't equipped to even consider interrupting the cycle of violence he'd experienced when he was a kid and, as a result, he carried on the legacy.

Nothing was more important to me than pleasing him. In my house, pleasing him meant, "Today, I won't be yelled at. Today, I won't be hit. Today, I'll get it right. Then maybe I can relax and just be me." But I couldn't relax because the more my dad would try to fix or control things, the more out of control he would become.

I went to bed almost every night feeling anxious, confused, and lonely. I woke up every morning worried about what the day might bring. *Do I look okay? Will I pass the test? Will I win the game? Who will judge me? Who will hurt me? Who can I trust? How can I please my teacher? Will I impress my coach? How can I make my family happy?*

The voices inside my head never stopped. And I was certain that I was the only one feeling the way I did.

I had the disease I now refer to as "terminal uniqueness" – I was so different I was sure it would kill me.

I had gotten so good at pretending, that I walked around with a fake smile and told myself, "There's nothing wrong with me or my family. I'm just fine." I tried desperately to believe it. Instead, I felt trapped between two worlds. One was the world of looking good, maintaining my image, accomplishing impossible goals, and pretending everything was perfect. The other was a world of judgment, self-doubt, violence and loneliness.

Although a few kids from junior high still teased me and talked behind my back, I wasn't being bullied anymore. But there were many times when I stood in silence, watching as my friends and teammates threatened and tormented other kids. I was there when they picked fights, called people names, and made rude, degrading, or sexist comments to girls. I hardly ever joined in the hurting, but in most cases I was too scared to stand up to my friends and tell them to stop. My biggest fear was that if I did, all their abuse would turn toward me and it would be just like junior high all over again.

I graduated with honors, and I received many awards, trophies, medals, and scholarship opportunities, but despite my successes, I wasn't okay with being me.

If you really knew me, you would know that I was ashamed of who I was.

It was my experience in high school that set the stage for how I would spend the rest of my life. I was determined to not repeat that shame, so in college I refused to stay silent. I found the courage to speak up for what I believed. I stood up for people, broke up fights in the dorms, and counseled my friends. By my sophomore year, I was chosen to be a resident assistant and peer counselor.

All along, I held onto a delicate but powerful gift I'd received from Mrs. Engelmann, my third grade teacher. I *knew* she really loved me. Somehow, that love had sustained me.

Fulfilling a dream spawned by the safety and love I received in elementary school, I became a teacher.

I committed myself to being the best teacher ever. I told my students, "You don't have to do it alone. I'm here for you. If you need anything, just ask." Almost every day, young people lined up outside my room seeking support to deal with many of the same challenges I had faced in school.

It became clear that I had a gift for building trust with as well as supporting young people. Passionate about helping kids in need, I decided to leave teaching and become a drug intervention specialist. Later, equipped with a Masters degree in clinical psychology and a license as a family therapist, I committed myself to making life easier for young people and their families.

I received a huge validation for my work when I was asked to open and direct two different adolescent drug treatment programs. One of those programs, an innovative hybrid group home/treatment hospital called Thunder Road, was based in Oakland, California. Ironically, it was close to the same street where my father had grown up. Serving upwards of 50 young people at a time, I felt especially proud to write and direct much of the program's curriculum.

As successful as the program was, my heart continually ached for the youth and their families whom we were unable to serve. I was plagued by the idea that somehow we had it backward. I began asking myself, "Why do young people have to be in trouble before they get the counseling, love and support they deserve?"

I felt determined to find a solution.

Yvonne

I was blessed to grow up in the ideal family. With a farm as our playground, my family and I spent countless hours in 4-H projects with our animals. We sang together, put on family shows, and built rafts to float down the nearby creek. To this day, we share a deep connection that I trust will never leave us.

However, had you come inside my house, you would have witnessed a lot of yelling, fighting, anger, and tears. It wasn't because we didn't love each other. It was because no one ever taught us *how* to love each other in any other way.

If you really knew me, you would know that growing up I had a lot of intense emotions and I thought I had to deal with them alone. I didn't talk about my feelings with my family and I never even considered sharing them with anyone else. It seemed as if everything happened *to* me, like I was trapped in a dunking booth waiting for the balls to hit the target and drop me into the frigid water.

One of my earliest memories is from the first grade. One morning, I woke up hungry. I wasn't just hungry, it seemed as if I was starving and no amount of food could ever fill the emptiness. At the time, I thought I was hungry for food. Now I know it was much more but I didn't know it then and in an attempt to fill my emptiness, I began eating *a lot* every day. By junior high, I was short, labeled as fat, and I wore braces. My mom topped it off by giving me an embarrassing homemade haircut. It wasn't a good combination, especially for a teenager wanting to fit in at school.

Because of the way I looked, I was constantly teased. My weight seemed to offer an open invitation for humiliation. I woke up every morning and prayed that the kids at school would leave me alone. One day, as our sixth grade class walked down the path to the library, the most popular girl in our school came running up from behind and shoved me down the hill. She started laughing, pointing, and shouting, "Watch the fat girl roll!"

Everyone burst into laughter. I wanted to disappear. Instead, I swallowed my feelings. I defiantly held back the tears, stood up, brushed off as much dirt as I could and climbed back up the hill. As humiliated as I felt for being laughed at, what hurt the most was the deafening silence from my friends. No one stood up for me or risked helping me.

At the end of my seventh grade year, in a desperate attempt to lose weight, I developed an eating disorder called bulimia. I began frantically throwing up everything I ate. I spent that summer with six cousins who knew nothing of my behavior. I was all alone in my secret world, stuck in a scary, dangerous, addictive cycle. My bulimia spiraled out of control and during that summer I lost a lot of weight.

When I went back to school in the fall, suddenly it seemed like *everyone* wanted to be my friend. As good as it felt to be noticed, ultimately it was far more painful to me than being teased for my weight.

I learned at a young age that we are treated very differently based only on what we look like on the outside.

In high school, because of my new, more acceptable appearance, I began experiencing one of my biggest dreams – I was one of the popular kids. I became a cheerleader, I was elected class vice president, and I had many friends. I finally knew I belonged, and people looked up to me. At the beginning of my senior year, the entire school voted me homecoming queen. Elated by the nomination, every part of me celebrated for that fat little girl who was once so mercifully teased. My celebration, however, was short lived. Just two days later one of my best friends, out of the blue, apologized for her part in all the rumors.

"What rumors?" I asked. "What are people saying?"

"Everyone is saying you are stuck up now that you won," she said.

Everywhere I turned, I heard the rumors and felt the separation they caused. I was devastated.

Prior to that time, I thought "those people" have it easy. The "popular kids" have it made. What I learned was that *no one* wins. It seemed that regardless of what you look like or whether or not you fit the "right" image, you *will* be judged. Apparently none of us are immune.

After graduation, addictions seemed to rule my world. In addition to food, I desperately tried other ways to fill the emptiness I felt inside. Shopping, drugs, stealing, sex, and alcohol only temporarily numbed the pain. I became so depressed that I hit bottom. I was walking the thin line between wanting to die and wanting a way out of my self-imposed prison. The cutting and self-mutilation I had been practicing suddenly took a turn when I intentionally injured myself and wound up in the hospital.

In the psych ward, I learned that things didn't happen *to* me, instead I had choices. I could live my life as a victim and spend my days blaming others, being angry and resentful, and then trying to numb out my pain. Or, I could choose to take 100% responsibility for my life and do the work it would take to heal. It was up to me. The idea of facing my biggest fears, of meeting myself in my deepest, most painful places, seemed overwhelming. But on a profound level I knew it was my only way of claiming personal power and real freedom.

I have come to realize that every experience contains lessons and gifts. Perhaps the most difficult times contain the biggest gifts.

Inspired by the lessons I received in the psych ward, I committed my life to passing on to others the tools I didn't receive growing up.

I spent years developing and implementing intervention programs for youth and their communities. I had the honor of supporting young people who had "problems," which for me simply translates to "young people developing their souls through intense life experiences." These experiences often showed up in the form of addictions, and many of the young people I worked with needed more support than I could provide in the groups I offered.

Word had spread about a newly opened drug treatment program called Thunder Road. Many people I trusted had spoken about the program's innovative, positive approach. I was cynical because most of the treatment programs available for youth at the time took the typical, "break them down, *then* build them up" approach. I wanted to skip the "break them down" part. I believed there was far too much of that already.

Despite my skepticism, I invited a colleague to join me on a tour of Thunder Road. I was cautiously excited about the possibility of a positive, supportive environment for teens, and I went to check this program out.

The moment I met Rich will remain in my memory forever.

When I walked into the hospital, I was struck by the welcoming atmosphere. Positive messages and inspirational posters and quotes filled the lobby. Suddenly, large double doors swung open and the program's clinical director, a smiling, handsome man named Rich Dutra, walked up and warmly shook our hands. Just then, a loud noise crescendoed down the hallway. He paused, wrinkled his brow and said, "I better take care of that. I'll be right back."

As he walked away, I immediately turned to my co-worker and blurted out, "I am supposed to be with that man!" I was stunned hearing those words come out of my mouth. Although I had never seen this man before, every ounce of my being *knew* what I had said was true.

When Rich returned to the lobby, it was all I could do to keep my composure. As we toured the hospital, both staff members and patients beamed with admiration for him. Some even jumped to their feet to hug him when they saw him. I found myself both surprised and impressed that Rich completely matched my passion for working with youth. His love for his work shined through his eyes. This obviously was not just his job; it was his life's purpose.

Over the next few months, we fell in love and began our journey together as professionals and as a couple.

Soon thereafter, we realized that the intervention and treatment work that we each had been doing separately dealt with *symptoms* of a deeper problem. Although alcohol and drug abuse, violence, depression, and eating disorders are serious issues that certainly need to be addressed and treated, we wanted to get to the root of the problem.

We formulated a dream to tear down the walls of *separation, isolation* and *loneliness* that young people experience, and instead, join them together in love.

We all experienced a moment of peace on earth.

A Dream Is Born:
Our First Challenge Day

**I think it really shows that no matter what you set
your imagination to, anything is possible.**

~ Michael Phelps

In 1987, we led our first Challenge Day in Livermore, California.

As the gym doors crashed open, groups of loud, laughing teenagers streamed in. They found seats in the circle, many of them staying together in their cliques, gossiping and trying to look cool. Others sat alone, appearing to be aloof, afraid, or menacing. Some cracked jokes. Some nervously drummed their heels against the hardwood floor. Some wore baggy jeans and baseball hats with skateboard logos. Others sported varsity letter jackets or punk band t-shirts. Some dressed like the pop star, Madonna, while others wore all black with heavy studs in their piercings. It seemed that we had achieved our goal to have every group on campus represented.

Once everyone had taken a seat and the doors had closed, we found ourselves looking out at a circle of nearly 200 unfamiliar faces. We were taken aback by the eye rolling, finger pointing, laughter and whispers. In a moment of fear we wondered, *What were we thinking? What if it doesn't work?*

The bell rang. For a moment, it seemed as though we were back in school ourselves.

We began by playing games intended to lighten the mood with laughter but also to challenge the participants to step outside their familiar cliques and groups. Our goal was to reveal the thread of humanity that ties us all together, and we used the tool most capable of penetrating the walls that divide us – our own vulnerability. With passion and tears, we shared painful stories from our teen years, which gave participants permission to do the same. The simple beauty of speaking our truth and "getting real" unleashed a ripple of compassion that transformed the energy in the entire room.

Suddenly, we felt held by something greater. Our fear lifted. A gentle confidence filled our hearts and guided our words. As though a miracle had just unfolded right before our eyes, our dream became a reality. Youth and adults alike, even those who had the most resistance, now seemed to hang on our every word. The tension and nervousness that had come into the room, now gave way to hope and possibility. For perhaps the first time in their lives, young people and adults from very diverse backgrounds connected and accepted one another. They stepped up as leaders and courageously shared from their hearts.

"I don't even know half of you," exclaimed a muscular young man wearing boots and a cowboy hat, "but I feel like I love you all!"

Nothing is more powerful than sharing our truth.

Then we gave them a chance to do something most of us never have an opportunity to do – start brand new. We challenged participants to find the people they had teased or hurt in some way, and to apologize for the things they had said or done. One by one, young people took the microphone and courageously expressed their sadness and sorrow to those whom they had been humiliating and harassing for years. Chills ran up our spines as we imagined how different our lives would have been if we too had been given this gift of compassion and understanding in school.

What happened in that room reinforced what we already knew – that every one of us has a place deep inside that remembers we are all meant to be connected. When young people feel safe, seen, and accepted, they remember who they really are and they rise to their fullest potential. Stereotypically tough-looking students, who prior to this day may never have shared their emotions with anyone, cried as they expressed themselves, telling their friends, parents, and teachers how much they loved them or apologizing for the pain they had caused. Every line of separation seemed to disappear. The room overflowed with hope, possibility, and love.

And we all experienced a moment of peace on earth.

One personally significant moment will remain etched in our memory forever. The captain of the football team and a couple of his buddies stood up and walked across the gym to a girl who had just cried about being humiliated and called fat. They stood in front of her, and with tears running down his cheeks, the captain said, "I'm so sorry for all the years of pain my friends and I have caused you. As long as we are here on this campus, we will make sure no one will ever hurt you again." Then he reached out and embraced her.

In that moment, the "fat little girl" and "scared, silent jock" that still lived inside us started to heal. We looked into each other's eyes and we knew that Challenge Day would be our life's work.

**Those who are crazy enough to think
they can change the world, usually do.**

~ Unknown

When we first created Challenge Day, the very people who had believed in and supported our work called us "crazy." They insisted that young people coming together, hugging, crying, apologizing, forgiving, and loving each other could never happen in a school setting.

We are proud to say that since 1987, in partnership with the people in our organization, we have touched the hearts and lives of many hundreds of thousands of young people and adults all over the world. Our work has been featured in the book *Chicken Soup for the Teenage Soul* and was highlighted as part of two nationally televised documentaries: *Teen Files: Surviving High School*, which won an Emmy Award in 2001, and *The Bully Solution*, which aired across Canada and won The Gold Ribbon Award from the Canadian Association of Broadcasters.

After Oprah Winfrey experienced the power of our work on her show entitled *Oprah's High School Challenge*[1], which first aired in November 2006, she tearfully declared in front of millions of people, "This is how we change the world!" She was talking about Challenge Day.

Then, in January 2007, prior to the second airing of the show, she proclaimed…

"I believe this show represents the very idea of Dr. Martin Luther King's dream fulfilled. It is the dream of giving hope a chance, giving peace a chance, and giving love a chance."

Needless, to say, most people don't call us crazy anymore.

We share this because we want you to know that if you ever have a dream or know in your heart that there is something you want or

---

1 http://oprahstore.oprah.com/p-1350-oprahs-high-school-challenge-11092006.aspx (transcript ONLY)

need to do, we challenge you to follow that dream even if people call you crazy.

**We are now at a point where we must educate
our children in what no one knew yesterday,
and prepare our schools for what no one yet knows.**

~ Margaret Mead

Our schools are a microcosm of the larger community. Many of us carry the very same stereotypes and hurts we learned in school into our adult lives – our relationships, our workplace, and everywhere we go. We talk behind one another's backs, form cliques, gossip, spread rumors, and then wonder why we feel just like we did in school – separate and lonely.

No matter who we are, where we live, how we look or dress or act on the outside, deep inside we all desire to be loved and included. We all want to feel accepted, respected, and celebrated for who we are, exactly the way we are.

We are all significantly more alike than we are different.

Although many people might argue otherwise, we believe that every single one of us does the best we can, given the experiences we've had and the support we've received. The truth is that no parent has ever said, "I want to have some kids and see if I can screw up their lives."

By the same token, no kid has ever said, " When I grow up, I want to get into fights, get kicked out of school, become an addict, go to jail, and someday feel depressed enough to kill myself." Moreover, no kid has ever said, "I want to grow up to be the one in my family whom everyone blames. 'It's all your fault, if it wasn't for you, this family would be fine!'"

So how do we prevent these scenarios? By creating peace from the inside out.

> **We can never obtain peace in the outer world until we make peace with ourselves.**
>
> ~ Dalai Lama

Much of our work, and certainly the focus of this book, is about shining a light on new ways of empowering you to become *the hero you've been waiting for.*

We believe that creating peace from the inside out means choosing to focus our attentions on the only thing we can control – *ourselves.*

Step 1 – Love and Accept Yourself

Self-acceptance and self-love are the keys that unlock the door to internal peace and personal freedom. Unfortunately, many of us look in the mirror with critical eyes or even disgust. We pick ourselves apart, put ourselves down, play small, and ultimately hide our unique beauty from the world. We replay over and over in our minds the things we think we've done *wrong* – our failures and our shortcomings. Our hearts filled with guilt and shame, we then go out into the world hoping others will love and accept us. Sadly, it doesn't work that way.

Peace and personal freedom start when you begin to learn how to love and accept every aspect of who you are. The key to self-love is forgiveness. We must have compassion first for ourselves, otherwise we will continually find fault in others.

Step 2 – Love and Accept Others

Everyone we meet has a gift for us. They reflect aspects of ourselves that we can either love or reject. Once we understand that everything we negatively judge in others is a direct reflection of something we dislike or have not resolved within ourselves, we are well on our way to internal and external peace.

The two most powerful forces in the world are love and fear. We see every interaction as a new opportunity to choose love. When we can accept, respect, and even celebrate all people, including ourselves, we take one step closer to creating peace on earth.

Step 3 – Live in Service

Many people think service is a selfless act that we do for others. In our experience, it's a gift we give ourselves. We all need to know we matter and that we make a difference in the lives of others. That's why we challenge you to feed your heart and soul by completing at least one intentional positive act of love or service each day. Every time you intentionally choose an act of love or service, you contribute to the healing and well-being of the planet. You also help to eradicate depression since it's hard for service and depression to exist in the same body.

The Formula For Change

A lot of people are waiting for Martin Luther King or Gandhi to come back – but they are gone. We are it. It is up to us. It's up to you!

~ Marian Wright Edelman

Rich

If you really knew me, you would know that two of my most memorable and life altering Challenge Day experiences took place immediately following national tragedies: the shootings at Columbine High School, and the terrorist attacks on September 11th.

On April 20, 1999, at Columbine High School in Littleton, Colorado, two angry students, outcasts according to those who knew them, packed gym bags full of bombs, knives, and semi-automatic weapons, and opened fire on unsuspecting students and teachers. A year in the planning, they had intended to kill hundreds of people and leave a legacy of having caused the most deaths in U.S. history. After thirty minutes of terror, thirteen people had been murdered and twenty-three more were wounded.

Just days after this horrific event, our good friend Justin Hilton organized a Challenge Day program that was open to both students and adults who had been affected by the shootings. More than 150 people signed up. As Yvonne and I entered the Denver Convention Center, we couldn't help but wonder if this time we were in over our heads. Surrounded by media, politicians, and other community leaders, my heart raced as I alternated between anxious doubt and calm certainty.

Before we entered the room, Yvonne and I held hands, locked eyes, and incanted our daily prayer, "God use us." Our goal was to trust, let go, and allow ourselves to be vehicles of transformation and healing.

This day, although clearly unique in scope, was in fact no different from every other Challenge Day we had hosted over the previous twelve years – it was a room filled with people in pain. Devastated by the tragedy, young people and adults created a sacred space in which they could tearfully share their experience and horror. One by one, they summoned the courage to speak out against the pain and hatred that could lead to such appalling violence.

And then something unexpected happened.

I handed the microphone to a petite, blond, young woman who was dressed in multiple layers of dark clothing. As she spoke, her voice cracked with emotion. She was clearly saddened by the senseless murders, but she was also overwhelmed with grief for the loss of her friend Eric who had been one of the shooters. Tears poured down her reddened cheeks as she exclaimed, "Eric never would have done what he did if he could have felt the love and acceptance we do today."

As I stood beside her, her anguish penetrated my heart and sent ripples of agony through my body. Every part of me believed that her words were true.

"All this pain could have been prevented," she said softly.

A deep sense of sympathy washed through me. I knew that I couldn't undo the past, so instead, in that moment, I became more committed than ever to making sure that tragic events like this one would never happen again.

Yvonne began to move toward us from across the room and, articulating what I was already thinking, she looked deeply into the young woman's searching eyes and said, "I am so sorry this happened.

And I will make you this promise. We won't stop doing this work until every child knows they are loved and accepted."

Two years later, on September 11, 2001, I was leading a Challenge Day in Toledo, Ohio, when the news came that the Twin Towers and the Pentagon building had both been attacked. When I relayed the information, the group's initial response was one of disbelief. Some even thought that I was joking. But as reality set in, many people reacted with anger and despair. I did my best to stay focused but I was fighting my own feelings of shock and self-doubt. Once again I had been entrusted with young hearts in the face of a national tragedy and I was being called to rise to the occasion. I found myself resonating with the words:

"If not me, who? And if not now, when?"

Just like everyone else around me, I was being called to become the hero in my own story.

I felt a surge of something rising within me, something far greater than myself. Suddenly, I knew that I was exactly where I needed to be. I am here to help guide people into realizing that pain and separation can be transformed into hope and possibility. I felt it. I knew it. And I embraced it. In a moment of uncertainty and confusion, I had uncovered a treasured piece of myself, a deep inner voice, and it has never gone away.

The day had left me completely exhausted, and as news of the mounting death toll and the growing devastation spread across our country, I felt vulnerable and alone, miles away from Yvonne and my kids. If you really knew me, you would know I cried myself to sleep that night thinking how I would feel if one or more of them had been killed in such a tragic way.

I returned home with a renewed sense of determination. But our world was changing and at times the despair seemed inescapable. Like an ocean of negativity, huge waves of anger, hopelessness, and fear seemed to be dragging our nation's schools and communities down with the undertow. Amid the terror alerts, school violence, and rising fear, we began to see a heartbreaking trend: so many young people living with a sense of powerlessness. And even harder for us to fathom was that even those who had been transformed and inspired by their experience of Challenge Day were being hit by the same overwhelming waves of fear and negativity once they returned to school.

We struggled to come up with a solution, and one night it came in a flash of insight. Yvonne and I both realized that we needed to create a bigger wave! *What if the seeds of hope, inspiration, and love that we plant at Challenge Day could be nourished by something bigger? What if there was a worldwide movement that could inspire us all to keep going?*

It was against this backdrop that both the Be the Change Movement and the Formula For Change were born.

Bursting with excitement, we took our ideas back to the Challenge Day staff. We sat in a circle eager to tell them about our new dream. It was as if providence was unfolding before us as Yvonne said the words that launched the movement. "People need to understand that no matter how frightening things get in the world, we can't give up. People need to know they can make a difference. Every one of us has the power to *be* the change. We can no longer sleepwalk through life. We need to wake up and *notice* what is happening. We need to know that none of us are victims, and that we are the ones who get to *choose* how we want things to be! People need to step into *action* and do something!"

One of our staff members, Garvin Deshazer, eagerly cried out, "That's it! You just named it! The Be the Change Movement." Then he added, "You not only came up with the name, you described the three steps for how to do it: Notice, Choose, and Act."

These three steps became Challenge Day's Formula For Change.

Perhaps it was a coincidence, but at that very moment a huge crow landed less than three feet from our circle and banged his beak against the tall window that separated us. The bird cawed repeatedly as it beat the glass with its beak. Shocked by both the noise and the bird's peculiar behavior, we all burst out laughing.

Apparently intent on getting our attention, this strange crow came back every day for months as we continued to formulate our ideas. Now, I consider myself to be an open-minded person, but I was truly astounded when one of our staff members looked up the crow in an animal totem book and revealed that the crow's message was to "caw your caw" or "speak your voice to the world." It seemed that our bird friend was onto something; it was clearly time to declare our vision to the world.

> **Change will not come if we wait for some other person or some other time.**
>
> ~ Barack Obama

Later in *Be the Hero* we will explore in greater detail the specifics of the Be the Change Movement, including its goals, its principles, and the ways in which you can participate. For now, though, it's enough for you to understand our Formula For Change. These three simple steps – Notice, Choose, and Act – have the power to completely change your life. Please believe me when I say that I don't make this claim lightly.

Yvonne and I have consciously applied these steps to every area of our lives. In our personal relationships, as parents, and at work we have used them to create policies and practices that help us build connection and teamwork. We use this formula to help us *notice* people and events and opportunities, so we can *choose* our dreams and goals and plans, in order to take *action* in our efforts to Be the Change – in our personal lives and in the world. As a consequence, we are definitely living the life of our dreams. And we know beyond any doubt that who we *be* and what we *do* makes a difference.

Throughout the rest of the book, we'll provide exercises for you to explore different ways in which you can Notice, Choose, and Act. For now, we'll start by outlining each step and providing helpful questions and activities to get you started.

Notice

To notice is to practice the art of observation. But for our purposes, it isn't casual or off-handed; instead it is focused and filled with intention. The first step in waking up is to become consciously aware of what is going on in your life. Before any of us can change something, we need to first notice that it exists. We've already said that creating peace from the inside out means focusing our attention on ourselves because we are the only thing we can control. Later on, we'll expand our observations to the world beyond us but for the moment, our challenge to you is to take a close look, without blame, at who you are right now.

Begin to become fully aware of how you are living your life and who you have become.

Going through this process can often be an emotionally vulnerable time of self-discovery. You will most likely find that you have collected a wide variety of traits, mannerisms, and habits. Be extra gentle with yourself. It's entirely possible that you may be taking an honest look at yourself for the first time.

Start by first noticing the parts of you that you like. We encourage you to journal about what you discover. Writing helps to focus your attention. Don't edit yourself as you write down your thoughts. We want you to really "empty the sponge" or let it all out without being critical of what you're writing. This is not meant for anyone else to read unless, at some point later, you decide to share it. So for now, write about yourself as if you were your only audience, as if this was the greatest gift you could possibly give yourself – the gift of putting your full attention on you.

Take time to be grateful for the qualities that you love and of which you are proud. Perhaps it's honesty, love, courage, commitment, patience, or the ability to forgive. Maybe it's a part of your body – your smile, your teeth, your voice, your laugh. Maybe you like your sense of humor or style. Perhaps there are compliments you've received that have made you feel especially proud. Look around your bedroom or your house for things that might help trigger your thoughts. Don't discount the smallest of things – your fingers, the lobe of your ear, a tiny thought or emotion that might not ever have been expressed.

We challenge you to really spend time looking and celebrating the learned behaviors, habits, and tools that have made you who you are today – the positive things that you would never want to change. We challenge you to silently acknowledge the people in your life who were part of you becoming you, and what they contributed.

It's crucial to remember that vicious self-judgment is a big issue for many people. As you continue your process of *noticing* and self-discovery, be careful that your self-judgment is not stopping you from truly acknowledging yourself, and instead running the show with negativity! We encourage you to find understanding, compassion, and loving kindness for yourself before you proceed. Going all the way through this process will help you obtain everything you need to create the life of your dreams.

Fair warning: This next step can be one of the most vulnerable and life-changing processes you will ever undertake. It is not always an entirely pleasant experience, so we encourage you to be gentle with yourself.

Now it is time to take an honest look at the parts of yourself of which you are not so proud. Maybe these aspects cause hurt or separation. Perhaps they show up as yelling, hitting, sarcasm, lying, cheating, spreading rumors, defending, stealing, being impatient, not keeping your word, constantly being late, letting people down, being in debt, or remaining in unhealthy or abusive relationships. Is it possible that you are abusing someone emotionally or physically? Are you a slave to your addictions? Are you taking the people you love for granted? And if they died tomorrow, would you regret anything?

Keep looking. If there are tears, let them out – they are a sign of strength, not weakness. When there are tears on the outside, the inside is healing and you are making room for lasting change. Keep looking.

How do you treat the people you meet? Do you like your relationships with the people closest to you? Are you proud of the way you live your life? Do *you* like *you*?

As you look, you may feel some embarrassment or shame. We urge you not to give up. Remember, you may have been asleep and unconscious for a very long time, so be patient with yourself. Try not to become paralyzed with judgment or self-hatred. You are beginning the process of awareness – the first step in creating change – so do your best to view your list of what you consider to be your shortcomings as opportunities for growth.

Take a moment to notice the ways you describe yourself. What are your "I am" statements? You might tell yourself, "I am loving. I am brilliant. I am beautiful. I am needy. I am inspiring. I am talented. I am a loser. I am a fraud. I am a good friend."

If we are who we say we are, it can get rather scary listening to the negative ways in which we describe ourselves or think about ourselves. You might be surprised to notice what you tell yourself when you're not fully aware of your thoughts and words.

What self-limiting statements, beliefs, attitudes, or behaviors have you allowed to define yourself? How do you keep yourself in a box? What excuses do you make for not achieving your goals? Be sure to journal about your discoveries. This is a powerful first step in changing your life. Don't short-change yourself.

Once you have set your intent to become more awake and you begin to *notice* more about who you are, it's time to *choose* who you want to become and how you will live your life now.

Choose

What's great about making choices is that they are rarely final. You can hardly ever choose the "wrong" course because even if you don't achieve your desired outcome, you set up an opportunity to find a better path toward it. If you miss the mark it doesn't mean that you failed, it simply means that there was more information you needed in order to move forward.

None of us are victims. We don't always get to control what happens in our lives, but we *always* get to decide how we respond. Once we realize that we have a choice, it's time to take 100% responsibility for our reactions.

Choice is one of our most powerful and important tools.

To choose is to begin to organize what you've noticed. That's why it's important for you not to edit or criticize yourself during the noticing process. First, you must simply get all your thoughts out, and then you can begin to evaluate your observations. You can start by putting what you've noticed into different categories. Some things you may not be ready to deal with, perhaps they'll go on hold. Other things you will want to keep as jewels and powerful reminders of who you are. Some things may require action. You will begin to choose a set of qualities and circumstances that you would like to do something about.

You don't even have to use your journal of what you've noticed, instead you can simply dream. At every Challenge Day, we ask people to discuss their biggest dreams. Now it's your turn. What are *your* dreams? What is your highest vision for life? How would you like things to be? If you knew that you could not fail, what would you *choose* as the most important elements in your life? If you were the hero you have been waiting for, what would your powers be?

To create something new in our lives, we need to start by having a vision, a clear picture of our goals, an imagined set of circumstances that we can aim toward. Since we have challenged you to start with yourself, begin to imagine the possibilities for who you can now become. *Feel* your vision in your heart. Imagine it living inside you. And then begin to help it grow. You can speak it, write it, sing it, dance it, sculpt it – whatever you choose, begin to shape it and give it form. *You cannot do this wrong!*

Yvonne and I recommend creating vision boards on a regular basis. Draw, cut, fold, and color; tear out words, symbols, drawings, and photos from magazines that depict your vision. Paste or tack them on a piece of cardboard that you can look at and focus on every day. Make sure that the specific qualities you are manifesting are clear and visible. We do this with our family. Our kids have vision board parties with their friends. At our retreats, we create vision boards with our staff. It's fun and it feels good because we are in it together. As a group, we focus on visions for the organization as well as for each of us as individuals. Put your vision board somewhere that you will see it every day. Remember, what we focus on grows. Believing that you *can* have the life of your dreams is the most vital ingredient in creating it!

Everything in our own lives – from our home and family, to Challenge Day and the Be the Change Movement, and even our appearances on television – once started as a vision. We had a dream and we began to pull it toward us. Even though there were times when people thought we were a little crazy, we started to talk about our visions as if they were true and destined to happen. Eventually, others became inspired by our excitement, they shared our vision and *together we made it a reality.*

Another great way of turning dreams into realities is to create an abundance of positive energy within you. Yvonne and I wake up every morning and turn our attention to what we are grateful for; we give voice to what we've noticed in order to help us continue to choose the direction our lives are taking. We start by completing the sentence "I am grateful for…." We are sometimes grateful for our health and our home, we are grateful for our children and the people in our lives and particular moments when they have expressed their love or their truth, we are even grateful for difficulties at times since they help us to learn and grow.

Then we set our intentions for the day. This is how we create our vision for how we intend to *be* – we choose moments and situations that we intend to act out during the day. We might say something such as, "I am loving today. I am expressing my love for my mother by calling her. I am patient with and listening to my co-workers. I am playing with my kids after work as if it's the most important thing I will do all day. I am exercising and pushing past my comfort zone." You can be as specific as you want to be. What we especially like to focus on are the things from yesterday that we wish we would have done differently.

Once you have envisioned something new for yourself, defined your vision, shaped it, and revised it, make sure that you have also chosen a plan of action that will help you achieve it.

Act

It's time to step into a whole new *you*! You do this by implementing your plan. Start small or go big, you decide. You can share your journal of what you've noticed about yourself with your friends, with your support group, or with at least one person you love and trust. If someone is reading this book with you, ask that person to share their list with you too, so you can see how very much alike we all are. Perhaps you can ask to describe each other. The people closest to you see you every day in ways that you cannot. Perhaps your partner will help you notice things about yourself you haven't yet seen.

If you weren't able to journal about your least desirable qualities, or even if you were, perhaps now is the time you decide to get support from someone you trust. Maybe you decide to get counseling for habits and behaviors you need help in changing.

If you've created a vision board, maybe you decide you want to share your dreams with everyone you can, or maybe you simply spend time looking at it and continuing to put your attention on the positive energy of it.

It's okay if your actions are modeled after someone else's actions. Many of us have teachers, relatives, or even spiritual role models we would like to emulate. Seek out people you admire the most and study them – make that part of your noticing. Then start becoming a new you by mimicking them. You might even consider, in some cases, telling that person what you are doing. Let them know that you like a trait or quality about them and that you are stealing it for yourself. They'll love it. According to Charles Colton, "Imitation is the sincerest flattery." We think he's right.

No matter how you've lived your life up to this point, you have the power to choose how you will act in this moment.

Create your new personality, leave your mark, follow your dream and *consciously write your own history or "her-story."* You get to say who you are. You are your own masterpiece! Who have *you* chosen to be and what actions are you taking in order to become it?

Make a commitment to do whatever it takes to make your dreams come true. Loving consciousness, diligent practice, and committed discipline are required to become whomever *you* choose. As often as possible, declare it out loud. Say it until you believe it, feel it, and become it. And "act as if." Some people call this the "fake it until you make it" part. The idea is simply that sometimes you have to try on a new coat before you know if it fits. In this case, try on your new self until it seems like it's really yours. Act as if you were already that person until it starts to become second nature.

As you take action, don't stop noticing and choosing and read-justing your course. There are no hard lines between the Notice, Choose, and Act process, so stay fluid and be open to the unexpected. Make sure that when you are met with surprises, you notice what's *right*. It's easy to see what's wrong and get trapped in negativity, so make it a conscious part of your notice process to create a space for what's right. We all know people who complain a lot. They've become experts at noticing and giving a voice to what's wrong. It's important to notice what's wrong but we believe that what you put your attention on makes it grow, and if you keep complaining you'll create more of the problem. On the other hand, as you talk about what's right, it helps you stay positive and increases your capacity for gratitude.

Also notice your mental roadblocks along the way. Almost daily the "critters" in my head tell me things like, "It's too hard; you don't have to; no one will notice; you know you don't feel like it." I call them critters because they are very much like the animals we had while raising our kids. Some of them were well behaved while others were out of control, peed all over everything, made lots of noise, and often left us feeling tense. Today, I understand that I am the master of my "critters." I can choose to be lazy, go unconscious, and let them run the show, or I can take charge and train them.

The bar Yvonne and I set for ourselves is incredibly high. For example, if you came to our house you'd see a question written in large letters across the top of our bathroom mirror. We borrowed this question from one of our favorite books, *Divinity in Disguise,* by Kevin Anderson. The question reads, "Is our relationship leaving God speechless?" As a couple, our goal is to be a living example of everything we teach.

If we remain numbed out, not only do we fail to Notice, Choose, and Act out the life of our dreams, we also don't experience the love of those closest to us and we miss out on feeling and sharing that love. We are all so hungry to *be* in life.

The good news is that we can change the way we show up in the world.

Today. This moment. Right now. Choose to *be* the conscious, open, loving hero you already know that you are. Try our Formula For Change. And as you do, please take note of this hugely important guideline:

Our formula is Notice, Choose, and Act.
It is not Notice, Beat Yourself Up, Choose, and Act.

There was a time in my life when I believed that if I beat myself up for the mistakes I made or the things I felt ashamed of, that somehow I would remember not to do those things again.

It doesn't work! I now realize that beating myself up lowered my self-esteem. Not only that, but because I was so hard on myself, I was also hard on others. Be *gentle* with you. Remember, it's a *practice*. We will be practicing this formula (or suffering the consequences of a numbed out life) for the rest of our lives.

Oh, and one last thing…

Remember to Celebrate!

For years we had successfully used our Formula For Change. Then we realized that if we constantly focus on what works and what doesn't work without celebrating our accomplishments, we miss out on a huge part of life – joy! Like many people passionately dedicated to changing the world, we realized we were on a treadmill of Notice, Choose, and Act. Despite succeeding in huge ways, we forgot to take the time to celebrate. That's why, at the end of every meeting in our office, staff members acknowledge the good they see and the successes of others. At the end of Challenge Day trips, our leaders celebrate the miracles they witnessed and the accomplishments of which they feel especially proud. On our reception desk we have a gong that staff members can ring in celebration of our daily successes.

So now, our challenge to you as you read the rest of *Be the Hero* is to apply our simple three-step formula to the lessons at the end of every chapter. And notice that I used the word *simple* rather than *easy*. It's one thing to read a book. It's another to actually take the lessons and use them to create the life of your dreams.

Everyday Heroes ~ Anne Fowler and Diane Cariss

 These two pioneering women had the courage to risk it all while supporting us in creating our dream. They went out on a limb and allowed us to showcase our very first Challenge Day program in 1987. Leaders in the field of education, Anne and Diane bring immense passion to all that they do.

Their partnership, as well as their faith in our leadership, has opened the door for more than a million young people and adults to know it's possible to feel safe, loved and celebrated in our schools. Masterful educators in their own right, both Anne and Diane have been honored for their innovative work, and for their uncanny ability to elevate the work and spirits of those around them. Recently retired, Anne and Diane now have the luxury of knowing theirs has been a life well lived.

Anne

If you really knew me, you'd know that in 1987 I felt helpless. Students everywhere were in pain, and there were no answers. I didn't see Challenge Day as a risk, but rather a vital obligation to our youth.

If you really knew me, you'd know that I have had a love-hate relationship with education. I strongly feel that every classroom should be physically and emotionally safe for all children, but sadly I have seen far too many teachers who created an unsafe and uncaring classroom. Conversely, I have been privileged to witness the miracles that happen when teachers embrace the principals of Challenge Day.

If you really knew me, you'd know that I see miracles every day – a lifetime of miracles that I may have missed had I not experienced Challenge Day, for Challenge Day helped guide me to live a life where I notice, choose and act, and I continue to Be the Change.

If you really knew me, you'd know that I feel proud every time I hear a student say, "Challenge Day has changed my life." I feel optimistic whenever I hear a teacher say, "Challenge Day has changed the way I teach."

Everyday Heroes ~ Anne Fowler and Diane Cariss

If you really knew me, you'd know that I have come to understand that we change the world one person at a time, and one positive act at a time...as we continue our quest; the future holds a positive critical mass created by the power of one.

Rich and Yvonne have lead the quest and they have been amazing role models for me and for millions of people who believe the world should and can be different.

Diane

If you really knew me, you'd know that I care deeply about people, and I want to help them. In 1987, I knew our young people (and their families) were hurting and needed help. I take big risks very carefully. I knew Rich and Yvonne well, and trusted them implicitly. I had the support and trust of the school district, and a community organization, "Livermore's We Say No Committee." By the time Challenge Day happened, I really didn't consider it a risk. My only fear for that first Challenge Day was that students wouldn't show up. We hadn't been able to tell them much about the day. That they came was a testament to how much they trusted us.

I love to play and have fun. I just never knew fun could include so much work, so many tears, and so much satisfaction until Challenge Day. I found miracles from the first – that we were allowed to do it, that students showed up, that students and adults had life-changing experiences, and that lifelong bonds were made – each and every Challenge Day. It is not a surprise that Rich and Yvonne's work is now getting the attention and acclaim that it deserves.

**Challenge
Days
in
action!**

If You Really Knew Me

The peaceful warrior's way is not about
invulnerability, but absolute vulnerability.

~ Dan Millman

It is one thing to know a person's title, accomplishments, successes or image. It is entirely different to connect to their humanity, to learn the intimate details about them that you would know if you really knew them. Many people are so afraid of getting vulnerable or, as we say at Challenge Day, "getting real," that they end up settling for superficial relationships and conversations rather than risking the possibility of sharing more personally, and then perhaps being rejected. People often compare their "insides" to other people's "outsides," and relate image to image rather than heart to heart. As a result, many of us spend our lives feeling separate and alone.

We believe one of the most courageous things any of us can do is to take the risk of "getting real."

Yvonne

If you really knew me, you'd know that in seventh grade I fell into a trap that would eventually take over much of my young life. If you really knew me, you would know that like most young people, I wanted to be accepted more than anything. I would sneak, lie and steal and no one, I mean *no one*, knew the embarrassing, desperate secret I carried with me every day.

By high school, I knew what image I needed to show in order for people to like me. However, if you really, *really* knew me, you would know that I was caught in the frightening, addictive cycle of bulimia. At first, I didn't even know what bulimia was. I certainly had no clue what kind of prison it would become, or how it would confine me. Like most people immersed in any addiction, I didn't think it could happen to me.

I'll never forget the day it began. It was Thanksgiving. Our family had just finished eating a huge meal, and everyone was stuffed.

My brother, whom I worshipped, jokingly said to me, "If I keep eating, I might end up with a belly like yours."

I felt devastated, but I just laughed it off. I waited a few minutes, then as casually as possible I went into the bathroom and burst into tears. I looked in the mirror and all I could see was fat. I hated myself. I felt sick inside, so disgusted that I wanted to vomit.

My face was flushed with fire from the intensity of my self-hatred. I had no idea how to deal with all I was feeling. Desperate to get the food out of my stomach, I stuck my fingers down my throat. At first, I just gagged. I continued to try over and over again. With a mixture of tears and sweat running down my face, all at once, I violently threw up.

Afterward, dizzy and light-headed, I noticed that the back of my hand was bleeding. I had scraped it with my teeth. Reeking with the smell of vomit, I washed my hands and face and brushed my teeth. I shut the toilet lid and sat down, cradling my head in my hands. As gross and as painful as the whole experience was, I was relieved that the food was gone, and that for at least one day I would not get fatter.

From that moment on, I secretly began to binge and purge. I would run water in the bathtub or sink so no one could hear me. I did this perhaps once a week at first, then daily. One day I realized it was no longer a choice. I couldn't stop. It had me. What I didn't know at the time was that when I threw up, my blood sugar dropped and then my body screamed for more. More food meant more throwing up. Gripped in this never-ending cycle, I felt completely alone and out of control.

With each day, my appetite increased. Soon the amount I needed to fill me was enormous. I began sneaking and even stealing food. I made up stories to cover my addiction. I would tell people I was having a party and that the gallons of ice cream, cookies, and spaghetti were for my friends. I learned that if I ate soft things, I wouldn't choke while I was throwing up. I ate so much at one time that I literately looked nine months pregnant. It was a vain attempt to fill the empty hole inside me and try to relieve my insatiable hunger.

Once completely stuffed, I plotted ways to throw it up. I needed privacy so no one could hear me or smell the vomit. I also needed time to recover. With my watery, bloodshot eyes and the violent impact to my body, I looked and felt like I'd been hit by a truck.

The obsession had taken over my life and left me terrified.

When my friends were going out in the evenings or on weekends, I stayed home frantically binging and purging in an endless cycle. I lied all the time to cover my tracks. At home, I explained away my time in the bathroom as a newfound interest in taking long baths. I blamed the missing food on my siblings or friends. I asked for extra money, saying that it was for field trips or special events. At school after lunch, I would tell my teacher I was sick, I had started my period, or that there was an emergency at home. I needed enough time to get to the bathroom while everyone was in class.

Lost in my addiction, my grades began to drop. I became moody and reactive toward everyone around me, especially the people I loved the most. Months turned into years. On the outside, I looked fine. Everyone thought I had it all together. However, I showed only a small part of myself to the outside world. If you really knew me, you'd know that I spent all my energy keeping the monster hidden, forever afraid someone would discover this horrible, shameful secret.

If you really knew me, you would know that it took over eight years to share my secret with anyone. I thought I was the only one living in this hell. Then one day, I was watching television with my boyfriend when a movie came on about a girl with a "disease" called bulimia. I was shocked – it had a name and I was not alone. It was as if I was watching my own story vividly unfold before my eyes. I froze with self-consciousness, fearing somehow my boyfriend would sense my feelings and guess that it was more than just a movie to me.

After the show, I spilled an hour of tears and, no longer able to contain myself, I did it, I revealed my horrific secret to a counselor. I finally found the courage to talk about my loneliness, my fear, my desperation. But I wanted an instant cure and it wasn't coming. My bulimia was so out of control, I couldn't stop the cycle, and in the depths of my pain, I became suicidal. With no other choice, my counselor had me involuntarily committed to the psychiatric hospital.

My healing began when I finally found the courage to end my isolation. I let go of my image, reached out for help, told the truth, and started to share my pain with others. With help, I learned I didn't have to do it alone.

Living with bulimia was one of the hardest times of my life. The truth is, it could have killed me. If you or anyone you know is trapped in this devastating and life gripping addition, I urge you to tell someone so you can get help.[1]

---

1 http://www.womenshealth.gov/faq/Easyread/bulnervosa-etr.htm - 1 800 994 9662

Live It!

What shames us, what we most fear to tell, does not set us apart from others; it binds us together if only we can take the risk to speak it.

~ Starhawk

One of the tools Challenge Day is best known for is an activity called "If you really knew me." Sharing my shame about bulimia is an example of what this activity might look like. Though most people don't start by disclosing their deepest secrets, completing this simple phrase has the power literally to transform shallow "chit-chat" conversations into an intimate, life changing opportunity for depth and connection.

Oprah called our work simple. And she's right. This tool and the others in the book can be used everywhere by everyone. We particularly like to use the "If you really knew me" tool at the dinner table with family and friends. We use it to open *every* meeting in our Challenge Day office. We use it to bring people close at parties and other social events. In our experience, the more open and honest we are willing to be, the more intimate and connected we become. The simplicity of this lead-in sentence naturally opens a doorway to a level of vulnerability, truth and understanding we all crave.

Dropping the Waterline and Getting Real

Many of us live our lives as if we are icebergs floating aimlessly in the sea of life, and largely submerged. We hide most of ourselves, and especially our most tender, secret places, below the "the waterline." Like a typical iceberg, we show only about 10% of ourselves, the part above the water. For the purposes of this discussion, let's call this 10% our image.

"Dropping the waterline" and getting real means facing most peoples' biggest fear – rejection. We're so afraid of being rejected, we often even hide who we really are from the people closest to us. For some, this looks like acting hard or tough, keeping secrets, being cool, being a jokester, or maybe even pretending we don't care about anything at all.

Many of us get stuck trying to live up to an image we believe will be acceptable to others. We fall into groups or cliques, and learn to label ourselves and other people in ways that seem to define how we should act and what we should let people see – jock, stoner, cheerleader, socialite, geek, loser, gangster, teacher, executive, coach, parent, etc.

I kept the secret of my bulimia plunged deep below the waterline. The hardest part was doing it all alone. I felt so gross, so crazy, so out of control, and so ashamed that I thought if anyone really knew me, they could never love or accept me.

If you never take the risk of dropping the waterline and letting people see who you really are, you can never feel all the love, celebration and acceptance you deserve. The only way you can experience authentic intimacy and connection with others is to risk exposing your true self.

What's your image? What secrets do you have? What parts of yourself do you keep hidden? How does your image keep you separate from other people? Do people know what you go through and what really matters in your life?

As you begin to drop the waterline and explore your depths, consider this thought. If we investigate the word intimacy, we find: Into – Me – You – See.

5 Steps for Building Intimacy and Connection

1. Choose people in your life with whom you'd like to be closer.

2. Be willing to drop the waterline and show them the real you.

3. Share yourself with them by completing the sentence, "If you really knew me…." Take the risk of revealing things that are vulnerable for you.

4. Invite people to join you by completing the same sentence, "If you really knew me…."

5. No matter what people share, be sure to appreciate them for taking the risk.

Be the Hero

**The more honest you can be (with yourself and with others)
about who you are and what you need to be fulfilled,
the more likely you are to create a life that's right for you.**

~ Dr. Suzanne Zoglio

Notice

In addition to the questions we posed earlier, consider these:

- Who in your life knows who you really are?
- Are there people whom you wish really knew you? What keeps them from knowing you?
- When was the last time you dropped the waterline and risked revealing yourself to someone who mattered? What happened? How did it make you feel?
- In general, how often do you drop your waterline – with strangers, with family, with a partner, with friends? Are you comfortable with how often you become vulnerable?
- What, if anything, keeps you from showing yourself and being vulnerable?
- Are there things you intentionally hide? Why? How might your life be different if you didn't hide these things?
- How much do you know about the people closest to you? Do you know who they *really* are?

Choose

- Among the people in your life who really know you, is there more of yourself you would like to share with them? Under what circumstances might it be possible?

- Are there people to whom you'd like to be closer? If you dream about the perfect relationships in your life, who does it involve and what does it look like?
- How might you become more vulnerable with the people in your life? What circumstances might have to be present in order for you to drop the waterline?
- Is there any support you need in becoming who you really are? Do you need a different set of friends? Do you need a therapist? Do you need more understanding from a parent?
- How can you create more opportunities for connection among the people you love?

Act

- Find some people you'd like to be closer to and share this chapter of the book with them. Tell them you'd like them to really know you, and ask them if you can tell them one thing about yourself that you keep hidden.
- Once you've gotten vulnerable yourself, ask them "What would I know if I really knew you?" Be patient with any resistance. Getting real can be uncomfortable, especially at first. A word of caution. Sometimes the question can feel like an ambush to people. Make sure you've dropped the waterline first before you ask someone else to do it.
- Use "If you really knew me" as a conversation starter to bring depth and connection to families, friends, school and work. We challenge you to try using this tool at your next family dinner or group gathering.
- Approach someone with whom you'd like to be closer. Try the model of Notice, Choose, Act by telling them one

thing you notice about them that you'd like to know more about; tell them how you envision your relationship deepening; and ask them if they would create a deeper connection with you.

- Start an on-going "If you really knew me" support group. Create time for people to get together and share the truth of who they really are and how they really feel. All that's needed is a timer and a group of people willing to participate.

- If you are dealing with secrets or any dangerous patterns, habits or addictions, reach out and get the help and support you deserve from experts or people you trust. Take the risk of sharing what you're *really* going through. You don't have to do it alone!

Celebrate!

- Take yourself to a movie, buy something special, take a long bath, treat yourself to an afternoon nap, proclaim your success to someone you love.

- Share your experience. Log on to www.challengeday.org/bethechange and tell us all about it.

Everyday Hero ~ Ray Ray

What you see is what you get with this powerful, loving man. He has miraculously transformed a lifetime of violence and fear into a life of love and service. Since overcoming a rough upbringing, Ray Ray has become a model of hope for thousands of young people and adults who have been gifted in witnessing the results of his personal transformation.

A committed husband and father of two, Ray Ray's family is the source of his inspiration, as he works to ensure that others won't fall pray to the traps of drugs, gangs and violence. As a Challenge Day leader, Ray Ray serves as a walking contradiction. Blending his tough guy image and experience with a profound level of hope and vulnerability, Ray Ray models new possibilities for men, boys and families everywhere.

Ray Ray

If you really knew me, you would know that I grew up very fast, having to take care of my three younger brothers. I was constantly asking myself why my father hated me so much, also wondering why my mother would never protect her sons from our father's anger. With the violence at home, my life became a lonely walk through Hell. My world at a young age was fighting, drinking, and taking methamphetamines every day and night. Once my high school days were done, I started to hang around gangs, getting involved in their activities.

Once I left home, my source of income and drugs came from collecting money or hurting someone just to send a message to let them know that they had screwed with the wrong person. I worked for many people, mainly drug dealers. To them I was known as "Pit." The things I've done and seen for many years finally came to a stop; I just couldn't stand the nightmares anymore. I continued using crystal meth every day to numb my pain. Also during that time, I got married and had two children. The addiction and pain I had, did not make a safe and loving home for my family.

If you really knew me, you'd know that I got clean, and instead of running away from the pain, I shared it with my wife. My children used to be afraid of me, and now they cover me with hugs and kisses. Being held and hearing the words, "I love you" didn't exist with my father and I. My son and daughter always hear those words, and no matter what age, I

Everyday Hero ~ Ray Ray

will hold my children. The communication, respect, and love we have for each other is incredible. One of the greatest miracles that has happened in my life is that I expressed my love to my father who rejected my love many times. I was 33 years old in 2008 when my father finally hugged me and told me that he loved me!

Challenge Day has helped me become a better person, not only for my family but for myself. I am also at peace with myself, and closer to my wife and children. I am able to control my anger, and express myself with words and not violence. Because of Challenge Day, I am a happier person.

There's No Such Thing as a Bad Kid: The Ache to be Loved

If you judge people, you have no time to love them.

~ Mother Teresa

Rich

If you really knew me, you'd know that in junior high I hated my life. I was picked on and harassed every day by three boys in particular. They were known as "bad kids."

The first time I met them was my very first day of school. I was on my way to gym class and I was lost. The bell had already rung. I was nervous about being late, and especially about standing out as being stupid, so I went outside to walk along the fence toward the gym. I neared three students who were gathered together by the building. They were all taller and bigger than me. They were dressed in dark clothing and wore headbands that could be seen underneath their black caps. As I got closer to them, I noticed that one of the boys was putting a knife into his pocket.

"Get the f--- out of here," he said.

I scurried past them to the gym and I thought that was the end of it. But it wasn't. They had noticed me. Not only did I know something about them that must have made them want to scare me into silence, but my deer-in-the-headlights expression made me an easy target.

Later that day, the three of them surrounded me in the hall and bumped me back and forth between them, laughing. It was a big joke for them but I was scared to death.

Rumors about these boys circulated. People told me that they'd been "jumped" into a gang. Because the boys were juveniles, some of the older members used them to do their "dirty" work. They stayed out late at night, they had guns, they shot people. I don't know if any of it was true but they began to seem ominous to me and I tried my best to avoid them.

Two friends from my summer baseball league, Mark and Rick, in many ways served as a lifeline for me. Knowing my situation with the three boys, they looked out for me and protected me when they could. But they, of course, couldn't always be around. Whenever I was alone, it seemed those boys would inevitably find me. They called me names, they followed behind me and slammed me against the lockers, they surrounded me in the parking lot and told me to get out of their way as they trapped me from escaping. They teased me about being small, the way I talked, the way I walked, the color of my skin, and anything else they could think of to embarrass me or belittle me or frighten me. When I resisted, it became worse. They all jumped on me at the same time, punched me, and kicked me. The torment continued for months.

I was too afraid to tell a teacher because I thought it would only get worse if I did. I was too afraid to tell my father because I thought it would make him ashamed of me. Even worse, I thought that if my father knew, he'd make me fight them, which is what his father made him do when he was my age.

One morning, my father came into the kitchen as I was finishing my breakfast. The table was a mess because my brother had left without cleaning up his dishes. But my dad blamed me for it. He got in my face, screaming, and told me to clean it up. It was another one of his unpredictable outbursts. Because I never knew what would trigger my father, I was constantly on edge.

I went to school that day feeling crushed. As I walked into my history class, one of the boys slammed into me from behind and I exploded with rage. Without even thinking, I grabbed him around the neck and slammed his head through the classroom window.

The intensity of my anger surprised me but what surprised me even more was seeing his face covered with blood. *Oh my God*, I thought, *what have I done? What if he bleeds to death?* It was a moment that lasted an eternity – the moment I realized I could have killed him.

I couldn't believe I could be so out of control; I couldn't believe I was capable of such violence.

I had stuffed so many of my feelings inside that they had created a volcano in me, raw emotions ready to blow up at any time. There we were, two boys from very different worlds, two boys who had become enemies without either of us having a clue about what the other might have been going through.

I learned years later that two of the three boys were brutally murdered in gang-related violence, one of them by being injected with battery acid. As much as I thought I had hated them, I felt sickened by the news. I now know that their bullying, at least in part, came from their own wounds. And I know that if we'd ever gotten to know each other below the surface we might have experienced some compassion for each other and even become friends.

As I think about it now, I can't help but wonder how our entire lives might have been changed if we'd had a Challenge Day.

What if we could have looked into each other's eyes, saw each other's pain, and discovered we weren't so different after all?

I say this because of Victor, and because of so many others like him whom we witness making courageous changes in their lives every time we lead a Challenge Day.

Just like the boys who tormented me, Victor was a "bad kid." That's the first thing I learned about him as I began setting up and preparing for the day's program.

One of the school coordinators pulled me aside, agitated, and pointed him out. "That kid is trouble," she said, nodding toward a burly looking boy at the back of the line. "Victor is the meanest kid in our school. He doesn't care about anyone."

She explained that the school's administration had assigned him to come to today's Challenge Day as an alternative to suspension. "I can't believe they made him come," she fumed.

I resisted the temptation to buy into her fears, and I reassured her (and perhaps myself) by sharing the belief Yvonne and I have. "There is no such thing as a bad kid," I said. "There are only kids who are badly hurting."

The coordinator seemed unmoved.

"I'll do my very best to reach him," I said.

The school was in a conservative, upper middle class neighborhood, and as the students began arriving, most of Victor's classmates appeared to have stepped right out of a clothing catalog. Designer apparel, perfect makeup, bright smiles and the energetic buzz of excitement and nervous energy filled the air. They bounced in, danced to the music, and playfully offered hugs or high fives as they made their way to their seats. Everybody, parents and students alike, seemed to be having a good time. Except Victor.

Unlike his classmates, Victor looked like a character from the Addams family. Long, jet-black hair hung over his entire face and down to his chest. The shoulders of his black leather jacket bristled with long, chrome spikes jutting out in all directions. Everything about Victor shouted "Back off!"

As he made his way to a seat in the circle, he pushed a classmate aside and made it abundantly clear he wanted nothing to do with our craziness. The chairs on either side of him stayed conspicuously empty. In a room bursting with people and energy, there he sat – angry and alone.

I knew what I needed to do. I promised myself that no matter how angry or resistant Victor might be, I would continue beaming him love and acceptance. I would do it on behalf of the boy in me, I would do it in memory of the boys who hurt me, and I would do it for this boy sitting across the room from me who clearly needed to be loved.

I made it my personal mission to reach his heart.

Every time I walked by him, I gently placed my hand on his shoulder and said, "I'm glad you're here."

At first he ignored me or smirked with indignation. As the day unfolded, however, Victor gradually began acknowledging my presence. My persistence was eventually rewarded by a mumbled, "Thanks."

Things shifted during the Power Shuffle, an activity in which participants stand on one side of a line and are asked to cross over to the other side when we read a statement that applies to them.

"Cross the line if you've ever been hurt or judged because of the color of your skin… Cross the line if you've ever been picked last in games or in sports, or if you've ever been left out all together… Cross the line if you've ever been labeled as a stoner, gangster, druggie, or told that you were a bad kid."

As we walked back and forth across the room, participants on both sides began shedding tears of compassion. Tension and fear slowly gave way to empathy and understanding. Both young people and adults began wordlessly reaching out to comfort and support one another. Always keeping his distance from the others, Victor seemed tentative, as though unsure of his place. It seemed as though every time he stepped across the line, he walked further into his world of anger and separation.

As if to say *I see you*, I moved in close to him. "You've crossed this line way too many times," I whispered. "Thank you for hanging in there." And then, through the silence, "I'm proud of you," I said.

In that moment, Victor let me in. Without even looking up, he softly answered, "I have no tears."

I wasn't sure I had heard him right. "Excuse me?"

Again, he murmured, "I have no tears. I can't cry anymore." Then he added, "Everyone thinks I'm a troublemaker and a loser. I go through this stuff every day – I just gave up."

I melted, touched by his vulnerability. I swallowed the lump in my throat. "Thank you for trusting me," I told him. He didn't lift his eyes from beneath his cloak of hair as I continued. "You're doing a great job just being you."

Later, as I made my way up and down the line of participants, I once again found myself at Victor's side. Without even glancing in my direction, he whispered, "Thank you for coming to my school."

I put my arm on his shoulder and softly responded, "I'm honored."

After the power shuffle, participants returned to their small sharing groups. This time, instead of pulling his chair away, Victor made sure he sat knee to knee with the others. Although his hair still completely obscured his face, his body language made it clear that he wanted to participate.

I watched as he took his turn sharing in the group. Although I couldn't hear what he was saying, his forward lean and the reactions he received from the rest of the group told me that he was speaking from his heart.

At the end of the activities, we give participants a chance to take the microphone and talk about what the day has meant to them. It is common for students to apologize to other students or even challenge each other to abandon hurtful behavior. Not surprisingly, Victor was at the root of much of the hurt people described.

Quietly, I made my way to his side and I asked if he would be willing to share with the group what he had told me. After a moment's hesitation, he agreed.

As Victor stood up and took the microphone, I asked for everyone's attention and introduced my new friend. The entire room turned in anticipation of his words. I publicly thanked Victor for trusting me and then invited him to share what he had whispered to me while crossing the line.

Speaking from behind his long black hair, seemingly disembodied, this courageous young man vulnerably declared, "I have no more tears."

The room fell completely silent.

"I go through this kind of pain every day," he said.

Moved by his words, a couple of students immediately raced over to stand by his side in support.

I can only call what happened next a miracle.

Acknowledging Victor's bravery and the support he had received, I gave him what might have been the greatest challenge of his young life. Reminding him that he was not alone, I pointed out the obvious, that he routinely pushed people away and handled every challenge in isolation.

Victor nodded in agreement.

"Are you ready to change that?" I asked.

He nodded slowly and whispered, "Yes."

I turned back to the group and asked people to raise their hands if they appreciated Victor's courage, and to keep their hands up if they would be available to listen if he ever wanted to talk.

All over the room, excited hands shot up.

I decided to push for another miracle. I faced Victor and posed this challenge. "Would you be willing to peek out from behind your hair and allow people to see you?"

Without hesitation, my new friend slowly separated his hair, exposing his gentle eyes and the tears streaming down his cheeks.

With thunderous applause, the entire room sprang to its feet.

Crossing the line that separates us

Live It!

Everything we do is either an act of love or a cry for help.

~ Marianne Williamson

All too often, people who look and act like Victor are stereotyped and judged. Falling into the trap of fear and negativity, many people unconsciously separate themselves from those who seem hard, rebellious, or distant.

Yvonne and I remain uncompromising in our certainty that *there is no such thing as a bad kid.* We believe even the angriest or hardest people to reach – both teens and adults – have a place inside that aches to be loved and appreciated.

Each one of us is born with a beautiful, glowing, shining heart filled with innocence, wonder, hope and dreams. Not only is this shining spirit in you, it also exists in everyone you know. It is sometimes easy to see that it exists in your mother, your father, your friends, your teachers, your boss, and your neighbors. It is less easy to see, though equally true, that a beautiful child also lives in the people who torment you, in our world leaders, and in every person who has ever lived – from Adolf Hitler to Mother Teresa.

Every one of us is born unique and exquisitely vulnerable. We count on parents and others around us to create a safe, supportive, and nurturing environment in which to grow. However, no matter how loving and supportive those who raise us are, inevitably there are times when our needs aren't met. Those unmet needs can create scars on the surface of our innocent, shining hearts. Worse yet, what happens if we are abused, neglected, hit, hurt, humiliated, or shamed? More scars, of course. Every wound creates another scar.

By the time we are in junior high, high school, or out in the adult world, our beautiful hearts are covered with a thick layer of scarring. We protect ourselves by preventing others from getting too close. Our protection can take the form of bad habits, addictions, or acting out, anything that keeps another person from getting close enough to our hearts to hurt us. The more scars, and the deeper they are, the stronger and thicker our defense shields become.

These defenses keep us from feeling connected to other people.

The good news is that the light inside our hearts never goes out. No one is intrinsically bad or broken. In our experience, when we consciously look for the good in others, we most always find it.

Philosophy of the Heart:
Some Things To Consider

1. You and every person you meet came into the world with a bright, pure heart.

2. Every person on the planet was once thought of as being cute, cuddly, precious, and even miraculous.

3. At some point, as part of our growth process, we are all hurt in some way.

4. Regardless of the origin, the severity, or the number of hurts we endured, every one of us naturally starts to protect ourselves and our tender hearts.

5. We create walls and barriers between our hearts and others to protect ourselves from further hurts.

6. These protections can take the form of shields of self-destructive behaviors such as drug abuse, eating disorders, excessive joking, negativity, violence, and even suicide.

7. The more we protect ourselves, the more we begin relating to others shield to shield instead of heart to heart.

8. We sometimes find ourselves connecting with others at the level of our scars because we allow our wounds to define who we are.

9. Regardless of our wounds and scars, and the protections we use, no one is intrinsically bad or broken.

10. Since the light in our hearts never goes out, it is always available to be discovered. Perhaps the discovery process is part of our soul's journey.

Be the Hero

Judgments prevent us from seeing the good that lies beyond appearances.

~ Wayne Dyer

Notice

- Has anyone ever labeled you as a bad kid or a bad person? If so, what behaviors of yours were considered to be bad? Can you link any of your behaviors to wounds or hurts you endured?

- In what ways do you protect yourself or keep yourself from revealing who you really are? How have the hurts you received both as a child and later in life affected how you act toward others?

- In what ways, if any, does your protection cause you to lash out at others? Do you make jokes or change the subject during moments of intimacy? Do you break eye contact with people first? Do you become aggressive? Or have you simply stood by and watched as other people have been tormented or humiliated? Notice moments that make you uncomfortable and see if you can connect them to parts of yourself that have also been hurt.

- What qualities or behaviors do you most want to change about yourself in order to allow others to see the beauty of your heart?

- Do you ever find yourself judging people based on the way they look or act, even if you have never met them? What qualities in others do you judge the most – either positively or negatively?

- Bring to mind someone you have judged as being "bad." Notice all the aspects of that person you don't like. Notice anything about the person you do like. Now, imagine you are that person. Think of things that could have happened to you that made you do the same things you judge the other person for doing.

Choose

- If there are people who have labeled you, judged you, and hurt you, can you imagine healing the hurt that keeps you separate from them? What actions might you take that would bring the wall of isolation down? You don't have to actually do them, you simply have to imagine doing them. These are actions that come from you, not from them.

- If there are people whom you have hurt, either by directly saying or doing something, or by indirectly standing by and watching, can you imagine apologizing to them? What would it look like if you did? Under what circumstances might it be possible to do that?

- What do you need to do to heal the scars that protect your heart? Dream about the ways in which you can be set free from the things that limit you. Consider what you have noticed about yourself, and imagine those things being healed. Who are you now?

- Envision a relationship with yourself in which you feel completely ecstatic and in love with who you are. Dream about being your biggest supporter and your best friend. How would you treat yourself differently? What new things would you tell yourself? What do you long for others to say about you? Is it enough for you to tell yourself those things in order to believe them, or do you need others to agree?

Act

- Make a Philosophy of the Heart poster for yourself. Draw a heart with bright yellow light beaming out at all sides. Fill the heart with wonderful words that describe who you are. Then think of all the hurts you've received in your life. For each hurt you think of, draw a dark slash over a word on your heart. Recognize that each slash represents a scar on your beautifully vulnerable heart.

- Consider for a moment what you have done to numb out or protect yourself from further scaring. Abusing drugs or alcohol, overeating, acting indifferent, or even over-achieving can all be ways to avoid further hurt and scars. List those on your poster. The final step in this process is to back away from the poster and just look. Notice – do you still see the light? The truth is that the light never goes out no matter how many scars we get. That is how we know that there really is no such thing as a bad kid.

- Over the next week, consciously fill people's hearts by pointing out the good you see in them. No matter how they act or what they do, your job is to beam acceptance and love. Notice what happens.

- Try dressing like someone you negatively judge. Spend a day walking in their shoes. Notice the reactions you get from people. Do people treat you differently? Do you act differently?

- Consider getting to know people you negatively judge in order to know their hearts and heal your own judgments. Approach them and drop the waterline with them.
- If you are negatively judged as being bad, choose a whole new you and start to take steps toward becoming it. Try tying a piece of string to your toothbrush as a reminder. Then, every time you brush your teeth, look at yourself in the mirror and send love to yourself. You must love yourself in order to heal. Begin by taking small steps and finding more and more aspects of yourself to appreciate.

Remember to celebrate!

Everyday Hero ~ Christopher Foster

Christopher brings a unique blend of street savvy and spirituality to all that he does. Raised in South Central Los Angeles, one of the toughest areas in the United States, Chris was lucky enough to have a family that was so full of love and support, he parlayed the positive energy into a lifetime commitment to serve others. Whether leading a Challenge Day program or preaching the Word to a congregation, Chris's passion to Be the Change shines through!

Christopher

If you really knew me, you would know that I collided with Challenge Day at the most devastating intersection of my life. Divorce brought about indescribable pain. My initial reaction was to build invisible walls to protect my heart, mind, and Spirit. I wanted to ensure that I would never feel that level of heartbreak again. I accepted the role of victim and isolated myself, while doing my best to maintain the image that everything was fine.

Challenge Day helped me realize that my method of protection was actually enabling past pain to exist in the present. I noticed I was allowing one negative experience to prevent me from loving others, feeling reciprocal love, and living a life with purpose. I chose to focus on God as my example, along with the principles of Challenge Day, which have empowered me to love and forgive, liberating me to rediscover my passion. I acted by becoming vulnerable again; although risk is involved, the reward far exceeds the risk. My desire is to be a conduit of love and to choose faith over fear always.

Challenge Day affords me the daily opportunity to experience substantial transformations in people who are strangers when I enter a room, but feel like family once I leave. On many levels, I am living the life of my dreams, and for this I am truly grateful.

The Cycle of Oppression

In the end, we will remember not the words of our enemies, but the silence of our friends.

~ Dr. Martin Luther King, Jr.

Yvonne

If you really knew me, you would know that my first dance in seventh grade taught me more about oppression than any book, class, or workshop I have ever taken.

I was eager to get home after school to try on my new outfit. My excitement about going to the dance overrode my usual insecurity about being fat. Wearing my new skirt and blouse, with matching red knee high socks, I turned on the radio and practiced my dance moves in front of the mirror. I was ready.

At 7:00 p.m., my mom dropped me off at the front door of the school cafeteria. "Have fun!" she said, with a goodbye kiss. "I'll pick you up right here at nine-thirty."

Flashing lights and loud music had transformed our humdrum cafeteria into a mysterious, enchanted wonderland. All the girls huddled together along one side of the room. The boys were as far away as possible. As one of my favorite songs boomed and echoed across the room, I made my way over to my two best friends.

For the next couple of songs no one moved. The boys stood stiffly on one side, talking and laughing loudly as they looked over at us. We acted as aloof and nonchalant as we could, waiting to see who would be chosen for a dance. After what seemed like an eternity, the "popular" boys began to cross the room and actually asked some of us to dance.

With each new song, more and more boys gathered their courage to approach the wall of girls. At some point, I realized that every girl had been chosen as a dance partner except me. Even my friend Sandy who was as picked on as me, was out dancing. It wouldn't have mattered to me whether a guy was popular or not, I would have been thrilled if any boy had asked me to dance.

I glanced down at my outfit. What a fool I was to think that anyone would ever want to dance with me – a fat girl with a mouthful of braces, a homemade haircut, and wearing the wrong clothes.

It was a mistake for me to have come in the first place. I sat down in the corner and prayed for the night to end so I could sneak out. Familiar tears began welling up. "Don't cry, Yvonne," I whispered fiercely to myself. "Whatever you do, *don't cry*." I just wanted it to all be over so I could go home.

After what seemed like an eternity, they announced the last song. Relief flooded through me. Then, in disbelief, I noticed Johnny, the cutest and most popular boy in the school, heading my way. As he kept walking toward me, my mouth dropped open. Until that moment, I didn't even think he knew who I was. He crossed the cafeteria into my corner of the room and came right up to me. I was shocked!

"Would you like to dance?" he asked, holding out his hand.

I could hardly breathe. Johnny had asked *me* to dance. Here, in front of the whole school, Johnny and I were going to dance the last dance of the night!

My heart raced. I jumped out of my chair, desperate to remember my oh-so-practiced dance moves. Reaching the center of the room, we began to dance. Then, without warning or even a clue, Johnny looked over at his friends and stopped dancing. All at once, they burst into jeering laughter, which echoed throughout the cafeteria. Stunned and humiliated, I just stood there in the middle of the dance floor with everybody laughing and pointing at me.

Johnny's best friend ran up and gave him a handful of wadded dollar bills. "Okay, you win," he said, rolling his eyes in my direction. "Here's your money. You earned it!"

Everyone in the room watched the transaction. As usual, no one – not even my best friends – said or did a thing. I was completely devastated.

Choking back tears, I ran out of the room and into the street. As I waited at the curb for my mom to arrive, it took all I had to act as though everything was fine. By the time my mom got there, I managed to put a smile on my face. I didn't say a word to my mom or dad about what had happened. Later, alone in my room, I cried myself to sleep. That night proved to be one of the longest and most painful of my life.

Having endured that kind of pain, you would think I would never do anything like that to another human being. Yet the following Monday as I rode the bus to school, Scott, the only kid on campus who was teased and humiliated more than I was, got on the bus and sat right in front of me. He turned around to face me and, with a gentle smile, said "Hi." Even now, more than 35 years later, I am crying with embarrassment as I write this story. I looked Scott right in the eyes and blurted, "Don't talk to me, you loser!"

Three days after the dance I was already passing on the hurt I had experienced.

Live It!

No one is free when others are oppressed.

~ Gandhi

We all know what it is like to have been hurt, teased, or humiliated, just as almost every one of us has, at some point, hurt, teased, or humiliated someone else. If not, we have undoubtedly stood by and watched in silence as someone else was being hurt. This is social oppression.

Rich and I define oppression as the systematic, routine, institutionalized misuse or abuse of power. Many of us have become so accustomed to living with it, it has become a part of "the way things are." Like toxins in the air we breathe, we don't even notice.

The consequences of social oppression are devastating. Throughout history we have created a long list of examples of the systematic abuse and mistreatment of certain groups of people. In many cases, potential allies have turned a blind eye or simply ignored the abuses. Racism, slavery, and the genocide of many tribes of people; anti-Semitism, the Holocaust, and Apartheid; sexism, the mistreatment and abuse of women, homophobia, and the ongoing targeting of gay, lesbian, bisexual and transgender people.

One of the most universal forms of oppression we have as a world community is the wounding of our children. Rich and I have a personal goal, which we've also established as the vision of Challenge Day, that every child live in a world where they feel safe, loved, and celebrated. Our society has a long way to go. There are those among us in great numbers who could be arrested if they treated adults the way they treat children. Under the guise of discipline, people regularly slap, hit, and beat young people. Discipline means *to teach*.

The Cycle of Oppression

At Challenge Day, we believe our best teaching tool is modeling. If we, as a society, accept hitting, slapping, and beating our kids as discipline, what are we teaching them to do? In addition, many children live daily with emotional abuse – yelling, shaming, humiliation. These are all generations of passed-on cycles of abuse that get handed to our young people simply by virtue of their age. Our babies, our tender, young souls are the recipients of our own pain, and they endure our outbursts without a voice and without a vote.

When we oppress our children, they often grow up to oppress or abuse others. And the cycle continues.

The abuse of power often runs rampant by those with more privilege and more opportunity. In school, the group with the most power is often labeled "the popular kids." These kids are often bigger and older; they wear nicer clothes or have more "stuff." They often tend to be better athletes, they're viewed as better looking, or they at least fit the stereotypes of our popular media. Often, they choose easy targets to carry out the cycle of oppression – the smaller kids, or the *really* big ones; those with less money, or with unique abilities; kids with different skin color, sexual orientation, or native language.

Consciously or unconsciously, kids with more power are sometimes stigmatizing these differences in order to enhance their sense of privilege. When Johnny humiliated me in front of the whole school, I doubt he was consciously thinking, "How can I hurt Yvonne the most?" To him, I was just an opportunity to boost his status with his friends and to maintain his position as the coolest and most popular boy in school. In fact, at the time, I didn't know that Johnny needed his popularity to hide his own pain. Years later, when he committed suicide, I realized that he wasn't a "bad kid." He didn't target me because he was vicious, he was simply caught up in the painful cycle that many kids have learned.

What happened? When we were born, we loved every part of ourselves.

From the top of our heads to the tip of our toes, we thought we were amazing. As little kids, we would tie towels around our necks, pretend they were capes, and fly around like our favorite Super Hero. When we found anything that looked like a microphone, we would crank up the music, dance around, and sing in the mirror. We were stars! Do you remember? We thought we were perfect. As little kids, we thought everyone around us was perfect, too. If they seemed different from us, our natural curiosity brought us together. We loved ourselves and everyone else.

Then we heard the lies, things like "You're ugly, you're stupid, you're too big, too small. Your family is bad, you live in the wrong part of town, you're a loser. Your skin is the wrong color, you don't speak 'right', you're 'gay', get away from me!" You know the list. Those targeted for oppression are left out, ignored, laughed at, teased, bullied, ridiculed, humiliated, picked on, beat up, or even murdered.

The idea that we can enhance our social standing by demeaning others becomes part of what Rich and I call "the cycle of oppression." It starts because some of us learned to build ourselves up by putting other people down. No one is born mean; especially when we were little, none of us thought it was okay to hurt other people. Oppression is *learned* behavior and it continues to reproduce and multiply as adults take their unresolved, childhood and teenage hurts from home and school, and carry them into the workplace and the community. The cycle also continues because people stand by silently and allow others to be humiliated in their presence.

Slowly, over time, we all learn to numb out in the face of constant oppression.

Almost certainly, the first time you saw anyone get hurt, teased or mistreated, you recognized the injustice. Maybe you even stood up to the person who was doing it, no matter how big or popular they were. Unless you were scared – and most of us were when we are small – you said something like, "Stop it! You can't say that!" Or you said, "Don't do that to me, that hurts!" Even if you didn't have the courage to speak up, you thought it and you resisted.

In spite of our initial resistance, as we grow up oppression continues to bombard us. We hear lies, we witness stereotyping, and we see cruelty virtually everywhere, especially on television. We repeatedly endure the pain of getting hurt, teased, or worse. We watch people we love and respect (or at least those we thought were popular and cool) do it. After a while, we forgot that it isn't okay. We either forget how badly it hurts or we find ways to numb out completely. Or worse, we pass the hurt on to those with less power than ourselves, like I did. As one of the least powerful kids in school, the only way I knew how to recover some of my lost status was to show that at least I was better than Scott.

We have all been oppressed. We all know what it is like to be hurt or mistreated. And we have all passed it on to others, even if only to our brothers or sisters. That is how oppression persists.

The good news is that anything we learn, we can unlearn.

However, we have to be vigilant about it. Because oppression is so insidious, we may not always be aware that it is happening. We have to stay awake and be mindful of it, especially if we are the ones with the power, and each of us has the power at some point. Many of us often get so lost in the realm of power that we don't notice who we are stepping on.

Once people in the power groups notice the cycle of oppression, it is relatively easy to change. Why? Because they have the power.

If you happen to be part of a target group on the down side of the power imbalance, Rich and I challenge you to join together with allies – people who support you – and never stop speaking out. What may be too scary to attempt alone becomes possible when you have the support of other people.

All over the United States and various parts of the world, Challenge Day graduates and others are standing up against oppression. Throughout history, allies have stepped up for the rights of others. The Civil Rights Movement and the Women's Suffrage Movement are two examples. In addition to ours – Challenge Day and the Be the Change Movement – there are so many others: Generation *We*, The Peace Alliance, The Non-Violent Communication Group, Oakland Men's Project, The Pachimama Alliance, *One* campaign, Books Not Bars, Center For Attitudinal Healing, Be Present, Youth For Environmental Sanity, Friday Night Live, The Season for Non-Violence, The Peace Corps, and countless other groups and individuals who are making huge strides toward ending social and economic injustice.

Oppression: A Game That No One Wins

1. None of us were born negatively judging or oppressing others.
2. Oppression is a learned behavior.
3. Anything we learn, we can unlearn.

Be the Hero

It is often easier to become outraged by injustice half a world away than by oppression and discrimination half a block from home.

~ Carl T. Rowan

Notice

- Can you pinpoint any times in your life when you have been hurt or limited by oppression? What happened? Maybe, like me at the dance, you were humiliated in some way. How did you respond? How did the situation affect your life?

- Who in your life, if anyone, has abused or misused their power or influence over you? How have these experiences affected your perspective and attitudes?

- In your life today, are you involved in any relationships at school, at work, or at home where you are being hurt in some way? What, if anything, are you doing to change your situation?

- Would anyone say they feel oppressed by you? Could there be any ways in which you are abusing or misusing your privilege or power? Is there anyone whom you are taking for granted or maybe hurting in any way?

- Are there individuals or groups of people whom you negatively judge or talk about? If so, how do your beliefs and attitudes affect the way you treat those people?

- When you hear others making negative, racist, sexist, homophobic, or otherwise oppressive remarks or comments about individuals or groups of people, how are you most likely to respond? Do you laugh along, walk away, interrupt, or add to the separation?

- Do you consider yourself an ally to those who are oppressed? Do you stand up against oppression? Do you speak out against injustice? Do you stand for equality? Do you get people's backs? List the moments when you answered yes to these questions.

- Has anyone in your life ever been an ally for you? Maybe someone has stuck up for you, made sure you were included and welcomed as part of a group. How did it feel? How did it affect your relationship with that person? How did it affect they way you felt about *you*? Does that person or these people know what a difference they made for you? If not, why not?

- Have you ever stood and remained silent as you watched someone hurt or humiliate another person? If yes, did you want to do something about it? What stopped you? What were you most afraid would happen if you said or did something?

- What groups or cliques, if any, are you a part of? Are there unspoken "rules" you follow: expected behavior, things you wear that indicate you are a part of that group? If so, do you like those aspects, do you agree with them? How does it make you feel to be part of this group?

- Are there any groups or cliques that you are not a part of that you wish you could be? If yes, why? How would you be different if you were a part of that group?

Choose

- Of the times you've felt abused by someone exerting his or her power over you, what other outcome can you imagine?

Under what circumstances would it be possible for you to drop the waterline with someone and ask for help?

- If you have ever watched someone humiliate another, what would you do differently if it happened again?
- If you are oppressing others or abusing your power, list the ways in which you can change your behavior or make amends.
- If you are negatively judging people, how can you learn more about that person or group of people in order to change your beliefs? Imagine yourself in their shoes and journal how you feel about being judged.
- Review the times when you've noticed oppression and done nothing to stop it. Now list all the ways in which you could have changed the situation, either in the moment or afterward. Under what circumstances can you imagine speaking with either the person in power or the person being oppressed in order to help heal the situation?
- Instead of wishing you were part of a different social group, can you create the conditions in your life that make you feel accepted and loved? What would that look like?
- If you are part of a social group that has tendencies to exert its power over others, list all the ways in which you can help your friends notice and change their behavior.

Act

- Make a list of all the areas in your life where you have power and influence over others. If you notice there are places and people with whom you've abused your power or taken people for granted, do what you can to rectify the situation or situations.

- Make amends with the people to whom you've been cruel, unfair, or mean. Apologize to those you've hurt by doing nothing in the face of oppression.
- The next time you make a decision that may impact another person, check in with that person beforehand to find out how your decision might affect him or her.
- For at least the next 30 days, keep a "Break the Cycle" log or journal. At the end of each day, write down the instances of oppression you've noticed and describe what you did about it. Remember to be gentle with yourself – simply being conscious enough to *notice* is doing something.
- Become an ally for a group that has been a target of oppression. Find a way to directly share your support. Choose a cause. Make a difference. Educate yourself about how oppression affects them. Wherever possible, ask members of this group to share their experience. Take time really to listen.

Celebrate by sharing your victories!

Log on to www.challengeday.org and blog your acts of positive change on the Be the Change link.

Everyday Hero ~ Shereef Bishay

A bright light committed to love and integrity, Shereef speaks his truth and models what it means to live and love with all your heart. First introduced to Challenge Day by his cousin Cherine Badawi, a Challenge Day leader, Shereef decided to commit himself to leading Challenge Days shortly after the attacks of September 11, 2001, because he aspired to make a positive difference in the world around him.

Shereef has also been a successful business owner and computer consultant, and has a dream to integrate his Challenge Day training and experiences into workplaces and corporations all over the world. In addition to being a committed husband to his wife Jolana who is also a Challenge Day leader, Shereef has recently stepped into balancing the joys and demands of parenthood with his passion for Being the Change. He is currently part of the team launching the Be the Change Leadership and Training Institute.

Shereef

If you really knew me, you would know that as I write this I can hear my one-month-old son in the other room. I want to tell you his name, but first I want you to know that I didn't know whether or not to give him an Egyptian name. I wondered if, by the time he's old enough to understand, people will treat him differently because of his name.

If you really knew me, you would know that I immigrated to the States when I was 22. My plane touched down a few days after they re-opened the airports after the attacks of 9/11. I was scared that day. I remember being the only one picked out of the line and taken to an "interview" room. I remember being searched, yelled at, and accused. I had no idea what they would do to me, or when I would be allowed to leave.

If you really knew me, you would know that the first woman I dated after I came to the U.S., broke up with me after her mom met me. Her mom saw a movie about an Arab man who stole his wife's kids. I reminded her of him.

If you really knew me, you would know that for every person who has been scared, I've met dozens who have blown me away with their kindness. Every day, people surprise me with their generosity and basic goodness. I know in my heart that there is no such thing as a bad kid, no such thing as a bad person.

This is why we call our son Selim. It's because I trusted that by the time he can speak, by the time the two of you might meet, the world will be a kinder place. Full of tenderness. Full of peace. That's what Selim means.

If you really knew me, you would know that I trust you, and I love you, even though we might never meet. And I am grateful for the hero in you, the one who will not rest until the world is a better place for all of us. My son included.

Shereef and his son Selim

The Comfort Zone

Be willing to be uncomfortable. Be comfortable being uncomfortable. It may get tough, but it's a small price to pay for living a dream.

~ Peter McWilliams

Rich

If you really knew, me you'd know that when I was in high school, I traded my integrity for silence.

I had been friends with Albert since elementary school. He sat behind me in class and we regularly shared innocent laughter, number two pencils, and snacks from our lunchboxes.

Our lives took separate paths in junior high, but the summer before high school, we reestablished our bond through Boy Scouts. In matching khaki pants and shirts full of merit badges, we'd follow each other through the forest trails and camp out with the rest of our troop under the stars. We'd all sit around evening campfires and recite the Scout Oath, "To help other people at all times; to keep myself physically strong, mentally awake, and morally straight."

On one of our camping trips, Albert and I were sitting at the edge of the lake sharing life stories. I was complaining about my dad, expressing the pressure I always felt from him, how hard I tried but how much I felt like a failure. I trusted Albert with my deepest thoughts and feelings. He was always such a good listener. Despite how different we were on the outside, on the inside we shared similarities that made me feel understood and supported.

On this particular day, Albert decided to trust me with his deepest secret. Like me, he said that he felt pressure to be someone he wasn't. He felt split between the person he *really* was and the person he had to pretend he was. And then he told me that he was gay.

It wasn't that much of a surprise to me. And it also didn't matter because I'd had an experience of Albert as being a good person and a good friend. I felt an immediate sense of compassion for him. I could feel his shame. Regardless of our circumstances, we both felt lonely, judged, and afraid. We were both imposters in our own lives, with bottled-up hurts hidden inside our secret worlds.

When high school started, Albert and I found ourselves in the same history class. We became partners on reports and school projects. When the class ended, we would see each other sometimes after school. I was on the football team and he often attended our games.

Then one day as I left the gym, I noticed two of my teammates harassing another student. "Fat-ass faggot!" they shouted as they shoved him against the lockers.

I could see the bullied student trapped between my teammates. It was Albert. He looked up at me with pain and anticipation in his eyes. I stood there, frozen. Then, I quickly looked away and kept walking as my friends continued to torment him.

I was so ashamed for not having the courage to stop my teammates and stand up for Albert that I began avoiding him. I'd look the other way if I saw him coming. Whenever I walked into a room, I'd scan the crowd to make sure he wasn't in it. I had unconsciously chosen my membership in a group over my friendship with Albert. I wasn't willing to jeopardize my place in the circle. That was my "comfort zone." I wasn't willing to stop trying to please other people and make choices that were right for me. I wasn't willing to help someone else at the risk of possibly targeting myself. The moral code I said I'd live by in Boy Scouts had been betrayed in a second. Afraid to make waves, my comfort zone became a place to hide. For the next three years, Albert and I lost complete contact with each other.

Then one day during my senior year, I heard some news that rocked my world.

Albert had attempted suicide. He couldn't bear the daily harassment and homophobic remarks any longer. As the rumors swept through the school, all I could think about was that moment in front of the lockers when I let him down. I was horrified to think I may have been part of the reason Albert had wanted to die. I wondered how things might have been different for him if I had found the courage to speak up.

For the next two weeks, he was constantly on my mind. I looked for him everywhere but I never seemed to run into him. I kept playing over and over in my mind how my two friends Mark and Rick had stuck up for me in junior high when I was being harassed. They protected me, and there were times when their friendship felt like it literally kept me alive. I had failed to give Albert the same gift. The safety I thought I had found while living inside my "comfort zone" of silence had actually caused a part of me to die. And I could no longer bear the guilt and shame.

I discovered that he had Spanish class before lunch, and so I sat on the bench outside his class waiting for it to end. Nearly an hour went by and as each moment passed I was certain that he would never forgive me. In fact, I didn't have the right to be forgiven. But nonetheless, I had to face him and apologize.

Finally the bell rang and the doors opened and there he was, walking toward me. He was looking at his feet. My body flooded with fear as I stood up. I couldn't imagine what he was going to say to me.

Almost every part me wanted to turn and run, but the part of me that wanted to stay was the part that needed to make this right.

Time stood still. *What can I possibly say to him?* I thought. *There's no way on earth I can ever make this right.*

He finally looked up and met my eyes. And miraculously, he immediately softened. Without ever saying a word, he already understood my intention. A tear began to roll down his cheek. He was welcoming me and I felt as though I didn't deserve it.

I fumbled for words. "Man, I just stood there. All I can think about is that moment. You were my friend, and I just, I avoided you." I swallowed hard. "I am so sorry I let you down. I should have said something. I promise you, it will never happen again."

He nodded, his lip quivering. "I might have done the same thing if I were you." He wiped tears from his face. "But that moment wasn't the worst part. The worst part was losing you as a friend."

I was surprised by how quickly he was ready to forgive me. I had never experienced that before. Ever. And it stunned me. I made a commitment to him that he could trust me, that I would have his back no matter what. We reconfirmed our friendship and promised each other that from that day forward things would be different.

This experience woke me up to a place in myself that I had long before buried. I realized that a part of me had chosen to numb out to avoid hurt and disappointment. It seemed that the only way I could feel my feelings was when something big happened. I knew the only way to rediscover the real me and become the person I really wanted to be was to allow myself to feel again. As it turned out, this was the first of many times I would come face to face with this realization. Still, it felt good to be me. I'd finally stepped out of my comfort zone by facing my fears, and I felt exceedingly proud of myself for doing it. I was determined that I would no longer play it safe, and that I would look for opportunities to stand up for others who couldn't do it for themselves.

Live It!

**To the degree we're not living our dreams,
our comfort zone has more control over us
than we have over ourselves.**

~ Peter McWilliams

There's a big, over-stuffed chair in our family room. When I sink into it, it's like falling into a cloud in heaven. I can sit there for hours reading a good book, watching a movie, cuddling with Yvonne, playing with our grandson or just taking a nap. I love that chair. Why? Because it's comfortable.

We all need to feel safe, relaxed, and secure in a comfortable place. However, if we stay there, comfort can start to imprison us and keep us from being challenged, from learning, and from growing.

It is only when a lump of coal is subjected to tremendous heat and pressure that it becomes a diamond. By the same token, how can any of us truly know how far we can go unless we have the courage to risk?

So many of us don't. Instead, we live safely nestled in what we call the "comfort zone."

The comfort zone is like a little box where we do the same things repeatedly and for the most part unconsciously, day after day. Hanging out with the same people, wearing the same clothes, listening to the same music, eating the same foods we grew up with – whatever we do to play it safe is living in our comfort zone.

Like my overstuffed chair, our comfort zones are supposed to be places to rest and recharge. The sad reality, however, is that many people live their entire lives in these comfort zones and become trapped there.

Outside the comfort zone is where we meet new people, have the courage to live, to love big, to apologize, to forgive, to stand up for people, to dance, to sing out loud, to play, to be seen for who we truly are, and to try new things.

If you want to leave your mark and create a lasting legacy on this planet, you must first step outside your comfort zone and risk judgment or failure. And when you do, it's vital you remember that success isn't defined by getting what you want; success is being engaged in life in a way that makes you feel proud. Winning isn't in the *doing*, it's in the *being*.

When you can truly *be* who you are, everything you *do* will make a difference – whether you realize it or not.

One of the things we do at every Challenge Day is have people clasp their hands together. Go ahead and do that now. What you'll notice is that there is a particular way in which your fingers seem to fit into each other, one of your thumbs rests on top of the other, and it unconsciously feels "right." But now, clasp your hands the other way, with the other thumb on top. It feels weird, doesn't it? It's not wrong, it just feels weird. And it only feels weird because you haven't done it. At some point, when you were a baby, you clasped your hands together in comfort and that became the way your fingers seemed to fit perfectly. By doing what we call "switching your thumbs," you begin to stretch past old comforts and into new realities.

That's where stepping out of your comfort zone starts. It can be the smallest gesture. It can be saying hi to someone you've always wanted to talk to or being so bold as to ask someone out on a date. Whatever it is, are your actions automatic or are they conscious? When you are aware of what you're doing, are you merely surviving or are you thriving?

When I was able to step out of my comfort zone and face up to my friend Albert, I felt so proud of myself that the experience changed my life. I began a lifelong journey of looking for more and more ways to find my sense of freedom. Today my entire life is lived on the edge, outside my comfort zone, and teaching others how to live life 100% fully alive. At Challenge Day, we teach kids to risk being themselves. I can tell you firsthand that the rewards are many and great.

In fact, in order to create Challenge Day, Yvonne and I had to live way outside our comfort zones. We thought that we might be seen as weird or crazy, we thought we might be isolated and shut down. And by some, we were. We expected to be judged since all leaders are judged. As Yvonne likes to say, it's a sign of visibility and courage. But thankfully today most people judge us as role models, heroes, and mentors, specifically because we are willing to risk, and step out of our comfort zones. At the end of each day, we know our lives are making a difference.

Now it's your turn. We challenge you to risk being and doing things differently. Have the courage to step outside your comfort zone and be a leader. Who knows, perhaps you'll inspire others to join you.

Thoughts On Emotional Risk Taking

1. Clasp your hands the other way for encouragement. Stepping out of your comfort zone might feel unnatural but it isn't "wrong," it simply means you have the courage to risk living life on your own terms.

2. Begin to differentiate between positive and negative comforts by recognizing if your sense of safety makes you internally feel trapped and limited, or if it makes you feel expansive and alive. Go in the direction that inspires and moves you.

3. Don't get halted by fear. Focus on who you want to be and not on how another person might judge you.

4. As you step outside your comfort zone, remember to be gentle with you. Risk taking can require great courage. Celebrate every positive step.

5. Don't evaluate success by the outcome. You win by living your life in a way that makes you feel proud.

Be the Hero

**There is no passion to be found playing small –
in settling for a life that is less than the one
you are capable of living.**

~ Nelson Mandela

Notice

- How has the "comfort zone" affected your life? Where do you play it safe, hide out or avoid taking risks? When was the last time you risked being uncomfortable? What were the results?

- In what ways do you play it safe or hide in your relationships with others – your family, friends, parents, classmates, teachers, siblings, partner? Do you hold back from being more intimate and "getting real?" Why? Do you ever just "go along" to please others? Do you ever say yes when you really mean no? And if yes, are any of these recurring patterns in your relationships?

- Are there places in your life where you have remained silent when you wish had spoken up? Have you ever stood by and watched when someone else was being hurt, humiliated or negatively judged? What was the cost of your silence or inaction?

- In what ways do you limit or hold yourself back from pursuing your dreams? Have you ever wished you could visit another country, try a new sport, learn a new dance, sing a song in front of an audience, or do something you didn't have the courage to do? What gets in your way?

- Do you consider yourself a risk taker? Are their certain areas of life where you live big? If so, why do you think that is and how does it make you feel?

- Are you living your life 100% fully alive? Are you living a life that you love and loving the life you live? Are you proud of yourself every day? If not, what's stopping you?

Choose

- In your observations of the ways in which you play it safe, how can you imagine doing it differently? If you could erase your limitations and inhibitions, who would you be?

- Imagine yourself living the life of your dreams. How are you different from the person you are now? What risks would like to take? How would you be in your relationships? How would you spend your days? In what ways can you imagine stepping outside of your comfort zones in order to bring you closer to the life you really want?

- If you could stop playing it safe in your relationships, what are some things you would change about the ways in which you interact? Do you have specific roles you tend to fill with certain people or as part of certain groups? Can you imagine sharing more truths, including expressing your true yes's and no's? Are you ready to let go of any "people pleasing" tendencies you might have fallen into, and how can you stop the cycle?

- If there are places in your life where you have been silent and you wished you had spoken up, how would you write a different ending? Do you owe anyone an apology? In the places you have felt there have been wrongs – either done by you or to you – what are the ways you can envision things being made right?

- Are there any new healthy risks you'd be willing to take? Any new goals you want to go after? What needs to transpire in order for you to get it?

- Perhaps you have friends and family members who seem trapped in their comfort zone. How can you commit yourself to be an ally and support them? How can you make a pact to join with them in taking healthy risks and living 100% fully alive?

Act

- Review your vision for the 100% life of your dreams. Choose a plan of action in which you risk achieving big and small goals. Start by taking at least one positive risk each day over the next week. Blow people away. Surprise yourself and others with your courage. Take special note of what you feel about yourself and how others respond to your actions.

- Give yourself and others the gift of speaking out against the injustice and mistreatment of others. The next time you see or hear someone being hurt or put down, take the risk of intervening. Or if it's already happened, express your support to the person who has been targeted and gently express your point of view to the person who has been the perpetrator. You might be surprised by how it makes you feel to become an ally or resource to someone else.

- Identify at least one person to help keep you accountable. Share your goals and commitments with someone whom you trust will support you in maintaining your commitments.

- Host a vision board party. Get together with friends and family to support each other in creating a vision of living your life 100%. Have people bring favorite magazines, art materials, scissors, paste, and other supplies. Once the group is finished, make time for each person to describe what they put on their vision board and why. Challenge your friends and family to join you in living 100% fully alive! Share your board with everyone you believe will help hold you to it. Finally, be sure to place your vision board in a prominent place where you will see it every day.

Celebrate!

Journal, share your successes with others, dance, proclaim your place in the world, and log onto the Be the Change website to blog about the miracles you've experienced www.challengeday.org/bethechange.

Everyday Hero ~ Jon Gordon

Raised in a deeply supportive home, Jon has committed his life to passing his blessings onto others. A graduate of St. Mary's College in Moraga, California, Jon went on to play professional soccer, which further supported his commitment to being a "team" player. Jon consistently looks for opportunities to lift up and empower those around him.

Prior to becoming a Challenge Day leader, Jon lived and worked in an orphanage in Mexico City, and returned to the United States and began work in a group home with teens who had been labeled as emotionally disturbed. Currently he serves as a Senior Challenge Day leader, and is an invaluable part of the organization's training and coaching department.

Jon

If you really knew me, you would know how humble I feel every day to be allowed to do this work. I grew up with strongly instilled beliefs about the ways in which we treat each other, and being respectful and accepting. I consider myself quite lucky to be in the family that I am in, and, through Challenge Day, I feel as though I am continuing the work that my parents and many others began long before me. There are many others who are working with us in this struggle, my sister and brother, our teachers, social workers, volunteers, doctors, and countless others. I'm just one of the lucky ones who gets to do it while wearing a cool red Challenge Day t-shirt, and running around a gym with more than a hundred teenagers and adults.

As an athlete, it is especially important for me to show that even in the competitive world of sports, these messages that I learned growing up of standing against oppression, and being true to yourself and open about your feelings, remain as relevant today. One of my favorite parts of Challenge Day is that it doesn't matter who you are, or what clique you associate yourself with, the program speaks to all of us.

If you really knew me, you'd know that I often have a difficult time explaining what it is that I do for a living. The answer changes depending on who I'm speaking with, but it usually involves a cheesy joke. For me, telling people about what Challenge Day does is vulnerable. As a man, the messages still ring in my head about what I "should be doing" and how I "should be acting." Even so, the moments that I am lucky enough to witness in these rooms doing Challenge Day, make it all worthwhile. There are countless stories. For now, I will leave you with this… During a Challenge Day recently, a young girl revealed some incredibly serious, unspeakable things that were occurring in her life. The school stepped in, and we were able to get her the support that she deserved. A couple of days later, this incredible counselor asked her why she never said anything. The girl said, "Nobody ever asked me."

That's why I do this job.

The F-Word

The world is changing and the physical barriers are down now. It's time for the emotional barriers to go down. And what better place to start than school?

~ Laura San Giacomo

Yvonne

If you really knew me, you'd know that all the hopelessness, helplessness, desperation, fear, shame, heartache, loneliness, and self-hatred that I experienced in my youth was *absolutely* worth the journey. My greatest victory is that I met myself at my center – in the eye of the storm – and I guided myself to safety. Like the alchemist who turns metal into gold, I transformed my pain into strength. And retracing my steps in order to show other people the way, has become my life's work.

One night, a few weeks after returning home from the psychiatric hospital, I woke up out of a sound sleep and found myself sitting up in bed. I could have sworn I heard someone talking. I turned on the light and looked around. I was alone. The clock read 3 a.m. I sat quietly for a moment, still half asleep. Although I never had any interest in writing before, I felt a strange compulsion to start. It seemed as though something had awakened inside me and now longed for expression.

I scrambled out of bed and collected a pen and some paper. Ready for the words to flow, I stared at the blank sheet, waiting. Nothing happened. I began arguing out loud with the voice that had awakened me, "You woke me up, now what?" And then, realizing that I was talking to myself, "Maybe I should still be in the loony bin."

Then, in an instant, it seemed as if a light blinked on. I could barely keep up with my thoughts as I wrote.

I saw myself as a child at a time when I was completely adored. In my earliest memories, I played with abandon, I believed in magic, and I dreamed that I could save the world. In fact, I *knew* that I'd come here specifically to change the world.

What happened?

I remembered that in the moments I felt hurt or sad or angry, I cried – but I cried with my entire body and with a no-holds-barred intensity as if my life depended on doing it: shaking, convulsing, kicking, screaming, and completely releasing every last drop of emotion. I remembered that when I did that, I eventually stopped. And then, like the sun bursting through the clouds, I felt better. Somehow, unleashing the storm was healing.

Throwing a childhood tantrum was exactly what I'd done in the hospital, and it was the first experience of healing I'd had since childhood; it was the first time I realized that I'm still here, I'm buried in emotion and crap, but I'm in here.

So what happened?

If powerfully releasing strong emotions is the way to heal, why did I ever stop doing it? …Because, like everyone else, at a certain age I was told in a variety of ways that it was wrong and bad. I was told to stop; I was called a baby; I was supposed to be tough; I was supposed to grow up.

I put my pen down. "OH MY GOD!" I shouted. And then, because it was still only 3 a.m., more quietly, "I am not broken and I am not crazy. I just have too many emotions that haven't been allowed to get out." I was so full of unexpressed emotions that I was like a balloon ready to pop. Despite trying to hold all my feelings inside, they'd leak out all over the place in unhealthy ways – onto people I loved and everyone else around me. I'd gotten to the point where I didn't know how to keep from "popping" without killing myself. But dying was the easy out I couldn't choose.

I was connecting the dots, and they weren't just mine.

"Everyone feels this way!" I said, still talking to myself. "Everyone feels insane, everyone feels trapped inside themselves, and everyone feels all alone."

I kept going.

Does anyone have a healthy family? Does anyone get to express their emotions? And is it really just that easy? I knew that obviously, we can't all just fall to the floor and lose control at any moment, so I wondered how grown-ups could have healthy tantrums. And then I imagined that if we created a world in which it was safe to express all of our emotions, *all of them*, we'd never be able to walk up to someone else and hurt them or kill them.

I was onto something. It excited me.

"We know how to do this," I said. "All of us were born with the ability to heal ourselves. We just forgot."

What I learned most powerfully in the hospital was that nobody outside of me was going to fix me. Initially I was disappointed about that, but now I was ignited.

Live It!

There is sacredness in tears. They are not a mark of weakness, but of power. They speak more eloquently than ten thousand tongues. They are the messengers of overwhelming grief, of deep contrition, and unspeakable love.

~ Washington Irving

As the weeks and months unfolded, I realized more and more that I was *not* crazy, or if I was, I was no crazier than anyone else *and* it was curable. As I began to explore and to understand what had happened to me emotionally, I gave birth to the "F-Word" lesson. By "F-Word," I'm referring to the eight-letter version – F-E-E-L-I-N-G-S – particularly those emotions that so many of us are taught not to feel, talk about, or show. Rich and I believe that many of society's problems, and much individual suffering, is the result of the consequences of the F-Word.

Until we were taught otherwise, as children we were totally open and free, and totally alive. We would often walk up to complete strangers and say hello or ask them if they wanted to play. We all once lived our young lives fully expressed, and we instinctively knew how to communicate our feelings. We screamed and cried, laughed hysterically with wide-eyed wonder, and became so full of love and excitement we would jump for joy. We didn't stop to think about whether we looked cool or weird, we just let our emotions out.

Also, as young children, when we fell down and scratched a knee, in a few days it would heal. Usually the only thing left from the scratch was a story to tell, perhaps a scar, but the pain always went away.

Rich and I believe the same thing is true about feelings – that everyone is born knowing how to heal. But then, at some point, we are taught not to talk about or show our feelings. Most of us heard some version of, "Grow-up! Don't be a baby. Stop crying or I will give you something to cry about!" This is true no matter how wonderful our families may have been. At one level or another, we were taught that our feelings aren't cool or even acceptable. The lessons come from everywhere – family, friends, school, and television.

In our work with young people, Rich and I always ask, "In what ways were you taught to keep your feelings inside?" They invariably spew out a litany of phrases that were drilled into their heads, "Children should be seen and not heard!" "Don't wear your feelings on your sleeve!" "What's said in this house stays in this house!" "Don't let them know it hurts you or they'll use it against you." "What will the neighbours think?" Many young people tell us that they were hit, slapped, or even beaten to get them to stop expressing their feelings. For some, the messages are more subtle. Although never directly told that their feelings were bad or wrong, they rarely witnessed the adults in their lives – their role models – openly expressing themselves.

Young men in particular are bombarded with messages that tell them "real men" should be tough and not show their emotions. You know the script. Grow up! Be a man! Big boys don't cry! Suck it up! Don't be a sissy! And, worst of all, don't act like a girl!

As we move through childhood and adolescence, the lessons never stop. By the time we become adults, the words have changed but the message is the same: be professional; be in charge; don't ever let them see you sweat; have all the answers; stay in control; and worst of all, don't act like a child.

Much of this training comes from the best of intentions. As parents, we love our children so much that we would do almost anything to take away their pain. This is why we try to stop our children from crying. But what if it isn't our job to keep our children from feeling the aches that inevitably come from living? What if the highest form of love is for a parent or caretaker to hold space for children as they dive deeply into the well of their emotions, knowing that this is part of their journey?

The way out of pain is to go into it, feel it completely, and come out the other side. I call this "following the thread in." At Challenge Day, we've learned that any feeling, including the deepest emotional pain, will shift when it is actually felt, all you need to do is follow it as it leads you more deeply into yourself. When we stop people from crying, we may be denying them this opportunity.

Though well-meaning adults usually don't *intend* to inflict emotional pain, they often still do. Have you ever heard something like, "You think you have it bad? When I was your age, I had to – *blah, blah, blah.*" Messages such as these imply that your pain is not as bad as somebody else's, and therefore it doesn't count. It's another way of saying, "Stuff it!"

It's not just negative feelings we have been taught to hide, but positive ones as well. Has anyone ever told you to be quiet and keep it together when you were ecstatically happy, excited, or laughing loudly? Were you ever told that if you celebrated yourself too much you were conceited or had a big head? Do you see how this works? So many of us were taught that we were not enough and, *at the same time*, we were told that we were too much! The solution was to become like robots. Don't show too much love, too much joy, too much excitement, or too much happiness. Don't be sad, don't grieve, don't be angry.

So many of us were taught that if we feel strong emotions something is clearly wrong with us. We learn how we are supposed to feel, to think, and to be, and what we need to do in order to be accepted. We are taught that if we don't listen to these messages, we might come across as one of those touchy-feely types – too sensitive, too loving, too nice.

As someone who should know better, I was always disappointed when I caught myself squashing the joy or excitement of my kids, purely out of habit. I will never forget the look of confusion and shame in my daughter's eyes on her fifth birthday when her friends arrived and she came running into my room screaming, "They're here, they're here!" Without thinking, I shouted back, "Be Quiet! Calm Down!"

Later, I wondered, why would I do that? Then I remembered that if I had come yelling and running through my house as a kid, the same thing would have happened to me. Without realizing it, I was perpetuating a cycle.

The Balloon

Feelings don't simply disappear if we choose not to express them. Instead, they get shoved deep inside, into a place Rich and I call the "balloon." We find this metaphor useful because balloons are flexible and they can endure a lot. However, if filled beyond capacity, balloons eventually pop.

My own journey is the perfect example. As a child, I was really close to my grandparents, especially my grandpa. When I was with him, nothing else mattered. My family used to call me "grandpa's shadow" because I followed him everywhere. I knew he loved me and I just wanted to be with him.

One day in junior high, we found out grandpa had cancer. Shortly after the diagnosis, he died. I was devastated. At his funeral, for one day, everyone cried, even the men. But from that day on, I never saw anyone grieve about my grandpa being gone.

I didn't want my mom to know how sad I was because it was her dad, and I thought my feelings would make her even more sad. So, for countless days after his death I would hide in my room all alone and blow my grief into my balloon. I'm sure my mom and the rest of the family did the same with their emotions.

In addition to all the sadness I was feeling about my grandfather's death, I remember looking in the mirror every day and hating what I saw – my pimples, my belly, my hair. I felt fat, ugly, and different from everyone else. I thought I was the only one who felt the way I did. I didn't know what to do with my emotions, so I blew them all into my balloon.

When I was humiliated or rejected in junior high, I added all those feelings of confusion, anger, and outrage to my balloon. In high school came addiction, sexuality, peer pressure with alcohol and drugs. I was accepted into the "popular" club and then rejected for being conceited. I had to begin to think about college, and to decide what to do with the rest of my life. All of that, and more, went unexpressed, stuffed into my balloon. I was trying to hold a lifetime of feelings so deeply inside that eventually I just wanted to die.

Full Balloons Can Be Deadly

My story is not unique. So many of us are walking around with huge balloons full of unfelt feelings, hurtful memories, and tension from unresolved experiences.

And just like real balloons, they eventually pop.

If we don't know how to express our feelings in healthy, positive ways, we can actually die from the F-Word. Medical research shows that lack of emotional expression can morph into stress, sickness, dis-ease, addiction, and even violence. Two of the most common ways young people die are through suicide and murder. When any of us attempts or succeeds in killing ourselves, we are essentially saying, "My balloon hurts so much, I'm just going to pop it myself."

Violence and mass murders on school campuses are a reflection of the silent suffering of far too many young people who never learned how to empty their balloons in a positive way. Lost and alone, often bullied, abused, or shunned entirely, they act out of desperation and pain.

Statistically, men tend to die at a much younger age than women. Could this be because men have less social permission to feel and emote? When men learn to be tough, to suck up their feelings and tears, the results can literally be lethal.

Perhaps you know someone who is dying to let his or her feelings out. Maybe you're one of them.

Leaking Balloons

In reality, our balloons don't pop right away. They are surprisingly strong. As our balloons get bigger and bigger, they begin to leak, much in the same way that air can leak out of a real balloon. The most common ways our emotional balloons leak is in the form of yelling and screaming, teasing, hurting, or otherwise lashing out at other people. Sadly, our feelings tend to leak out primarily on the people we love the most and on those who are closest to us, including family, friends, teachers, and co-workers. If you are a parent or a teacher, sometimes your balloon will leak out on your own children and students.

If you really knew me, you would know that even though I teach this lesson regularly, I still sometimes find my balloon leaking, mostly on Rich or the people closest to me. This practice of emptying my balloon takes commitment. It's a never-ending process.

Numbing Out

To those of us trained to "read" feelings as they leak out, it becomes clear that these are signs of a balloon filled beyond capacity. Anyone whose feelings are leaking out is unconsciously saying, "These feelings hurt too much!" For young people, they may also be saying, "If the adults knew how I was feeling, I mean *really* feeling, they would probably be scared to death, or they'd get angry at me, or they'd tell me to get over it. So I'm going to have to figure out a way to deal with these feelings by hiding them or avoiding them completely."

During every Challenge Day we hear students openly share that they smoke, drink, sleep around, do drugs, or gamble. They feel addicted to shopping sprees, texting their friends, watching television, and playing video games. They join gangs, fight, steal, hide in their rooms, or go off all alone. It is frightening to hear that they regularly tease and bully other kids, and that they consider or even attempt suicide. Though our society teaches that young people who engage in such behaviors are "bad," Rich and I fervently disagree. We believe they just haven't learned how to let the emotions out of their balloons.

Fix This Bad Kid!

Parents looking for support with their kids often call our office. They say things like, "I hear young people really trust you a lot, and I need help with my son or daughter." Or, "Would you please tell me what I need to do to fix this bad kid!"

We understand how helpless adults might feel when their kids are running away from home or thinking about suicide. They see their children eating a lot, not eating at all, or eating and throwing up; their kids don't talk to them anymore; they see scars from cuts or burns on their teenagers' skin; they smell smoke or alcohol on their clothes or breath. To us, these are all clear indicators of young people with balloons about to burst. They are trying their best to deal with all the feelings and emotions they carry around, usually all alone.

These young people are unconsciously holding up a great big sign that says,

I don't know how to say this, but please help me and my family!

We don't agree with the idea that their "acting out" means that they are bad kids. They are not saying, "I want to be judged, kicked out of my home, sent to a different school, or become a statistic in the juvenile court system." And they for sure don't want to be told, "If it wasn't for you, this family would be fine!" They are saying, however, "Help me deal with these feelings that I carry with me every second of my life," and they are also often saying, "Help my family!" Because if one of us has a problem, no matter how small, we all have a problem.

Positive Ways To Empty Our Balloons

Rich and I developed Challenge Day because young people – and in fact *all* people – need to relearn and to practice emptying their balloons in positive and safe ways. Since as children we innately understood that expressing feelings helped them heal, we wondered what would happen if we allowed our child-wisdom to endure. Our goal has been to re-establish a culture that encourages everyone to cry, to express, and to open up, rather than hide, repress feelings, and pretend to be tough.

In our experience, many young people *do* know how to empty their balloons. When we ask them to give positive, safe examples, they offer many brilliant ideas. The most popular include talking to someone they trust, singing, or allowing their feelings to flow while listening to or playing music. Students often share that they play sports, exercise, journal, write poetry, go to counseling, dance, laugh, play, scream, shout, hit pillows, pray, meditate, do art, or perform drama. All of these activities support them in releasing their feelings in healthy, non-destructive ways.

These techniques do not apply just to young people. We all need to learn how to deal with releasing our emotions fully, and in healthy ways. No one is immune to the F-Word.

Dealing with Anger

Most of us know what it's like to act from a place of anger. When we do, however, we often regret it. Imagine how different our world would be if we had safe ways to release our anger before we blew up.

For example, when I'm angry, I like to hit pillows. It is so satisfying to hear the intense "pop" of the tennis racket hitting the bed while I allow my feelings to explode out of my balloon. Sometimes I find a place where I can scream or cry, or I ask a friend to hold me. I have also kicked cardboard boxes; that works particularly well. I'm willing to do whatever it takes to get my feelings out so they don't leak out onto my kids, Rich, or anyone else! I like to think of it as having a "feelings storm." The goal is, as in nature, to unleash all the "bad weather" until the dark clouds pass and the sunshine returns.

I often wonder how governments would function if politicians found appropriate ways to release their emotions. I imagine how different our world might be if they retreated to their offices, took time to breathe, and then released their anger on pillows or boxes, instead of taking it out on each other and the rest of the world.

One of the best ways we've found to help people release anger is through a tool we describe in Chapter 11.

Tears are Strength, not Weakness

Tears are a birthright. They are an invaluable tool that is part of our humanity. If we have the courage to allow them to flow, our tears can cleanse us throughout our entire lives. At Challenge Day, we teach that when tears are on the outside, the inside is healing and the heart is opening up.

I have found that when I grieve, my tears are similar to waves; they rush in and then they dissipate; they crash onto the shores of my consciousness and then foam away.

We believe that when we cry we *do not* fall apart; we actually fall together.

Tears emerge from lots of experiences, not just sadness and grief. Think about it. Have you ever cried when you felt ecstatic joy, connection, or love? Have you ever cried while watching a movie, witnessing your team win, or listening to a favorite song? We cry not only at funerals, but also at births; not only at divorces, but also at weddings; not only from losses, but also from victories. Have you ever laughed so hard you cried, or cried so hard you laughed?

When we feel our feelings fully, we not only change our entire vibration, but afterwards we *think* more clearly. No wonder so many kids are having such a difficult time in school. It is hard to think when we are bursting with suppressed emotions. Expressing our feelings is a fundamental and necessary part of our humanity.

Those who do not know how to weep with their whole heart don't know how to laugh either.

~ Golda Meir

The "F-Word" in Short

1. Each of us is born fully expressed – from laughter to tears we hold nothing back. Our full expression gives us the natural ability to feel joy, and to release and heal our emotional pains.

2. Society teaches us to keep our feelings inside. This is unnatural and unhealthy.

3. The emotional balloon is the place people store unexpressed feelings.

4. When our emotional balloons are overly full, they often tend to "pop" or at the very least "leak" on the people closest to us.

5. In an attempt to protect ourselves from emotional pain and discomfort, many of us choose instead to "numb out" in self-destructive ways.

6. Young people and others who numb themselves out or act out their pain are often labelled as "bad" or told there is something wrong with them.

7. Emotional health, personal freedom and real connection come only when we find positive and dependable ways to empty our emotional balloons and fully express the depths of who we are.

Be the Hero

The best and most beautiful things in the world cannot be seen, nor touched... but are felt in the heart.

~ Helen Keller

Notice

- Are you comfortable expressing your emotions? Are you comfortable being with the emotions of others? If not, what do you think gets in the way?

- Do you live and express yourself 100%? Like a child, do you laugh out loud, play, sing, and dance? Do you express your feelings of love, joy, happiness, excitement, and bliss? If not, why not? Where did you learn to hold back?

- When others are dancing, laughing, playing, or expressing their happiness, how does it make you feel? What do you tend to do with those feelings? Do you join in?

- Are you comfortable with what some would call our more "challenging" feelings including sadness, fear, grief, and anger? If not, why not? How do you handle these emotions – in yourself and in others?

- As you notice your feelings – how you express yourself and what you hold back – what emotions have you blown inside your balloon? How have these unexpressed feelings affected your life and relationships?

- Does your emotional balloon ever leak on the people around you? Have you ever hurt someone with your anger, pent-up emotions, or silence? Has anyone's balloon of emotions ever leaked on you?

- Are there ways you find yourself protecting or numbing out your emotions? How do these habits or behaviors affect your life and relationships?
- Do you have people or places in your life where you feel safe to fully express your emotions and to be who you are? If so, who are those people and what is your relationship to them? Do you consider yourself a safe place for others to express themselves?

Choose

- Imagine yourself being totally free to express the full range of your emotions. What do you see yourself doing? How have you held yourself back in the past and how can you rewrite those moments? When you first imagine a different way to express yourself, you can then consider expressing yourself differently in the moment. Spend time dreaming about your full self and the freedom that comes with you being you in every moment.
- If you can, close your eyes and imagine going inside your body. Start with your feet and move up very slowly. Can you imagine that there are trapped emotions in your muscles and organs and bones? Where might you feel that you've stored these emotions and filled yourself up like a balloon? See if you can discover ways in which your body can release the emotions – dancing, running, yelling, or otherwise.
- If you have noticed that your relationships with people have been affected by your stored emotions, are there ways you can imagine changing your behavior in the future or

talking with that person (or someone else) about creating a different connection?

- Imagine a totally safe haven in which you fully express yourself. Now imagine inviting the person or people who feel safe to you into that space. Then dream about what you will say or do in that safe space with those safe people.

- Imagine yourself being a source of safety for someone. Who would you choose to invite into your safety zone so that that person can release his or her feelings? What would that other person say or do, and how would you react?

Act

- After you have dreamed about healthy choices to express yourself fully, make a list of those that you can and will commit to doing as a way of emptying your emotional balloon. Post your list as a daily reminder to express your emotions. Music can be a powerful tool. Make a playlist of songs that help you feel. Use your list to help you keep your balloon as empty as possible.

- For at least the next thirty days, practice paying close attention to any ways you perpetuate society's messages that you or others should keep their feelings inside. Once you notice the old attitude or behavior, choose an alternative that invites healthy, full expression. For example, you can change the phase "don't be a baby" to "it's okay to cry."

- Approach one person that you have "leaked" your emotions onto, apologize to that person for having done so, and ask him or her to help you recognize if it happens again.

- Find one person whom you trust to be your safe haven. Share this chapter of the book with them and ask them to help you co-create new forms of expression for yourself and each other.
- Find one person and be the safe haven for them. It can be the same person who is your safe haven.
- Attend personal growth workshops such as Challenge Day or Next Step to Being the Change. These and other workshops can help you open up and reclaim the full expression of your emotions.

Remember to Celebrate!

Everyday Hero ~ Kris Carlson

Like few people we've ever met, Kris is a living example of courage and vulnerability. A gifted and passionate woman, Kris spent most of her early adulthood partnered with her best friend Richard Carlson. Together, Kris and Richard created a life of love and connection that served as a model to friends, as well as to millions of readers with whom they shared their stories around the world. *Don't Sweat the Small Stuff* became more than the title of their book series; it became a way of life.

Then, in December of 2006, Richard unexpectedly died of an aneurysm, throwing Kris's life and the lives of their two daughters, Jazzy and Kenna, into a tailspin full of devastation and grief. Courageously, Kris reached out for support, and dove head first into the agony of her pain and loss. The extraordinary void allowed her to feel her deepest aches while finding the strength to move through the ensuing challenges with unprecedented grace.

A committed mother and friend, Kris has continued to move forward in her work as a bestselling author, and to inspire all of us to love fully in the moment through her book *An Hour to Live, An Hour to Love*. Kris's journey into herself, and the gifts she continues to share with the world, are nothing short of heroic.

Kris

If you really knew me, you would know that we had it all; we were the Hollywood version of the perfect family. Richard and I met in college, fell in love immediately, and built a life together sharing our love and relationship with two amazing daughters. Then, after twenty-five years, it was suddenly over. Richard died at fifty thousand feet, and in that moment it was like I was tossed out of the airplane with my only parachute being my faith in life and love. Gripped by a tsunami of grief, I didn't have a choice that Richard died, but my choice was in how I moved forward.

Having been blessed with amazing friends like Rich and Yvonne, and many others, I had a tremendous amount of community support, and Rich and Yvonne, practically neighbors, were always ready to support me and hold my space as I grieved. I had served on the Board of Directors of Challenge Day, and both Richard and I served on the Global Leadership council. I attended many Challenge Days, Next Step workshops, and participated in many Board Retreats. All of this, along with the work that

Everyday Hero ~ Kris Carlson

Richard brought to the world, and much earlier inner work I had done, now seems like it was preparation to teach me how to dive into my grief process. Ironically, years earlier while attending Next Step, I said in a circle that I had nothing to cry about – life was good. I even asked Yvonne once if she could teach me "vulnerability."

Heartbroken, I lay spread eagle on the floor as my balloon filled, and the feelings inside built to a crescendo. I screamed a primal scream of death and surrender as my arms and legs flailed wildly like a fish out of water on the floor. My heart pounded as I gasped for air, and then as the wave began to subside and take me to shore, I felt an opening. As I learned to fully embrace grief and all the feelings, the expression of those feelings became a pathway of love out of my abyss of sorrow. Grief is an undeniable response to loss but has the power to heal all our wounds if we have the courage to feel our feelings, and cry our tears of sweet surrender. Then, something akin to bliss comes as we feel to heal.

The Gift of Listening

**Listening is an attitude of the heart, a genuine desire
to be with another which both attracts and heals.**

~ J. Isham

Rich

When I first met Yvonne, I didn't share her certainty that we were destined to be together. What I did know, however, was that her embracing, full smile and her clear, blue eyes captivated me. I wasn't just taken by her extraordinary beauty, I also found her to be one of the most profound human beings I had ever met. When she spoke about her vision for the world, her philosophies on life and parenting, and most of all her love of young people, her face lit up and, in fact, the entire room buzzed with her electricity. Even though she was only five feet three inches tall, she seemed larger than life to me. The wisdom in her words built a bridge from her heart to mine. She was clearly a mirror for my own dreams and philosophies, and it seemed I had found my professional match.

"You're hired," I said, not long after I'd met her.

"What do you mean?" she replied. "I'm not even looking for a job."

"I'd love you to do some training with our staff and work with me to run our new support group. Why don't you think about it for a couple of days?"

Less than a week later, our destiny began to unfold.

Before long, we were falling in love.

Though I've always been a talker, when I became a counselor I also took great pride in listening. Yvonne, however, took the art of listening to a whole new level. She would look deeply into my eyes and ask probing questions. At one point, she asked me to share my entire life story. Not sure how much to tell or if she'd really be interested, I started with surface things like, "I was born in Oakland, and I have one brother and one sister…." But as I spoke, her compassionate gaze invited me to go deeper into myself.

"What else?" she said every time I paused. Her eyes were always completely fixed on mine, encouraging me to continue.

My heart melted in her presence. Yvonne was so good at coaxing me inward that I was actually able to discover places inside myself that I had never explored. Very few people in my life had ever asked how I was really feeling, let alone took the time to listen.

I can't say how long I spoke without interruption or how many times Yvonne encouraged me to continue. What I do know is that when I was with her I felt like the most important person on the planet. Never before had I felt so seen and heard.

"Listening is the best gift any of us can ever give another person," she would say. "And it doesn't even cost a penny."

I was so hungry to be heard that I hardly noticed how out of balance our conversations had become.

It wasn't long into our relationship that I woke up to the fact that Yvonne knew much more about me than I did about her. I desperately wanted to learn how to listen as well as she did, and when I asked her why she was such a great listener, her response blew me away!

"They like you when you talk," she said. "But they love you when you listen."

If you really knew me, you'd know that although I can be an excellent listener, it takes practice for me to stay awake and to be conscious of how well I am really listening. Sometimes I have to remind myself simply to *listen*, not to wait for someone to stop talking so that I can answer, offer coaching, or share my point of view.

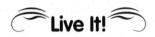

Live It!

The first duty of love is to listen.

~ Paul Tillich

Yvonne and I believe that "feeling heard" is the single most important aspect of any healthy relationship. Respectful, compassionate listening can be the difference between conflict and love, confusion and understanding, separation and connection. Full and open attention has the power to heal hearts. Listening is the key that opens the door to deep and lasting relationships.

Communication is not just two people talking – it is two people taking their turns listening. We believe that the ultimate goal of all communication should be to "commune," meaning to connect with another person. No matter what it is we are trying to say, if the other person can't hear it, we have failed to communicate. That's why effective communication takes (at least) two willing and active participants.

Listening seems to have become a lost art.

In the maelstrom of our fast-paced, high-tech, multi-tasking, results-orientated society, listening has often taken a back seat to making our point or winning the argument at any cost. As a result, whether we're still in school or out in the world, many people find themselves feeling unheard, misunderstood, unappreciated for who they really are, and hopeless. Young people and adults who fail to receive the gift of listening from those closest to them often seek connection elsewhere. For better or worse, we move from place to place and relationship to relationship looking for someone who will take the time to really listen *and* understand.

This letter was read aloud by a young man at a retreat I was facilitating back in 1983. I believe it has an important message for all of us.

Dear Mom and Dad,

Thank you for everything, but I am going to Chicago to try and start some kind of new life. You asked me why I did those things and why I gave you so much trouble. The answer is easy for me to give you, but I am wondering if you'll understand.

Remember when I was about six or seven and I wanted you to just listen to me? I remember all the nice things you gave me for Christmas and my birthday. I was really happy with the things I got for about a week or two. The rest of the year, I didn't really want presents; I just wanted you to listen to me like I was somebody who felt things, too. Because I remember even when I was young, I felt things. But you said you were too busy.

Mom, you are a wonderful cook, and you had everything so clean. You were often tired from doing all those things that made you busy. But you know something, Mom? I would have liked crackers and peanut butter just as well if you had only sat down with me for a while during the day and said, "Tell me all about it so maybe I can help you understand."

And when Donna came, I couldn't understand why everyone made so much fuss. I didn't think it was my fault that her hair was so pretty; or that she didn't have to wear glasses with such thick lenses (like I did). Her grades were better, too, weren't they?

If Donna ever has children, I hope you will tell her to just pay attention to the one that doesn't smile very much, because that will be the one who's really crying inside. And when she's about to bake six dozen cookies, tell her to make sure first, that the kids don't want to tell her about a dream or a hope or something. Because thoughts are important to small kids, even though they don't have the words to use to tell about how they feel inside.

I think that all the kids who are doing so many things that grown-ups are tearing out their hair worrying about, are really looking for somebody that will take the time to listen for a few minutes. Someone who'd really treat them as if they we're grown-ups – who might be useful to them – and you know, be polite to them. If you folks had ever said, "Pardon me!" when you interrupted me, I probably would have dropped dead.

If anybody asks you where I am, tell them I've gone looking for somebody with time, because I've got a lot of things I want to talk about.

Love to all,

Your son (a boy with a record as a juvenile delinquent)

Intentional Listening

Knowing how important listening can be in any relationship, Yvonne and I commit ourselves to creating *intentional listening* time every week. To really listen means that we focus all our attention on "getting" the other person. When we listen with our ears *and* our heart, we find it easier to feel compassion. For us, "date night" has become code for the times when we lock out the world, and honestly and vulnerably place all our focus on listening and really getting each other's experience.

Date Night Using Intentional Listening

Yvonne

Save the flowers, candy, and big expensive presents. Although I love fine dinners out, showers of compliments, massages and intimacy, they all fall second to Rich giving me the gift of listening.

Soft eye contact and a genuine desire to listen without interruptions creates one of the most sacred gestures we can ever offer. When practiced intentionally, hearts open, magic happens and miracles occur.

Rich

What if every person in your life could feel fully heard by you? How might that change your relationships? What if you felt fully heard by the people you love? How would that affect the way you listen?

If you are truly listening to another person, they will undoubtedly come closer and reveal more. Like a flower unfolding before our eyes, those who feel heard are more likely to expose their most vulnerable parts. This is where our closest emotional connection occurs. I like to ask myself if my listening is making it safe for this person to share the truth of who they really are.

The good news is, no matter how poorly any of us may have listened in the past, it's never too late to change. It takes courage to face the places where we have fallen short as listeners and understand how we may have actually harmed our relationships. By noticing who you are as a listener, you take the first step toward being the hero you've been waiting for. Starting today, give yourself and others the gift of listening.

10 Tips for Great Listening

1. If you are listening, you are *definitely* not talking.
2. When listening, remember not to fix, give advice, or otherwise interrupt.
3. Maintain eye contact so the person knows you are honestly interested in what they have to say.
4. Listen with your ears *and* your heart. Listen so well you can actually *feel* what the person is sharing with you.
5. Remember that nothing you have to say is more important than "getting" the other person's experience. Make understanding the other person even more important than being understood.
6. Practice Active or Attentive Listening. To insure you are really getting the other person, reflect back what you heard. You might say something such as, "What I heard you say was …" then repeat what you heard a couple of sentences at a time. The other person can tell you that you got it right or they can correct your understanding. This exercise is particularly helpful when the communication is emotionally charged.
7. Demonstrate empathy. You might say something such as, "I imagine that must have been really painful for you."
8. Be an invitation for emotions. Many of us are so uncomfortable with tears that we want to "fix it" and make them go away. We assure you that tears *are* a part of fixing it. To support someone who's crying, simply look them in the eyes, listen and allow yourself to feel compassion. Depending on your relationship, gentle touch can also be a powerful tool.
9. When the person seems to have finished speaking, try asking, "What else?" (You'll discover more about this in the next chapter.)
10. Remember, "They like you when you talk, but they love you when you listen."

Be the Hero!

Deep listening is miraculous for both listener and speaker. When someone receives us with open-hearted, non-judging, intensely interested listening, our spirits expand.

~ Sue Patton

Notice

- Who are the people in your life with whom you can really open up and talk? Do these people practice "intentional" listening? Do they stop whatever they're doing, look you in the eyes and just listen? How does it feel when someone really listens to you?

- Do you consider yourself to be a good listener? Are you able to keep your full attention on the person to whom you are listening? Or do you find yourself thinking about how you are going to respond instead? Do you really feel them? Do you ever find yourself wanting to "fix" the other person or change how they are feeling in any way?

- How do you think people would describe you as a listener? Would you say that the people you consider closest to you believe their hearts and their feelings are safe with you?

- Are there people in your life who might complain that you don't listen? If so, are these people with whom you would like to have a closer connection? What can you do to show them you are interested in what they have to say?

- How often do people choose you as someone they can trust with their emotions?

- When people are angry or frustrated with you, are you able to hear them? If not, why not? What gets in the way?

- Have you ever started talking with someone about an experience that was emotionally charged for you only to have the listener turn the focus of the conversation to them? How did it feel? What did you do? How did it affect your relationship with that person?

Choose

- If there are people you would talk to more deeply if they practiced intentional listening, can you imagine how it might change what you would say? Journal the difference between what you do say and what you would like to say. Then, imagine re-doing that conversation.
- If you have moments when you realize you have not been an intentional listener, journal about the times you tried to fix or change the speaker's feelings, and then imagine having a different response. This is a great way to bring awareness to your thoughts and actions.
- Review the 10 Tips For Great Listening. List the moments when you have accomplished each one. Then list the moments when you did not. This is another great way to bring awareness to your listening skills so that you can choose a different course of action in the future.
- Imagine yourself as the most trusted listener and confidante among your friends. Make a list of all the imaginary things they say about your best qualities.

Act

- Consider having another conversation with someone in which you held back what you were saying. Tell that person what you need from them in order to open up more fully. Perhaps you need to not be interrupted. Perhaps you need to feel more understood. Whatever it is, be clear about what you need and ask for it.

- Review your list of moments when you think you could have been a better listener. Approach at least one person who was talking, and tell that person the ways in which you wish you would have reacted as s/he was talking. Ask that person if there is anything they have held back in saying.

- Ask a friend, parent, or partner how you might be a better listener. Consider sharing this chapter with them and discussing what you each need from each other in order to more fully communicate and be understood.

- For the next week, make a conscious effort to really listen to people. When they finish talking, ask, "Is there anything else?" Notice what happens.

- Set up interviews with your parents, grandparents, and other family members. Ask them to share their life histories, or the most important moments, lessons and experiences in their lives. When I did this with my grandmother, I used a videotape. (Note: this can be a beautiful way to honor both the person you are interviewing and your heritage).

- Set up a "date night" or "date day" with a person or people closest to you in your life. Take turns giving each other the gift of listening. Then do something fun together.

Celebrate!

Find a mirror, look yourself in the eyes, and celebrate all the ways you have been a great listener. Be sure to listen to *you*.

Everyday Hero ~ Kristy Brodeur

Simply said, we would trust Kristy with our lives. Her simple, unbridled love has the power to touch hearts, open minds, and transform her every relationship. One of our longest tenured leaders, Kristy first stepped up to the role of Challenge Day leader following the horrific attacks at Columbine High School in Littleton, Colorado.

As a senior Challenge Day leader, Kristy serves as a positive example of all that we teach in our organization. A loving and committed mother, partner, and friend, Kristy brings her deeply compassionate and effective listening skills with her everywhere she goes. With a Master's Degree in Social Work, Kristy has taught at JFK University, worked to eliminate domestic violence, and has spent 14 years as a part-time Forensic Interview Specialist sharing the gift of listening and healing with young victims of child sexual abuse.

Kristy

If you really knew me, you'd know that one morning, around 5 a.m., I got a call from Rich who said that Yvonne was really sick, and could I please help him lead a Challenge Day in two hours. "What, me? What will I be doing? How will I do it? I won't be able to say it like Yvonne…" I think that was my response.

Very calmly, Rich assured me that I would be fine, and it would be great!

Well, it was great. It was amazing. It created a warmth in me that I would not forget for a long time. After that, I continued my life. I finished graduate school, earning a degree in Consulting Psychology, got a full time job working with victims of crime and interviewing suspected child abuse victims, got married, and had my first baby. It had been a long time, maybe seven years since I even thought about leading Challenge Days.

If you really knew me, you'd know that the day that changed was the day tragedy fell upon Columbine High School on April 20th, 1999. When I heard of the tragic shooting, I was stunned; I felt impaired and dazed. I got a call from Yvonne and together we cried for the young people, their families, the survivors, the community, our hopelessness, and our helplessness. Yvonne started to really drop the waterline and talk about how hopeless she was feeling, that there was so much need to get Challenge

Days into every school, in every town, in every state, in every county, and that her fear was that she and Rich could not do it all alone anymore. I remember telling Yvonne how important their work was, and that they were changing the world. I remember asking her, "What can I do? What do you need from me? I will do anything to help you continue doing this work." I remember that in a soft, tearful voice she said, "I need you to become a leader." Holding my breath, knowing in that moment my life was about to change, I said "Okay." My training and transformation began in July of 1999. My first day as a Challenge Day leader came that September in Casper, Wyoming.

If you really knew me, you would know that when I first started leading Challenge Days, my goal was about empowering the young people, having empathy for what they were going through, and being an older sister to listen to them and be their ally. Now, although all those are still true, I step out into the middle of the circle, and it has now become about loving those young people, and holding them with mama love and energy. Now it is about possibly saving their lives. As a parent, Challenge Days are so different for me to lead. I want to make sure that every young person I meet gets home after school, that no parent has to visit them at the cemetery or in a hospital. I make a commitment to myself before each start of a Challenge Day that I will look into every young person's eyes so they feel noticed and seen, and I will hug as many as I can, so maybe some will get at least one hug that day. And after a long day of hugging and loving, I get to come home to my own two children, and look into their eyes, make sure they are seen and noticed, and give them as many hugs as I can before bed. Sometimes I forget, with the hectic life of a working parent, but I am so blessed to have days like Challenge Day to remind me.

What Else?
The Gift of Listening, Part II

> Suffering cheerfully endured, ceases to be suffering
> and is transmuted into an ineffable joy.
>
> ~ Gandhi

Yvonne

It was one of those weeks. My fifteen-year-old daughter, stressed beyond capacity, kept snapping at everyone. I reminded myself that anger is always a cover for other feelings and, in an attempt to help, as well as to move the rest of the family out of the crossfire, I asked her if she wanted a "session."

A session combines the tools of "emptying the balloon" and giving "the gift of listening." Rich and I use this technique with our families, with each other, and in the Challenge Day organization. In fact, giving and receiving sessions is a very important part of the training that each person goes through in order to become a Challenge Day leader.

At first my daughter just mumbled, "No," which I took to mean, *I want to, but I'm really scared.* Finally she released breaths of fire and reluctantly followed me into the most private room in our house.

My goal was to stay open and be ready for anything in order to support my child in her journey through the pain of her unfelt feelings and into the discovery of a new part of herself.

I stood approximately four feet away from her and looked into her eyes. This gave her plenty of space to breathe, feel, stomp her feet, and move her body like any child who naturally remembers how to collapse into a tantrum. I did my best not to look anxious or "weird." My highest chance for success was to be open with no agenda, and instead just listen and trust the natural process.

As she breathed deeply her face reddened and it seemed as if she was contemplating blowing me off. I imagined it took courage for her to trust me enough to go into her feelings instead of shutting down or numbing out. I guided her by suggesting, "Why don't you finish the sentence, 'I am angry that…' "

That did it. Tears began flooding her eyes and rage exploded through every vein as she yelled, "I am angry at you!"

I silently reassured myself. *Okay, here we go, she is going to start with me. Don't get hooked, just listen.*

She continued yelling, her voice growing louder with every state-ment, but she still seemed a bit tentative, as though checking in to see if I was truly ready to hold her anger. Then, blasting through her doubts, she shouted, "I hate that you are always gone! Every child in the world is more important to you than your own!"

She'd triggered my defensiveness, and my mind searched for rebuttals. *When I am home, you are always busy with your friends and you rarely have time with me anyway.* But I kept silent, remembering that the only way this session could end with me feeling proud would be for me just to listen – no matter what. I stayed with her and asked softly, "What else?"

She upped the ante and took her best shot, screaming, "I hate you!"

My ego grew horns, but I managed to keep quiet. I told myself to keep my body in a relaxed and open posture while I let her hostile energy just flow through me.

She continued with a full head of steam, "You like Loren more then me! You baby her all the time!"

My mind raced, my heart pounded, and I suppressed the urge to protect myself. Instead, I held onto my goal of being as non-reactive as possible.

Then we got past her testing point and off she went. "I hate my life! I hate my sisters! Dad doesn't listen and he never trusts me! You are always nagging me, and it seems that my room being clean is more important to you than all the stress I am under!"

I breathed, softly but deeply, internally complimenting myself for being able to listen without reacting.

She kept going, showing no signs of slowing down. "I hate school! I don't know why they teach us half this stuff anyway! I feel so stupid! I am retarded and it is so embarrassing being in Special Ed!"

Now I wanted to take care of her and reassure her that she was brilliant. I wanted to list all the geniuses in the world who had forms of dyslexia. Yet I knew she just needed to feel, not be saved. I asked, very softly, "What else?"

She immediately responded. "I feel so ugly, I am so fat, I hate my body!"

I wanted to tell her about how our media portrays women and intentionally launches us on an endless cycle of hating our bodies in order to buy things in the hopes of looking prettier or thinner. But I resisted, remembering how fat I felt at her age. In my mind, I relived my desperate, secret life with bulimia. Strong waves of understanding rippled through me and I allowed some tears to spill – not so many that she would have to turn off her feelings and shift over to taking care of me but just enough to let her see that I got it.

My daughter was not just talking about her pain, she was fully feeling it.

As she continued emptying her balloon, she literally resembled a woman in full labor. "I have no clothes that fit me! All the other kids have nice clothes with brand names. Why do I have to be the poor kid with hand-me-downs?"

My parent's version of "You think you have it bad," rolled through my head, though once again I chose to ignore it. I actually felt excited that she was doing what I call, "following the thread in." I knew that her only true way out of this "feelings storm" was to go all the way into and through her emotions.

I kept encouraging her by repeating, "What else?"

With an intensity that shook the entire house, she wailed, "I can't do this anymore! I can't do this anymore!"

I felt proud for being able just to listen, which overrode any temptation to give advice, defend myself, or fix her.

Then it came, every parent's biggest fear.

She screamed in agony, "I hate my life! I want to die! I want to kill myself!"

This was my final test. If I could be here with her through this, I could do anything!

I flashed back to what seemed like a lifetime ago, when I was in the mental hospital. Beads of sweat surfaced on my forehead. My inner cheerleader – what I think of as my higher self – chimed in by asking, *What would you want your mom to do?*

The answer came fast and clear. *Just listen and love.*

I vividly recalled the terror I had felt at her age when I was certain that I was going crazy. My compassionate tears flowed freely as I said, "What else?"

Her sobs intermingled with screams as her body contracted in spasms. Her movements reminded me of a three-year-old fully expressed in her body.

She cried for what seemed like an eternity, though in reality it lasted maybe twenty or thirty minutes.

I simply stayed in her eyes as I softly invited more. "What else?"

Gradually, her anger moved into what appeared to be sadness and grief.

At some point I said, "You are doing great."

She responded with a withering glare that I translated to mean, *Don't patronize me!*

I hoped that my off-track encouragement would not stop her release, and I remained totally present, allowing time for her emotional balloon to completely empty.

Then her breathing softened and she relaxed.

Instincts are particularly important in this part of the process and the mother in me knew that this was the moment to gently reach out. I took her hand in mine, and without interrupting the flow, I gracefully made my way over to a nearby chair and guided her into my lap.

She wrinkled her nose, which I was sure meant, *Oh mom, I'm too old for that.*

"Humor me," I whispered.

I had proven my safety. She allowed herself to fall into me, tucking her head into my shoulder as I began to gently rock her. For a few minutes, her crying increased, though it came from a more peaceful place. I was in no rush. Where else was there to go? What could be more important than this moment? I held her as we rocked.

Then, as if nothing had happened, she looked up with a giggle and said, "What's for dinner?"

In that moment, I knew she was complete. We had done it!

What an honor it was to midwife my daughter as she gave birth to herself through this session. Waves of pride spread through my body as I continued to say *I love you* in the most intimate way I could – by simply listening and holding space for her as she felt all of her feelings.

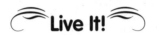

Live It!

What the caterpillar calls the end of the world, the Master calls the butterfly.

~ Richard Bach

Being a teenager can be extremely challenging. Adults tell you what to do and where to go. You have to make major decisions that can affect your entire life, at the same time that your body is changing, your hormones are raging, and your feelings are often running the show.

As the mother of four, I have repeatedly learned that the best gift I can give to my children is to remember that their feelings are simply feelings. The greatest way for me to say *I love you* is to be able to hold the space and listen to them as they move through their emotions – *without* taking it personally. Most every parent would agree that it is considerably easier to listen to other people's kids than their own, especially when the kids are ready to explode. So, throughout this process the only thing a parent needs to remember is to listen, love and ask, "What else?"

Giving a session is an art, requiring that one person intentionally listen while the other empties his or her emotional balloon. To do that, it's best to set a "container" solely for the session. The container serves two main purposes: the first is to establish a mutually agreed-upon time boundary for when it will end; the second is to be clear that in this container, and *in this container only*, the person "sessioning" has explicit permission to share *anything* and to express *all* of his or her feelings in healthy and safe ways. The *only* thing the one offering the session needs to remember is to listen, and *if needed*, genuinely ask, "What else?"

When I give a session, I kind of split myself in half. One part of me is the outer or human part that just listens, while the other part is my higher self, the wisest part of me who silently coaches me through the process. It can be difficult not to chime in with my stuff or to jump in and fix things. I need my inner voice to remind myself that my job is to listen.

I remember this particular session with my daughter because of the many times I wanted to stop her pain and make her feel better. I longed to say, "You are not fat! You are not dumb!" At the same time, I struggled to keep myself from getting too defensive. I had to allow her to attack me and hold firm in knowing that I would be more proud of myself by taking it than by becoming defensive, *no matter what*. In the end, my daughter was able to break through because I had proven that I was a safe refuge in which she could completely release.

I liken this process to the difference between pulling the weed out with the roots versus just cutting off the top. I went for the roots. My daughter was able to vent all of her feelings and completely empty her "emotional balloon." And I was able to let her know she'd done it perfectly by holding her when she was finished. That was one of the things I craved during difficult times as a teenager. I wanted to be held and rocked but I never asked because I thought I was too old or too big. Still, I longed for that kind of nurturing. The phrase, "Just humor me," has become a great tool. Saying it then allowed my daughter to surrender as I tenderly rocked and mothered her.

I feel so blessed every time I have the privilege to vulnerably support or midwife someone into, and completely through, their feelings. It's the same kind of emotional breakthrough that happened to me in the psych ward and ultimately saved my life. If you really knew me, you'd know that each time I do it with someone else, I picture a butterfly.

Butterflies are a miracle of nature. In order for a caterpillar to complete its journey through life, it must spin its own cocoon. Once inside the cocoon, miraculously, it allows itself to completely melt down into "imaginal" cells. The caterpillar melts in order to transform. Out of this natural, spectacular process of metamorphosis, a magnificent butterfly soon appears, ready to soar off into its new life.

What if, like the butterfly, we are also born with the ability to transform our lives?

If you have ever deeply and courageously "followed the thread" of your emotions to their origin and then emerged out the other side, you understand exactly what I mean. It can seem as though you are literally melting down and transforming.

Many people have certainly had the experience of being overfilled with feelings as their emotional balloons explode. But without someone listening and holding a "sacred space," it's all too easy to hurt ourselves or others, emotionally or physically, along the way. The melting down part takes place but the transformation is missing.

We used to inherently understand how to do all of it. But ever since we threw our first tantrum, many of us have been forcefully taught not to go there, that to express strong emotions is wrong. Children are punished for their tantrums and adults are shunned. As a result, so many of us never empty our balloons.

We need to be responsible for our feelings. Just as we care for ourselves by eating healthy, exercising, and having a spiritual practice, it's vital to fully express our feelings in order to grow as human beings.

The key is to intentionally set a safe container. In my ideal world, people would understand this process.

Ideally, our families would lovingly demonstrate unconditional listening as we rollercoaster through the full gamut of our emotions. Unfortunately, without access to the tools of setting a safe container and sessioning, most of us have been stifled, shamed, punished, or perhaps even physically hurt as a way to shut us up. Regardless, no one is a victim here. If we are avoiding our feelings, we are continuing a cycle that has been passed down from generation to generation. Now, however, we can become more conscious and notice what we're doing so we can make a different choice, and then act on that choice.

Accountability Buddies

Rich and I feel enormously proud that everyone in the Challenge Day organization practices the tools we teach in this book. And to make sure we all have the support we deserve, everyone in our organization creates a personal growth plan, including the selection of an "account-ability buddy" who cheerleads and supports them in creating the life, job, and relationships of their dreams. On a regular basis, these buddies check in to hold each other accountable in achieving their stated goals. Accountability buddies offer encouragement and, most importantly, "sessions" to help each other empty their emotional balloons.

One of our basic beliefs is that, with enough love, we can all naturally heal. All we need is someone who is not afraid of us respectfully expressing strong emotions. Our buddies give us the gift of listening as we find our way back to ourselves.

Because our work as Challenge Day leaders requires that we hold the emotions of countless youth and adults, every leader commits to a minimum of at least one emotional release session per week. By giving each other the gift of listening and emptying our balloons on a regular basis, we prepare ourselves to hold the onslaught of emotions that can come our way.

People often ask, "What happens if the timer goes off and you are right in the middle of an emotional storm?" When that occurs, and it often does, we recommend the tool of "attention-out." This is a simple and common technique used in many forms of counseling. It means asking a question that causes the person to move from *feeling* to *thinking*. Some examples are to recite the names of vegetables that start with the letter "C," or to list the names of the Seven Dwarves, and state which one you like the most and why. Lists can be a great tool to attention-out. One of my favorites is to ask the person to start listing the things they are grateful for; this not only helps to attention-out from the big emotions but also ends the session on a positive note of gratitude.

Questions should make the person *think or be funny*, or they should be *open-ended* and require more than a one word or a yes or no answer. The funnier or more outrageous the attention-out questions are, the better the results. The goal is not to complete the answer as much as it is to bring the person out of his or her feelings and back into their rational minds.

10 Steps for a Session

1. Find a partner who has read this chapter or understands how vital it is for people to fully feel all of their feelings.

2. Create a container by choosing a safe and private place, and setting a timer. Make sure you've got plenty of Kleenex on hand.

3. For the person in need of the session, commit yourself to allowing all feelings to be expressed. The listener commits to accepting those feelings without defensiveness, fixing, or responding.

4. As the listener, you can begin the session by asking a simple question such as, "What are you feeling?" Remember, the best gift you can give someone who is having a session is to encourage them to fully empty their emotional balloon.

5. A powerful tool to get an anger session rolling is to evoke emotion by having the sessioner match your volume and energy by completing the sentence, "I'm angry that …!" This tool can be used as needed throughout the session.

6. Ask "What else?" if the sessioner seems complete, gets stuck or needs reassurance that you are still there and willing to continue listening.

7. After the timer goes off, pause, breathe, and allow the emotions to settle. Then validate your partner for his or her courage. Remember, do not respond to anything that has been said.

8. If necessary, "attention-out" with questions that move the sessioner from the heart to the head. You want to prepare the other person to either leave the session or switch to your turn, knowing their feelings are simply feelings, and that they can go back to school, work, or life without their emotions running the show.

9. If your partner has sessioned about someone else and that relationship is not complete, make sure the sessioner goes directly to the person to clear up anything that is between them. Then have your partner come back to you and let you know when that has been completed. Refer to our Rumor Elimination Model in Chapter 13, if necessary.

10. What's said in the session stays in the session. It is crucial to keep all shares confidential. The only exception is if someone is in danger of physically hurting him/herself, hurting others, or being hurt by another. In any of these situations, seek professional help and get your partner the support he or she deserves.

Be the Hero

There's no easy way out. If there were, I would have bought it. And believe me, it would be one of my favorite things.

~ Oprah Winfrey

Notice

- Is there anyone in your life whom you trust to hold you during your strongest emotions? What about these people makes it safe for you to express yourself? What is it about the way they listen, their body language or attitudes that tells you to keep going? When was the last time you allowed them to come through for you? Did you allow yourself to cry and scream until your balloon felt empty? If you did, how did that feel?
- When was the last time, if ever, you had a good cry or anger session? How did it feel in your body? What effect did it have on your attitude and behavior? Were you able to think more clearly? Did it help you make better choices?
- When, if ever, have you held or supported someone while they expressed deep grief, anger, or rage? Were you able to keep your attention on them? How was it to be present with intense emotions? Did you feel compassion? Did your support allow them to get to the bottom of their emotions? How did the "session" affect them? Did you notice any changes in the person's attitude and behavior afterward?
- As a child, do you ever remember having a tantrum? What happened? How did people respond? Do you remember being yelled at, shushed, or told to go to your room? What effect, if any, did people's reactions have on you and the way you would later express your feelings?

- How often does your "emotional balloon" leak out on the people around you? Have you ever hurt anyone with your anger? How often do you say things you regret?
- Have you ever been physically or emotionally hurt by someone else's anger?
- Have you ever made dangerous or unhealthy choices as a result of your unexpressed emotions? If so, what did you do and what were the consequences?
- Is there anyone in your life that you would trust to be an accountability buddy for you? Someone whom you believe might help you create the life of your dreams, listen when you need it, and hold you accountable for living your 100% life?

Choose

- Think about a time when you held back strong emotions about something. Perhaps you can think about something you are currently holding inside you that has gone unexpressed. Now choose the person with whom you would like to release these emotions and imagine completely emptying your balloon. What does it look like? What do you say and do?
- Can you imagine allowing someone to have this same sort of session with you? Envision yourself "holding the space" for someone else to completely release his or her emotions. How do you encourage that person to empty everything that's inside?
- If you have noticed times when your emotional balloon has leaked onto others, plan a course of action to fully express your emotions and then plan the steps you would need to take to make amends for any words or actions you regret.
- If you have been hurt by someone else's actions or words, how can you imagine feeling better? Would you need to have a session to get out your feelings? Or would you need to address

the situation with that person in some way? List all the things you might do in order to feel better.

- If you have made unhealthy choices as a result of unexpressed emotions, are there any ways in which you need to address those choices? What action can you imagine taking in order to fully heal?
- Envision the perfect person as your accountability buddy, and then list all the ways in which you might support each other.

Act

- Share this chapter and these tools with your family members, friends, co-workers, and other people in your life so that you can support one another in having sessions when needed.
- The next time you notice someone in your life has a full emotional balloon, offer him or her a "session." Find a safe place, set a timer, and let them know they have permission to share whatever they are feeling. Practice the steps listed for having a session. If at any point they seem stuck, try asking the question, "What else?"
- Find someone you trust to become your regular "session buddy." Create time each week to empty your emotional balloons. Using the tools in this chapter, exchange time crying, screaming, yelling, laughing, and expressing yourself fully so that your emotional balloons don't leak onto those you love. Notice how alive and free you feel afterward.
- Apologize to someone you feel you have hurt with your words and actions.
- Get help in healing any unhealthy habits you may have as a result of a full emotional balloon.

Celebrate!

Give yourself permission to laugh out loud and celebrate the freedom you feel.

Everyday Hero ~ Christian Dean

A young woman filled with passion and fire, Christian has overcome a lifetime of hardship. Abandoned by her father at a young age, she has spent her time in school doing her best to make her mother proud. After being introduced to the work of Challenge Day in November of 2005, Christian became passionate about Being the Change. Speaking in front of hundreds of people at Challenge Day's annual fundraiser in 2008, she tearfully celebrated her graduation from the quiet girl in the back of the room to the powerful and passionate young woman she had become.

Christian and her mother Keva were asked to be part of an Oprah Winfrey show focusing on the emotional issues behind teenage obesity. Since both Christian and her mother have had lifelong struggles with their weight, this test would prove to be especially challenging. Once again, Christian shined as one of the brightest and most passionate lights in the room. Her undeniable courage, and the fire with which she spoke her truths left no doubt that this young woman had come into her own. Christian powerfully exemplifies what it means to take responsibility for Being the Change in her own life.

Christian

If you really knew me, you'd know that my weight was my hiding place most of my life. I was teased and tormented because of my size, besides the fact that I was uniquely different. Kids would call me names, and I let that condition me into thinking I wasn't worthy, pretty, or good enough. As a result, all through my schooling, I'd let the things that were said to me, put me in a box and quiet me.

If you really knew me, you'd know that I've learned to quiet the voices in my head that tell me I'm not beautiful or talented. Even though my mother would always say, "You're beautiful, talented, and intelligent, and don't let anyone, including yourself, tell you otherwise," I didn't begin understanding this until my junior year in high school.

If you really knew me, you would know that the work of Challenge Day has tremendously changed my life. I was able to dig deeper into my emotions and deal with the reasons why I felt the way that I had. With the tools that Challenge Day and my family have taught me, I've blossomed into a confident young leader.

Christian and her mom, Keva

Communication and Relationships

Seek not so much to be understood as to understand.

~ St. Francis of Assisi

Rich

It wasn't until we were in the midst of writing this book that I realized Yvonne and I had similar transformational moments, and that they had happened for each of us at nearly the same time in our lives.

Yvonne's experience in the psychiatric hospital allowed her to meet herself in a profound and life-changing way. After she had screamed and cried and raged and released her bottled-up storm of feelings, she was finally able to hear that still, soft voice within her saying, "I'm in here. And I'm okay."

I had my own experience of hearing a quiet voice deep within me come to the surface. The moment is strikingly different from Yvonne's, but the message is nearly the same.

As an undergrad at St. Mary's College in Moraga, California, I was required to take a theology class. After exploring my options, I settled on a class called The Good News. At the time, "good news" was the last thing I expected to hear about God. If you really knew me, you'd know that I had given up on God. I had searched for Him in high school but I decided that God was merely a reminder of guilt and shame, and I wanted nothing to do with Him – or at least my understanding of Him.

On the first day of class, the instructor, John Dwyer, stood before us and boldly stated, "God loves you, no strings attached."

Although his words were something that I wanted to believe, I'd already made up my mind about that nonsense. My hand shot up; I was ready for a debate. But John wasn't interested in debating whether or not God exists, his only goal was to pose a series of what-ifs and let me figure out the rest.

"What if there's no accident that you're alive? What if you lack nothing and everything you need already exists inside you? What if you don't have to manipulate people to get what you want from them? What if you absolutely knew that you never had to *be* anything or *do* anything in order to become a perfect you?"

My head was on fire with a thousand responses. And then came the question that rocked my world and finally took hold.

"God loves you, no strings attached. Do you have the courage to live as if it's true?"

He was asking me if my thoughts could change my actions. He was asking me to bring a different kind of consciousness into my *being* to see if it changed anything I was *doing*. It was a perfect question because without realizing it, I was a "human doing," someone so wrapped up in my outward accomplishments that I had no real awareness of who I was.

The question halted me and reverberated through me for weeks. *What if God is holding me right now?* I'd ask myself over and over again.

Then one day, I was playing baseball and something just clicked. It was my most memorable game ever, not because of what I was doing but because of the extraordinary feeling inside me. I felt fearless and alive. And I was surprisingly unattached to anything I was doing. In fact, in my first three times at bat, I'd struck out.

On another day I would have been devastated, but on this day I somehow didn't care at all.

As I stood at the plate and faced the pitcher for the fourth time, I felt completely at ease. When the pitch came toward me, I connected, and the ball sailed over the back fence, as well as the scoreboard, for a home run. I rounded first base when it struck me: this was perhaps the first moment of absolute freedom I could really remember. I'd spent so much time trying to prove myself, trying to please someone else, and feeling disappointment in everything I did – no matter how successful it seemed – that I'd forgotten what it felt like to be still inside. The realization was so jarring that I began to cry.

Until then, I didn't know what it felt like to stop trying and just be me. Before that moment, the last time I remembered feeling truly amazing, I was a child.

As I rounded second base, every cell in me began releasing the years of self-hatred that had piled up and buried me in insecurity. Tears of joy streamed down my cheeks as I tried to navigate my body around the infield. By the time I hit home plate, my tears had given way to a deep sense of peace. I was welcomed with high fives and hugs of congratulations from my teammates who were celebrating my feat; little did they know that I had actually made a personal breakthrough.

I didn't know it at the time, but a new foundation of self-love had been laid. And it wasn't until that happened that the experience of fully loving someone else could ever be possible.

Yvonne

Joining in love with another person in the deepest sense becomes significantly more likely once you have met yourself first. Unless you have experienced some version of "I'm in here, I see me, and I love what I see," then you cannot truly look upon another person through the eyes of love. We all begin our journey seeking outside of ourselves in an effort to be understood. But we cannot have the experience of being understood by anyone else until we understand ourselves first.

After leaving the hospital, my hunger for food shifted to a hunger for healing. I was able to stop binging and purging because I discovered an entire world of support I'd never known existed. I was eager to fill myself, and the empty hole within me, with books, workshops, 12-Step meetings, and classes. I began to explore various religions and spiritual teachings from around the world, and whatever else pulled me toward the deepening process of waking up, opening to more love, and learning more about myself. I had spent most of my young life trying to figure out how to stop my flood of emotions, and now I wanted to know more about them.

The more I looked, the more I discovered that all of my sadnesses were connected, and as I tied them together, following the thread inward, I knew that the power of healing was in my hands. The path had been lit, and there was a light at the end of the tunnel.

What I began to understand is that wherever there are strong emotions, there lies great opportunity for growth. That's why relationships are so powerful. We are both drawn toward and repulsed by the people who are most capable of igniting us.

Relationships, romantic or otherwise, are sacred temples of higher learning.

However, if you really knew me, you would know that I thought painful yelling matches followed by emotional distance was a normal part of families and relationships.

Rich

When I met Yvonne, I was a superstar. I'd completed both undergrad and graduate school ahead of schedule, and I was excelling at nearly everything I attempted. I was a hero in most everyone's eyes. I gave people permission to be who they are – to laugh, to cry, to get real. I witnessed the miracle of what happens to people when they feel safe and loved and celebrated – they blossom.

While I was expending so much energy on everyone else's healing, what I didn't realize was that I had erected walls around my own heart. Because of my family history, I'd made an unconscious decision to not let myself ever get hopeful about love. Without knowing it, I had decided not to risk investing my heart with anyone. So, although I was becoming a master at knowing how to give, I didn't have a clue about how to receive. I was so happily entrenched in my comfort zone of giving, that I didn't even know there was anything else… until I met Yvonne. She was the first person who ever got past my protective guard and showed me that I could have what I was giving away.

When Yvonne and I first got together, we hardly ever fought. We were so in love that everything felt easy. Inevitably, I suppose, the honeymoon had to end. In our case, the closer and more vulnerable we got, the more attached we became to our respective points of view. We began fighting as passionately as we loved.

My family's history of conflict, combined with the fact that both Yvonne and I had previously been divorced, left me afraid that every fight would be our last. Though I tried not to show it, a part of me feared that one of us might give up on the other at any time. Yvonne and I really loved each other and neither of us ever wanted to fight or break up. Unfortunately, we lacked some of the tools we needed to compassionately and effectively communicate our hurts, needs, and desires.

The question became, would we rather be right or would we rather be in love?

Yvonne and I promised that as long as we remained committed to growing and learning, we'd never give up on each other. That promise, and the depth of our love, led us to seek out every resource we could that might help us create the relationship of our dreams. We went to counseling, joined separate support groups, and read every book we could find to improve our communication.

Yvonne

We were both opening to allow more love and happiness into our lives. Every day felt like a new opportunity to practice our new tools, to practice being "us." But still, there were times when, for no apparent reason, my positive outlook on life suddenly disintegrated. I would wake up and everything looked bleak. Rich went from being the man of my dreams to my biggest nightmare. But I realized that he hadn't changed a bit; it was me. I had somehow unconsciously fallen into "victim mode" and I couldn't seem to make myself care. I felt disgusted with myself and I blamed everyone else for how I was feeling. I would fall into cycles of negativity and tell myself, "See, this stuff doesn't work, it doesn't last. I can't change my life after all." It was even harder now because once I'd tasted joy, love, growth, consciousness, and authentic passion, the pain felt worse.

That's when I began to embrace the idea that failure is part of the process. Changing habits and learning new skills takes time and practice. I had to learn how to have compassion for the person inside me who wanted to run before she knew how to walk. I had to give myself permission to be a beginner.

And more than anything else, I had to remember to look myself in the mirror, meet my own eyes, and love me, too.

Rich

If you really knew us, you'd know that the communication tools we outline in the following pages form much of the foundation for our deeply fulfilling and passionate marriage. We've learned that our relationship must come first – before work, the kids, and the needs of the world. In fact, we spend one night each week, which we call "date night," where we apply these tools in an effort to deepen our partnership and connection.

As we've mentioned, *attentive listening* is the first step, since effective communication is not just two people talking, it is two people taking turns listening attentively to each other. However, we can greatly increase our chances of being heard, if we can also learn how to express ourselves more effectively.

Yvonne and I now use the following communication tools not just in all of our relationships, but in our programs, and in every other area of our lives. We guarantee that, when faithfully applied, these tools really do work.

Live It!

Did you ever notice how difficult it is to argue with someone who is not obsessed with being right?

~ Wayne W. Dyer

We are all communicating all the time. Both consciously and unconsciously, we express our thoughts, feelings, attitudes and re-actions through our body language, facial expressions and, most of all, the words that we use. When we interact with each other, there are always at least two kinds of communication going on – rational and emotional. Rational information is usually conveyed through language, while emotional information is usually transmitted non-verbally.

As an example, here is a typical conversation between a parent and a teenager. The parent inquires, "Is your homework done?" The parent may feel that this is a simple question and expect a simple yes or no answer. The teenager, however, responds to the raised eyebrow, the sharp tone of voice, and the pointing index finger, by saying something like, "Why don't you ever trust me?" Clearly the teenager is responding to the emotional rather than the rational content of the message. Sound familiar?

As we grow and develop, we learn how to communicate, both verbally and non-verbally, through our family members, teachers, peers, and all the individual successes and failures that are an inevitable part of life. Over time, we learn what works and what doesn't based on the reactions we receive from those around us. Often, however, we settle for habitual ways of being and relating with others, even though we may be unhappy with the outcome. Many of us get into a pattern of trying the same things over and over again hoping for different results. Sometimes we are so focused on changing what we say in order to be heard, that the other person is left feeling "talked at" rather than understood. In many ways, we feel some degree of the same thing – that we fail in our attempts to connect with others. Sound familiar?

If effective communication is at the core of every healthy relationship, how can we increase our chances of success?

Rich

Speaking for myself, I know that most every failed communication in my life has involved some level of fear – the fear of being misunderstood, used, hurt, abandoned, judged, or otherwise rejected. In most every case, I focused my attention nearly completely on what I wanted to say, the point I wanted to make, or what I wanted the other person to do. In short, my focus was on me. I discovered that no matter what I was trying to say, if the other person couldn't hear it, I had failed to communicate.

Yvonne

For me, the biggest obstacle to communication has been the perfectionist voice inside me, the demeaning "critters" that live in my head – the ones that tell me *I should be this* or *I should do that*. My own self-judgment can cause me to come across as judgmental or impatient when I attempt to communicate with others. My own fears and discomfort make it harder for me to be vulnerable and communicate what is truly in my heart.

Learning To Commune:
The Challenge Day Communication Model

Remember that the ultimate goal of all communication is to "commune," or to connect with another person. In Chapter 10, we explored how to connect with others through the gift of listening. Now we want to delve deeper into what it means to commune, in this case, to be in a state of heightened, intimate receptivity. This model isn't just for romantic relationships, it is for every relationship you encounter, which, in our eyes, is more fulfilling if it is vulnerable and intimate.

Step 1 – Set a Container

Have you ever had something important that you wanted to say to someone? Have you ever just walked up and started talking without first checking to see if they were available to have a conversation right then? How long did it take for you to notice that the person you were speaking to wasn't really listening? Maybe you even found yourself feeling hurt and frustrated, perhaps blaming the other person for not hearing you?

When this happens, many of us just give up and walk away hurt. Why would any of us continue to do this? What are the odds of having a successful conversation if one person isn't participating?

That's why the first step in our model is to set a container for the conversation. This might sound a little formal or even weird, but it simply means making sure the person you are speaking to has the time and interest to listen in that moment. Setting a container can be as easy as telling the person you have something you'd like to speak with them about, and then asking if he or she has a couple minutes to listen. In essence, you're just checking in to see if it's a good time.

When you ask if someone has the time to listen, it is important that you wait for the other person to answer. In order for this step to work, you have to be willing to hear a "No," or a "Not right now." At that point, it's time to negotiate for a win-win by asking, "When would be a good time?" When both people agree on the container – in this case, a time and place – you have set the conversation up for success. For example, I might ask, "Will you please just listen to me for ten minutes so I can get all of my thoughts and feelings out?"

Yvonne and I often use a kitchen timer to create a specific container for listening. Since Yvonne describes listening as the most important gift I could ever give her, I'm here to say the timer has been an invaluable tool that has contributed greatly to the success of our relationship. Timers work well for both one-way conversations, where just one person wants to be heard, or two-way conversations, where both people get a turn. Using a timer helps both the speaker and the listener know there will be a boundary.

Additionally, setting the timer means the listener has agreed just to listen for a set amount of time. This is especially useful for difficult conversations where one person might be tempted to interrupt, get defensive, or worse, attack back.

We highly recommend using a timer.

Step 2 – Get Vulnerable

When we want to communicate something important, especially if we are upset, it's easy to be harsh, abrupt, or even aggressive. My goal is to stay humble by reminding myself that anything I may be mad about with someone else, I have done myself. Being humble and vulnerable increases the odds of another person really hearing us.

Being vulnerable simply means getting real, dropping the waterline, and letting the person know how you are feeling. It means saying things such as, "I'm sharing this with you because I love you and want us to be closer," or "I feel nervous telling you this because I really care about you." You can even add, if it is true, "I know I have done it myself which is why I'm able to see it in you." This step increases the chances that the person you are speaking to understands that the intention behind your communication is to get closer, *not* to make them wrong. The more vulnerable you are, the more likely you are to be heard.

Step 3 – Use "I" Messages and Avoid "The Finger"

Before I teach about "I" Messages, I want you to think about "The Finger." Have you ever had a finger pointed in your face with an accusatory "you" message behind it? Examples of such messages include, "You *never*...," or "You *always*...."

Now, honestly, have you ever put your finger in someone else's face with a similar energetic message behind it?

The truth is that most of us have been on both sides of the finger countless times. We often find ourselves bruised by what we call "You" wars. For example, have you ever heard or said, "You are always late!"

"You never think of anyone but yourself!" "You are so selfish!"

Using accusatory "You" messages is like being stuck on a hamster wheel; they simply don't work!

When we use "You" messages, it's as if our finger is literally in the other person's face. We are telling the listener about *them*. Because so many of us have been raised with or hurt by "You" messages, the listener often feels blamed, attacked, or put down, and usually becomes angry or defensive. In cases like these, the listener's response will often be to shut you off, pull away, or even attack back. The challenge is to take the finger out of the other person's face and point it back at yourself. Keep your attention on you, on what you feel, want, or need in a given situation. The goal is to take full responsibility for your own feelings using an "I" Message.

Using an "I" message helps the speaker to keep the focus on what they want, need, or feel. Practice starting sentences with words such as "I feel…" when this is said or done. But be careful not to say, "I feel like, or I feel that."

The hardest part for many people attempting to use "I" messages is the "F-Word." Because our culture does not promote the authentic communication of emotions, many of us lack words to describe what we are actually feeling.

In order for "I" messages to work, we must have feeling words to insert. Examples of feeling words include sad, mad, happy, angry, afraid, jealous, embarrassed, or frustrated. We are never wrong when we keep our attention on the truth of what we are feeling regardless of the situation. Once we share how we feel, we can then add "I need___," or, "I want___," to complete the communication.

Here is an example of how to change a "You" message into an "I" message.

"You" message:

"You never clean your room! It looks like a pig pin!"

"I" message:

"I love you and I don't want to nag. I notice I'm feeling frustrated and angry that our agreements to keep your room clean haven't been honored. I would love it if you would clean your room now or let me know when you will get it done."

Watch for hidden "You" messages

It's all too easy for a hidden "You" message to sneak out. It might sound something like, "I feel frustrated and angry that *you* never clean your room."

This is a good attempt at an "I" message, but *you* slipped out.

It takes practice to communicate with "I" messages. Most of us were raised on "You" messages, so be patient and keep working at it. It will be worth it!

Step 4 – Share Below the Waterline

The joy of putting the "commune" in communication is the ability to say what really needs to be said and to know the other person will hear what really needs to be heard.

Often people are afraid to tell the truth to someone they care about because they don't want to hurt the other person's feelings. Some people are afraid of conflict and possibly reliving or experiencing unsuccessful communications from the past and so they keep quiet. Others don't think it is "that big of deal." However, when we fail to speak our truth, we cheat ourselves out of the intimacy that can be created by dropping the waterline and being truly vulnerable with another human being.

When this happens, we begin to fill our balloons by holding these feelings inside. It also creates separation because the unspoken truth becomes emotional baggage in the relationship.

Here are four types of communications below the waterline that many of us are reluctant to share honestly:

- **Withholds/Grudges** – Hurts, feelings, or resentments we have been holding back which keep us separate from others.

- **Feedback/Coaching** – Honest, supportive suggestions focused on assisting the other person's growth. These may include ways in which each person can contribute to making the relationship better.

- **Amends/Apologies** – Saying "I'm sorry" and correcting mistakes. We talk more in-depth about how important these are in Chapters 17 and 18.

- **Validations/Appreciations** – Shifting our focus to seeing the positive and taking time to vulnerably tell others what we like or love about them. There's more on this in Chapter 16.

As you approach sharing anything below the waterline, it is important to let the listener know what you want to do when you set the container by saying, "I would like to clear a withhold with you." "Are you open for some feedback?" "Are you open to a little coaching?" "I would love to share an appreciation with you, are you willing to hear it?"

Setting the container helps ensure that the listener is in the proper mindset to receive your communication.

Two Helpful Hints

Be Prepared for the Listener's Reaction

Until both parties are comfortable using this model, listeners often react. They may bat your communication away with phrases such as, "Oh, I was just kidding when I said that." "Come on, I didn't mean it." "But you don't understand." If the listener is caught off guard, or they're not ready to hear what you are saying, they may get defensive and lash out at you (the speaker), especially if they feel threatened. It is important not to beat yourself up for trying to communicate. Be patient and don't give up. Remember, you are an expert on you. You can never be wrong if you are not dumping or attacking, but your goal instead is to truly "commune" by using "I" messages and vulnerably tell the truth about what *you* feel, think, or experience.

The Ideal Listener Response

As you become comfortable using this model, you will be able to listen without getting defensive. Remember, this is as much about allowing people to get their feelings out as it is about hearing what someone else has to say. If you are the listener, give the speaker room to feel his or her emotions. Once that person is complete, we recommend a simple, "Thank you." The thank you means, "Thank you for caring enough about me and our relationship to share this." If you have ever had anyone respond with a sincere thank you after you cleared something yourself, you would know how fabulous it feels to just be heard with no response or reaction. You may also want to validate the speaker for having the courage to be vulnerable by sharing what is really going on.

Once the communication is complete, take some time to reflect on what was said. Is there any truth to the person's communication?

Most often, much of what you heard consisted of emotions and the other person's "stuff." You don't need to fix this. You just need to be present while the other person lets go of it. If there is a grain of truth in what the person was saying, you can choose to act appropriately.

More Information

For more communication tools, we recommend you look into the work of Marshall Rosenberg. His pioneering work with Non-Violent Communication has helped create peace in relationships all over the world. Go to www.nonviolentcommunication.com or www.cnvc.org for more information. His seminal book, *Nonviolent Communication: A Language of Life*, is excellent.

For educators or parents, we recommend his book, *Life-Enriching Education*, aimed at helping schools improve performance, reduce conflict, and enhance relationships.

If you are a parent looking for better communication with your kids, we also recommend one of our favorite books, *How to Talk So Your Kids will Listen and How to Listen So Your Kids Will Talk,* by Adele Faber & Elaine Mazlish. We always had one on the back of the toilet while raising our kids. When things got heated we could take a "time out" for ourselves and quickly find suggestions for when we returned.

Be the Hero

The spoken word belongs half to him who speaks, and half to him who listens.

~ French Proverb

Notice

- Do you find yourself getting defensive or angry when talking to people? If so, what are they saying that has you react that way? Are you more defensive with some people than with others? If so, why do you think that might be?

- Do people tend to get defensive or angry when you are trying to communicate your wants or needs? What role, if any, do you think you play in their reactions?

- Is there anyone with whom you'd like to have a better relationship? Where in your life could you be a better communicator?

- How often do you catch yourself talking without knowing if the other person is interested or really has time to listen? If you don't know, practice noticing it.

- As you communicate with others this week, notice if you focus more on making your point or on creating connection between you and the listener. And notice how often you find yourself using a "You" message.

- Knowing it's often far easier to see others than to see ourselves, is there someone in your life whom you trust receiving coaching or feedback from that might help you be even more amazing? What do you want help with and who can you approach to get it?

- Is there anyone in your life who deserves an apology? Where in your life could you clean things up or make things right?

- Do your friends really know how you feel about them? Are you carrying any resentments or grudges that cause you to hold yourself back or distance yourself from others? Are there things you've withheld because you don't want to hurt their feelings? Conversely, were you afraid to tell them how much they mean to you because you were embarrassed? What holds you back or stops you from sharing your truths with these people?

Choose

- If you notice that you become defensive or angry with some people more than others, or that certain others become defensive with you, imagine yourself having a different dynamic with them. Under what circumstances might you be able to forge a better style of communication? Imagine at least three things you might do to take responsibility for your part in changing things for the better. Is there coaching you need? Is there coaching you would like to give? Are there withholds you want to clear? Imagine what you would say and how the conversation would go, and then consider doing it.
- Make a list of the people in your life. Include the issues you think inhibit your relationships with them. Choose the tools that might help you improve them. Then plan a course of action you might take.
- Imagine yourself approaching someone you love with something important to say. Consider a few things you could do to ensure you have the best chance of being heard.
- If you've noticed yourself using "You" messages or not listening as well as you might, rewrite the same conversations. Practice doing it better in your imagination because what you conceive, you can achieve.

- If you feel as though you'd like to receive coaching from someone, first imagine yourself coaching someone else. Find the words you think might be most effectively received. Then, make a list of the ways in which you are best able to hear feedback. Being clear about the ways you might shut down to listening to what others have to say is the first step in being able to open and communicate your needs.

- Consider the last time you found yourself on the receiving end of a "You" message. How did it feel? What are you willing to do as your part to make sure others don't feel the same way? Translate any "You" messages you've heard or have used into "I" messages instead.

- How generous are you with your appreciation and compliments? Is there anyone in your life who deserves more appreciation from you?

Act

- Approach one of the people with whom you'd like to change your relationship. Apologize, make amends, express an appreciation, or reveal the ways in which you feel you inhibit your relationship. Notice how it went, make any necessary adjustments in your course of action with another person, and consider doing it again.

- Approach a loved one with something important you want to discuss. Set a container. Use your tools. Commune with that person.

- Ask someone for feedback or coaching on an issue that's important to you.

- If you've used any "You" messages in a conversation with someone, apologize and make amends.

- Choose one person every day this week and express an appreciation you have.

Celebrate!

Learning new tools and achieving better communication with the people you care about is cause for real celebration. Look in the mirror and brag to yourself about how amazing you are.

Everyday Hero ~ Bathsheba Harambe

Bathsheba has a fire that burns deep in her heart. She courageously speaks her truth and chooses love in all she does. A passionate educator and parent, Bathsheba spent most of her early professional career working to educate African American youth. She has always loved education, and wanted to model the incredible positive influence that her teachers had on her. Bathsheba created Umoja Camp with her husband, and founded an African-centered school because she wanted African American children to have a place to learn and be proud of their cultural heritage. Bathsheba's mission is to inform all children they are powerful. Once introduced to the work of Challenge Day, Bathsheba continued to express her passion, by training and educating people from all cultures.

Bathsheba

If you really knew me, you would know I was born and raised in the St. Bernard Projects in New Orleans, LA. And I felt ashamed of where I lived. Due to this shame I remember always pretending to be someone else, making sure everything in my life looked like I wasn't poor. I had the latest clothes, hairstyles, you name it. I was often teased about where I lived, but my mother taught me in those difficult times a powerful message: "It's not where you are from, it's where you are going." Since then, I have been on a mission to inform African American children to love themselves and honor their culture, regardless of circumstances and where they live.

If you really knew me, you would know that when I first came to Challenge Day I had worked in an all-black environment for eleven years. My experience with diversity was limited. I came to the organization with many judgments and false myths about people from other cultures. Challenge Day opened my eyes and heart so that I am able to meet and embrace many wonderful people throughout this continent.

At one of the first Challenge Days I led, I met an amazing young white man in Washington State who had no interaction with African American people in his life. At the beginning of the day, he would not talk to me or even dare reach out to shake my hand. As Challenge Day progressed and the barriers started to drop, he began to vulnerably share what his life was

Everyday Heroes ~ Bathsheba Harambe

actually like living in his community, and how he wanted something different. By the end of the day, this young man walked up to me, grabbed my hand, and asked me to dance with him in front of his all-white school of friends. I learned that acceptance is love. We must honor the differences. Thank you Yvonne and Rich for loving me the moment you saw me.

Rumors for Better or Worse

I resolve to speak ill of no man whatever, not even in a matter of truth; but rather by some means excuse the faults I hear charged upon others, and upon proper occasions speak all the good I know of everybody.

~ Benjamin Franklin

Yvonne

When I was a junior, my high school was plagued with rumors about a girl named Cecilia. Her supposed promiscuity kept every "popular kid" from being seen in her presence for fear of losing status.

My pain from being teased in junior high had begun to fade. The only reminder of the humiliation was my secret shame of bulimia. School was a joy for me now and, as one of the popular kids, I had power.

Because of my past experiences, I understood the power of popularity and I was determined to use it as a tool for good. I intentionally spent time trying to connect with other students from all over the school. I made it a point to get to know those who were being ostracized – whether it was because of the size or the abilities of their bodies, how much money their family had or didn't have, the color of their skin, the languages they spoke or could not speak – no matter the reason. As a result, my circle of friends was vast and colorful.

Knowing how much rumors play a role in high school life, I decided not to fight the practice but to use rumors as a way to bring people together, rather than as a way to divide them. You might have called me manipulative; if so, I wore that label with pride.

Having the "in" on the people who were being judged or viewed as "less than," I began spreading positive, true rumors about them.

"Do you know how nice Carol is?" I would tell people. "She came out of her way to help me push my car when it broke down."

Knowing my best hope for making headway was to merge instead of hitting head-on, I said things like, "I used to judge Mike, but now I know him and I really like him. I even saw him stand up for some kids who were being teased, and do you know how much he has to deal with at home in his family?"

At the time, I was head-over-heels in love with Louis, my first "real" boyfriend. His hand had been chopped in half in a farming accident when he was young, so he too had compassion because he understood what it meant to be different or "not normal."

When we heard the rumors circulating about Cecilia, Louis and I decided to get to know her. We would hang out with her during lunch and share life stories. The more she revealed her heart, the easier it became to like her, and we all soon became close friends. Because Louis and I were popular, our friendship with Cecilia became a doorway for others to see her with new eyes and include her in their circles.

Then came one of the biggest parties of the school year. I had to take my sister home after drama practice so I arrived at the party late. After talking to a few people, I excitedly asked if anyone had seen my boyfriend. One of my friends pointed to the backyard and said, "I saw him walk outside with Cecilia."

I made my way to the dimly lit yard, and weaved through clusters of people who were talking and laughing aloud at one another's jokes. Some turned to say hi, and I acknowledged them briefly as I continued to search for Louis. Then out of the corner of my eye, in the shadow of a huge oak tree, I saw the silhouette of him with his arms wrapped around Cecilia.

My body surged with jealous anger as my imagination filled in the blanks. I was certain they had betrayed me, and all I could think to do was leave. As I made my way back into the house, my rage had become a poison that I injected into everyone around me. The more I spewed, the more my story bloomed. Soon it had become, "I think they were kissing."

I spent nearly an hour seething and gathering allies to my side, an army of angry friends who enthusiastically jumped to my rescue. Cecilia's former reputation made it easy for people to believe that she had influenced my boyfriend – that he was innocent and she was the perpetrator. There seemed to be an undercurrent of almost eager delight and satisfaction in some of them to have new material for gossip, and I felt justified having so many of them carry my toxic words home as they left.

Then the room went silent as Louis and Cecilia walked into the house. I felt righteous in my anger and aligned with the many people who turned their heads in disgust. Unaware of the toxicity in the room, Louis and Cecilia brightened when they saw me and rushed toward me. The purity of their energy made me question my initial impulse. As they approached, I noticed that Cecilia's eyes were red and swollen. When she reached out to hug me, I knew I had been wrong and I was suddenly filled with the fire of shame.

Cecilia explained that without warning, her father was taken from their home and forced to return to Mexico. Her entire family was devastated. I suddenly understood that what she needed most was love and support, and my boyfriend was simply being a good friend by holding her as she cried.

I was mortified. Even though I had made Cecilia my friend, and I knew her heart, I had allowed the negative stories that had been circulated about her to color my perception of what was happening out near the tree. My unconscious impulse was to inflict the same kind of pain onto someone else that I had once experienced myself. Because of fear and jealousy, I had created my own negative rumor that deeply hurt two of the people I cared about most. It took months of one-on-one conversations, complete humility, and multiple apologies, combined with my friend's gracious forgiveness, to clean up the fall-out of my unconscious actions.

Live It!

Trying to squash a rumor is like trying to unring a bell.

~ Shana Alexander

I imagine almost every person alive carries painful memories caused by rumors. Whether the memories are from being the spark that started the rumors, or of being the target, we share the hurt. Negative rumors can spread like wildfire, and they inevitably cause separation, and often leave lasting scars.

Unfortunately, negative rumors have become almost an expected part of teenage life.

On a daily basis, as Challenge Day leaders we hold students as they openly express the loneliness and devastation caused by the never-ending cycle of rumor spreading. I would be willing to bet that many young people graduate from high school remembering more about the art of spreading rumors than any subject they studied.

Although rumors can often have such a demoralizing effect on so many teenagers' lives, it is a rare thing for a school to take the time needed to create awareness and to address the consequences of this issue.

One of the biggest challenges Rich and I had to endure as parents was witnessing our children's distress brought on by the pain of the daily rumor mill they experienced at school. Life would be going just fine, and then all at once, someone, often a friend, would spread an excruciating, untrue rumor. I remember numerous tearful mornings when one of our daughters would refuse to go to school. Afraid to face the looks and whispers, or risk being shunned or left out completely, she would plead to stay home.

Not only young people live in the realm of rumors. Adults also have an intimate relationship with the separation and hurt rumors can cause, whether it is in our own families, at work, in our places of worship, or in our circles of friends.

From a very young age, we practice the art of talking about people behind their backs. Even though we know the hurt that lies and gossip can cause, our desperate desire for acceptance often leads us to join in and continue to spread them. Ironically, many seem to derive pleasure from the short-term satisfaction of these unholy alliances. They get hooked on the drama created by rumor spreading and the importance of being included in another person's "secret."

Because rumors are so insidiously embedded in our daily lives, if we want to end the practice, we need to stay very awake to prevent even subtle rumors from sneaking into our conversations.

To help break the excruciating cycle of rumor and counter rumor, we developed an effective way to intervene when it is happening. We call it the Challenge Day Rumor Elimination Model. When you use this model, you are committing yourself to support only win-win, positive communication, and become a bridge to better relationships for yourself and the people around you.

There are three important issues this model addresses. First, it stops people from continuing to spread rumors either intentionally or by silently standing by and letting it happen. Second, it provides a container to deal with all of the emotions that people may be feeling because of the story that's going around. Finally, it encourages people to confront the source of the rumor and gives them some support for the process.

In the Challenge Day organization, this is one of the tools we use regularly. Years of experience with it lets us know that the model can really work if you are willing to use it.

Challenge Day Rumor Elimination Model

Step 1: Attempt To Interrupt

If someone comes to you speaking *anything* negative about another person, recognize that it is a rumor! Our first challenge is to stay awake and conscious enough to *notice*! Then do your best to interrupt it. Say something like, "Why don't you go talk to that person directly?"

Step 2: Listen

If the person speaking is too upset to stop talking or to take responsibility for going directly to the person they are spreading rumors about, offer a safe place for them to empty their balloon. We talked about how to conduct a session in Chapter 11. Remember to listen and share compassion for the speaker's feelings *without* adding to the separation or agreeing with unsubstantiated judgments. You have an opportunity to create resolution and peace if you don't collude.

Step 3: Get a Commitment

Confirm that the speaker will stop talking negatively or is willing to go directly to the person they have judgments or concerns about. Confirm a time when the person is willing to clear up their concern directly with the person they were speaking about. Offer to support them if it seems appropriate or necessary.

Step 4: Check Back

Hold the person accountable. Ask them to report back and let you know when they have completed their conversation. *This is very important.* Care enough about both people to make sure the process is complete.

Step 5: Never Repeat

Let the rumor end with you! Do not pass on what you hear to others. Remember, there are always two sides to every story.

Positive Rumors

I will be the first to admit I am an expert at spreading rumors, and today, I am proud of it! Since so many of us have refined the art of rumors, Rich and I suggest instead of completely unlearning the skill, have fun using it. One of my favorite Acts of Change has become to intentionally share positive, true rumors about people. I especially enjoy passing them on to people who negatively judge or don't like someone. It is so fulfilling to know I have been a part of having people shift from judging someone to seeing them in a beautiful, celebratory light. Take pleasure and enjoy seeing how much love and connection you can create by directly saying, "Let me tell you a great rumor!" Then truthfully gush about what you see, know, or love about someone else, and eagerly invite people to pass it on.

How many of these rumors can you spread today?

Be the Hero

A rumor without a leg to stand on will get around some other way.

~ John Tudor

Notice

- Spend time reflecting on how negative rumors have affected you or the people around you. Have you ever experienced pain or loss because of a rumor? In what ways, if any, have rumors affected your relationships with others? Have you ever lost a friend? Have you ever prejudged or avoided anyone because of things you heard about them?

- Consider the ugliest rumor you've heard about another person, true or not. How did that rumor affect your beliefs and feelings about that person?

- Has anyone ever spread negative rumors about you? Why do you think they did it?

- Have you ever spread rumors about someone else? What was your motivation? How did the rumors affect that person? How did you feel afterward and why?

- Take an honest look at yourself. When you hear a negative rumor about another person, what are you most likely to say or do? Do you jump in and add on, or do you interrupt? Perhaps you don't even recognize the negativity. How often, if ever, do you find yourself spreading or initiating rumors about others? When it comes to negative rumors, are you a part of the *problem* or a part of the *solution*?

- Have you ever believed a negative rumor about someone only to find out later that it was a lie? What, if anything, did you say or do after you discovered the truth?
- Have you ever spread a "positive" rumor about someone? Maybe you shared how nice someone was to you or how thoughtful someone is? How did it feel to spread the "good news" about this person?

Choose

- Assuming you've experienced or witnessed pain or loss due to negative rumors, the next time you hear a disparaging rumor about another person, how would you like to respond? What, if anything, might you say or do? If you could rewrite any of your previous experiences, how would you change things?
- Where in your life might you be more diligent at interrupting rumors? What course of action might you take with someone or with a group of people?
- The next time someone spreads a negative rumor about you, what are some ways you might feel proud of dealing with it?
- Assuming you want to be a positive part of the solution, consider some ways you might see yourself helping to interrupt negative rumors or stopping ones that are circulating now.
- Is there someone in your life whom you have wrongfully judged? Is there any way you could change the situation or see yourself making things right?
- When it comes to rumors, what kind of family member, friend, or co-worker do you choose to be? How will you incorporate the lessons of this chapter into your life and relationships?

- The next time you notice, think, or hear something nice about someone, what are some ways you might consider spreading the "good news?"

Act
- Identify at least one person in your life who seems to have a problem sharing negative rumors. Share this chapter with that person and do your best to support them by gently interrupting their habit.
- Make a conscious inventory of all the people you've heard or spread rumors about. If possible, do what you can to find out the truth about them and then make a point to spread the "good news" about them.
- Make it your daily practice to interrupt any negative rumor you hear.
- Spread *positive rumors*. Consciously look for opportunities to spread positive rumors and pass on compliments.
- Find one person whom you've negatively judged or even helped to perpetuate rumors about. Apologize and promise to help end the rumor mill.

Celebrate!
Share your experiences and triumphs. Log on to the *Be the Change* website and blog about your successes: www.challengeday.org/bethechange.

Everyday Hero ~ Kushal Naik

Kushal is a unique combination of brilliance, love and commitment. He was introduced to Challenge Day following a series of suicide attempts involving students at his high school. As part of his leadership class, Kushal became a founding member of his school's Be the Change Team, which was instrumental in helping to launch a school-wide Be the Change effort that included peers, administrators and parents.

Following his graduation in 2006, Kushal became the youth representative on Challenge Day's Board of Directors. Currently, Kushal is attending medical school at The Medical University of Silesia in Katowice, Poland, where he continues to keep in active contact with the Challenge Day organization.

Kushal

If you really knew me, you would know that Challenge Day took my high school by storm following a number of tragic events, which changed the lives of everyone involved forever. Challenge Day, for me, was initially just another day, but as our school started to accept the values and ideas presented, the atmosphere changes were awe-inspiring. I am such a strong supporter of Challenge Day because I have personally faced oppression in many forms, and I have experienced so much struggle in my attempts to overcome it.

I am dedicated to supporting Challenge Day because it shows people around the world that oppression is all around us, and that we can even be guilty of oppressing others ourselves. However, most importantly, the Be the Change Movement shows a way to fight back against oppression to better their lives, and the lives of others around them.

The Be a Man Box

The male stereotype makes masculinity not just a fact of biology but something that must be proved and re-proved, a continual quest for an ever-receding Holy Grail.

~ Marc Feigen Fasteau

Rich

One unforgettable day when I was four years old, I got to go to work with my dad. He was an after-school recreation director, and as we walked hand in hand across the playground where he worked, I felt like a movie star. Everyone seemed to know him and like him, and I felt especially proud to be his son.

The playground was filled with kids who were older and bigger than me. They were all playing basketball, climbing on the monkey bars, swirling on the merry-go-round, and whizzing down the slide. My eyes widened with excitement and I raced over to join my new friends.

The more I played, the more courageous I became, and I decided to try the big slide. It was a blast. I'd climb expertly to the top, position myself on the metal slide, and let go, laughing all the way to the bottom. Then I'd run around to do it all over again. On my fourth trip up, I was surprised to discover a girl coming up from the other side. She'd crawled up the front of the slide and we simultaneously reached the top of the ladder. Urgent to take her turn, she pushed me backward just at the moment my little hands let go of their grip, and I went tumbling downward. As my body hit the ground, the impact momentarily knocked the wind out of me. And then, I burst into tears.

I'm not sure how long I lay there or how loudly I had been crying before some kids ran to get my father. What I clearly remember was how frightened my dad seemed when he asked if I was okay. I wanted to put on a good face for him. I knew from experience that my dad was uncomfortable with tears. I worried that he would be disgusted or ashamed of me. I also didn't want to let him down by telling him a girl had shoved me and I couldn't hang on. So I told him that I was fine. That seemed to make him feel better. He sat me up, patted me on the back, and said, "Shake it off, you'll be alright."

I choked back my tears and did my best to pretend that nothing had happened. Already, at four years old, I knew it wasn't okay for boys to cry.

As my dad and I started walking toward his office, suddenly a shooting pain tore through my neck and shoulders, far more than my little body could stand. I began crying uncontrollably, unable to stop the flood. My dad had no idea what I was feeling so he comforted me in the only way he knew how – by continuing to pat my back. I cried out in pain as he tried to console me. "Come on Rich, shake it off. Shake it off!"

I wanted to please him, so I did all I could to stop crying. By the time we got to his office, I had stifled my tears. He sat me on a hard, metal chair and I shifted back and forth, fighting the throbbing ache and trying to get comfortable. I wanted to be a "good boy." I sat quietly listening to Motown tunes while I waited for my father to get off work.

On the drive home, we hardly spoke. I was proud of myself for being able to make it all the way to our house without crying. I felt like a real man, like my father, stoic and in control. But as soon as my mom opened the door and asked if I was okay, I burst into tears. Moments later, I was in the car heading for the hospital.

The x-rays revealed that I'd broken my collarbone in two places. I was fitted with a huge cast that looked like a pair of shoulder pads. I was relieved that something was wrong with me. Having a cast meant that there was a good reason for my tears. Maybe now my dad wouldn't think I was such a baby.

Live It!

A man's sense of self is defined through his ability to achieve results.

~ John Gray

Collectively, our culture shoves boys into an invisible, life limiting, emotionally restrictive and often dangerous place that at Challenge Day we refer to as the "Be a Man" Box. Everywhere we turn, our fathers, coaches, friends, and popular media pass on stories of what it means to be a man: "Big boys don't cry!" "Grow up!" "Be tough!" These are just a few of the destructive messages many men hear from the time they are little boys.

Although this training varies from community to community and from culture to culture, the underlying message is that there is a right way to be a man. Strength is measured in emotional detachment, heroic physical accomplishments, and most of all, self-sufficiency. Confined to a life sentence inside the Be a Man Box, men are allowed only two basic emotions: anger and humor.

As far back as elementary school, I felt attracted to girls but I had no idea how I was supposed to act around them. When I reached high school, I seemed to be popular and my dad made jokes about me being a "lover boy." I enjoyed the attention and the status he had given me, so there was no way I could jeopardize it by asking him about relationships or how to be with girls.

When I watched how other men and boys were behaving, I compared myself to them and I wondered if I was doing it right. On the outside, I looked as though I already knew how to be a man. I was great in sports, I had many friends, and I said and did all the "right" things. On the inside, however, I felt lonely, confused, and unsure of myself most of the time.

I wondered what was wrong with me, but I was afraid to talk to anyone about my feelings. Instead I watched men on television, and I just did my best to act the way they did.

Whenever we ask men in our workshops what happens if they step outside the box, they speak about being ignored, teased, rejected, alienated, labeled as gay or girly, or in some cases beaten up and even killed. For many of us, our biggest fear is that we will be disrespected by other men and rejected by women, so that ultimately we will be all alone. Many men would rather be trapped in the "comfort zone" of a limiting box, than separated and isolated outside of it.

In addition to making men feel like frauds, the Be a Man Box seriously distorts men's relationships with other men as well as with women.

The Consequences Are High

Many men are taught to relate almost exclusively through playful banter, jokes, teasing, competition, rough housing, drinking, cussing, and sexualizing women. As a consequence, many of us find ourselves feeling separate or competitive with other men. Even more damaging to both men and women is that the most offensive put-downs assigned to men are to be called a woman, a woman's body part, or any word implying we are homosexual.

Among all the other messages that these labels convey is that we shouldn't get too close to other men.

This *homophobic* thinking (homo meaning *same*; phobic meaning *fearful*) often prevents many men from creating close, supportive relationships with other men, including our brothers, fathers, and grandfathers.

However, if being a *real man* means we can't hug or share our emotions with other men, then we become almost completely dependent on women for intimacy and closeness. This distorts our relationships with them. Some men become so unconsciously afraid of their dependency and need for women that they aggressively control or dominate the women in their lives. For other men, women become little more than trophies to be displayed and then discarded, especially if they threaten to get too close. Taken to the extreme, this fear can lead some men to desperate and intolerable acts, including verbal and physical abuse, and sadly even rape or murder.

While it is clear that not every man who receives this training automatically distances himself from other men, or becomes an aggressor, an abuser, or a rapist, the problem is that it's difficult to completely escape the grasp of the Be a Man Box. As males, no matter how much we are loved or how much permission we are given to share our hearts and emotions, at some point we all come face to face with the tragic consequences of this training.

Whether you are male or female, or even if you don't identify with either gender, your life is still being impacted by the Be a Man Box. It's possible that every war on our planet has at its core the essence of this training.

Breaking the Cycle

The good news is that this lesson is not about our destiny as men or as a civilization. Rather it is intended to open our eyes to choice. By shining a light on the inhumanity of this systematic training, it is our hope that men everywhere will ultimately be liberated from the cost of its limiting and painful lessons.

As men, we need to wake up and decide for ourselves who we choose to be and how we wish to live our lives. The challenge is to avoid looking to the media or even to our friends for guidance on what it means to be a man. We need to look into our own hearts. The goal is freedom – freedom to be who we are, freedom to love, freedom to learn, and freedom to ask questions when we don't know.

We must recognize that we are part of something bigger than ourselves. Over the years, that has often meant joining the military or becoming involved with sports and similar institutions. Lacking any formal rites of initiation into manhood, many men have turned to self-reliance, isolation, and competition as a means of asserting their manliness. As the men's movement takes hold, more and more things are changing. The Mankind Project, the Million Man March and other groups are providing us with the opportunity we all need to redefine what it means to be a man.

By turning our attention from competition and aggression to brotherhood and connection, we, like many of the women in our lives, now have the opportunity relate on a deep level as friends, supporters, and teachers for one another. It's time for fathers to hold fathers, brothers to hold brothers, and fathers to hold and nurture their sons. It's time we support one another in healing past hurts, unlearning stereotypes, and allowing for a balance in our lives. It's time we raise our sons in new ways, completely honoring the masculine, more aggressive and directive aspects of ourselves, while also welcoming the feminine, more receptive and nurturing aspects of ourselves. It's time we all wake up to the choice we have – to choose our destiny as men and to stop living our lives as victims limited by the training of the Be a Man Box.

What's Good About Being A Man

In spite of all the hardships and challenges we've faced as men – the training of the box, our expendability in war, and the expectation that we are to be providers, financial caretakers, and emotionally self-contained – I am still grateful to be a man. Because of the training we get as men, it's easy to fall into the trap of male bashing and blame. It is easy to find agreement, among both men and women, that stereotypically as a group, men are less emotionally available, horny, self-centered, and at times rude. Even I have noticed my own arrogance in assuming that I was just an exceptional male. When I came across men who, in addition to being hardworking, strong, athletic, and dependable, were also sensitive, supportive, and trustworthy, I would often fall into the trap of thinking I had found a gem, a special man, one worthy of my trust and friendship.

Now after fifty years of life, I know that I was sorely mistaken. I can now honestly say every man I have ever met is worthy of my love and respect. Down deep, in spite of the training, every man who walks this planet is capable of and desires depth and connection. I now know the only thing that ever stopped me from trusting other men was my own fear that I would get hurt or let down. Trapped in the cycle of oppression and the training we get as men, many of us believe in the limitations we are given and we stop reaching for our own greatness. We stop soaring. We stop developing the fullness of ourselves and instead settle for less than we are capable of being. Seen as having immense social power and privilege, we as men begin to subtly agree that our privilege inevitably comes with a price tag.

A Look At The Other Side

I have had the gift of a strong, healthy, physical body. I have walked the streets unafraid of whether or not I could protect or take care of myself. I have been an athlete and a teammate to countless other amazing men committed to a common goal. I have had opportunity after opportunity to step up as a teacher, manager, director, and founder, and in every case I was seen as an exceptional leader. I have been honored by male peers as a powerful, compassionate role model. I have shared the gift of lifelong friendships with male friends who have accepted and celebrated me with all of my short-comings. I've climbed mountains, taken camping trips, rafted rivers, and won championships with boys and men who have overcome incredible odds. I have been a men's group facilitator, as well as a participant with other men who have joined me in facing the depths of our deepest emotional pain.

When I am with men, I notice that I feel completely at home – I am free of all "trying" and I find it easy to laugh. My male friends seem to understand me from our unique male perspective. They are completely flexible and forgiving about my business obligations; they let me know they care about me without being needy or making me feel guilty. I love the fact that I am encouraged and appreciated for my power, my love, my ability to speak, to take charge and to be vulnerable. I am grateful for the opportunity I get on a regular basis to look women in the eyes and blow them away with the power of my love and appreciation, without hitting on them or expecting a response. And I am especially lucky to have spent close to half my life in love with the woman of my dreams.

The Be a Man Box comes with limitations but it also contains gifts, and I was blessed with a committed, well-meaning father who coached my sports teams and passed on his best lessons. As a result of my father, I learned that service and care for people should always take precedence over individual accomplishments. I learned the value of hard work and fair treatment, and the ecstasy of physical strength.

As a man, I have been provided with numerous opportunities to earn a living and create a life of abundance. I have been allowed to be a sexual being with complete permission to express the fullness of my passions. I have been blessed with doing my part to create the miracle of life. And I am grateful to have had the gift of watching my kids being born, rocking them in my arms as they fell asleep on my chest, and being celebrated as someone they called, "Daddy."

Compassion and Forgiveness

Whatever we believe or feel about the men who served as role models and teachers – whether they were present, absent, or down-right mean – they all did the best they could given the training they received and the hurts they carried. No man ever lives his life intentionally disconnected, defensive, angry, or cruel.

For years, I spent a lot of time being hurt and afraid. I blamed my father for much of the insecurity and doubt I felt growing up. I blamed him for being violent, for making demands on me in sports, for pushing me to excel in school, and for rarely letting me know how much he believed in me. In my mind, I felt that he loved me more for what I did than for who I was.

Then, after participating in several men's groups and personal growth work including the Hoffman Quadrinity Process, I found the path to my personal freedom. I was finally able to drop my resentments and ask my dad about his childhood. For the first time, I began to see life through my father's eyes. Hearing his stories opened me to a deep sense of compassion for the daily rage and violence he'd had to endure. I realized that he'd gotten it far worse than I ever did. Both my father and I learned the hard way what it meant to live stuck inside the nightmare of the Be a Man Box.

Then, after years of both of us allowing ourselves to step outside the box and express our feelings with one another, my dad was even able to apologize to me for the pain I had suffered on that unforgettable day when I was four years old.

If you really knew me, you'd know that I felt particularly vulnerable writing this chapter. It was hard for me to celebrate my own masculinity, and to focus on the gifts and advantages of being a man. While I felt compelled to shine a light on the insidious training that can so often separate us from each another – men from men, men from women, and fathers from sons – I also wanted to open new doorways into what is possible for men to exemplify in the world… but I didn't really know how. I kept finding myself bumping up against the same limitations we all face on a daily basis. It's time we confront those limitations and truly band together to create a safer, more loving, and compassionate world.

Yvonne's Perspective on the Be a Man Box

Growing up, the men in my family seemed larger than life, and I spent many of my most memorable moments with them. As a child, I was referred to as my grandpa's little shadow because I followed him everywhere. My brother and I spent hours in our tree fort, and I can still remember the excitement that surged through my body as we fought off our make-believe enemies from our plywood perch. I can also still smell the scent of horses grazing and feel the wind on my face while I sat tucked into my daddy's lap riding high up in the tractor for hours as we plowed the field on our family farm. I loved my mother and sisters, but my grandpa, my dad, and my brother were my heroes.

Unfortunately, by the time I became a young adult all that changed. As I endured years of hurt and humiliation from boys and men, my balloon was overflowing with anger and I began to believe that every man was "the enemy."

I had a huge list of "good reasons" to be angry with them. In school, after I had dangerously lost weight and achieved the stereotypical image of beauty, I faced the routine harassment of being whistled at, called derogatory names, and often pushed past my boundaries on dates when my "No" didn't seem to mean no. Later, I was beaten up and raped. I even had a boyfriend try to kill me for breaking up with him. My experiences may sound extreme but they are not unlike those of so many women I knew, and I became furious about the disrespect and violence that we're forced to endure. Consequently, I wanted very little to do with most men.

I spent much of my time colluding with my girl friends about how horrible men were. We marched in the streets of San Francisco at night, aggressively claiming our safety, dignity, and freedom. A part of me saw all men as potential villains and therefore subject to the fire of my fury.

Carrying so much pain, having very few tools, and not knowing that someday this poison would actually turn into medicine for my work with teens, I did the best I could with all the feelings I carried in my balloon. Even in the times I was able to release my emotions, my anger and resentment kept me judgmental of, as well as separate from, half the population.

How My Perspective Changed

After suffering a lifetime of pain, it took just one day to completely transform my perspective. The miracle happened when I first learned about the Be a Man Box during a youth summer camp I was part of staffing over 25 years ago. Harrison Simms, my friend and teacher, divided more than a hundred campers into two groups. Young women were seated on one side of a taped line on the floor, with young men on the other. Then Harrison, a large, beautiful, fully bearded black man, powerfully described what happens to boys born into our culture. He cried freely as he and all the young men discovered and revealed the horrors of this life-limiting and often-deadly training.

I was spellbound, listening to men vulnerably share the loneliness and pain of being imprisoned by the box. I heard them describe how they were told not to cry, how they were hit and beaten and then told they were not able to hold or support one another. In the course of a few transformative hours, I woke up to the realization that men were not the enemy. Their courage to speak gave me compassion, and a window into the innate innocence of every man in the room. I began to immediately re-channel my deeply embedded rage toward men, into understanding the dangerous training men and boys are drenched in on a daily basis. My newly found empathy created an additional purpose for my life. I committed to not only continue my efforts to empower women, but I also dedicated myself to compassionately healing the separation and wounding caused by the Be a Man Box.

Understanding the cause of men's disrespect and acts of violence, however, didn't automatically empty my balloon of all the hurt and resentment I carried with me, so I intentionally set out to heal and release the pain from my past.

Although much of my healing took place in support groups with women because so much of my anger was at men, it was especially helpful when men stepped up as allies. I'll forever be grateful to Rich, my counselor Jeff, and all the other men who generously offered to listen and to hold space as I emptied my emotional balloon. With their permission and a safe container, I had many sessions where I yelled, screamed, cried, hit pillows, and spewed out the poison from my past.

After an enormous amount of emotional release work, my ultimate healing happened in a most unexpected way.

Men are not the Enemy

Ten years ago, an opportunity arose that profoundly tested my capacity to love. Rich and I have some dear friends whose dream was to have a baby. After much heartache, grief, and many unsuccessful attempts to get pregnant, doctors finally told them that it was impossible for my friend's body to carry a baby. And so Rich and I, together with our kids, decided to support them in making their dream come true. We decided that I would carry their baby for them as a surrogate. For nine months, this miracle child developed inside me, and I nourished it and loved it as if it were mine.

You see, Rich and I raised four kids of our own, *all girls*. But this time, after thirty hours of labor, when our friends' baby was born, *it was a boy*. I held him in my arms, looked into his eyes and realized that he was every bit as precious, beautiful, and pure as our baby girls. There was no difference. By giving birth to a baby boy, I experienced a profound healing. I immediately understood that all the anger and resentment that I, and many women, held toward men should not be aimed at them, but rather at the training of the Be a Man Box.

Today our work to eliminate this destructive box takes on added personal urgency. Our first grandchild was born in 2007. He is a boy. My love for him has ignited renewed inspiration. The purity of Rocklyn's smile and the innocence in his eyes has further deepened my commitment to do everything I can to end the hurt and educate others to the dangers of the Be a Man Box.

Playing
with
our
grandson
Rocklyn

Be the Hero

The ultimate measure of a man is not where he stands in moments of comfort and convenience, but where he stands at times of challenge and controversy.

~ Dr. Martin Luther King, Jr.

Notice

- How have you or the men in your life been affected by the training of the Be a Man Box? In what ways, if any, have your life and relationships been limited by this training?

- Whatever your gender, take a moment to consider what you see or experience when the men in your life relate to the world around them. What do you notice about their interactions? Are there any men in your life whom you wish could more easily show their emotions?

- Which, if any, of the following comments have you used or heard? "Be a man, don't cry, toughen up, don't be a wimp, a queer, or a fag." How do you think these words affect people?

- Examine your relationships. Of the people closest to you, how many are men and how many are women? What about these people or your relationship makes them so special to you? Which, if any, of these people would you say you feel more emotionally safe with and why? Do you notice any patterns?

- Have you ever been in a group of people who were bashing men or complaining about the way they act? What, if anything, did you say? Did you go along? Did you interrupt? What, if any, effect did those comments have on you or the way you look at the men in your life?

- Have you ever found yourself being quiet about the behavior of men around you when you wished you had spoken up? Have you ever made, experienced, or heard sexist remarks toward women? Have you ever done something you were ashamed of because you feared hurt, ridicule or rejection from men?

- Of the men in your life, are there any whom you feel especially close to or supported by? What about these men makes them so special to you? Do they know how you feel? Have you let them know how important they are?

- When was the last time a man impressed you, inspired you, or emotionally touched your heart? What about that man, or the circumstance, moved you? Does he know how he impacted you? Did you tell him? If not, why not?

- Over the next week, consciously observe the male role models in your life. Include family, friends, media, sports personalities, and other men you see in everyday life. Notice how they act and what you admire about them. Use these men to help you decide how you can break out of the Be the Man Box.

Choose

- If you have identified ways in which you have been affected by or limited by the Be a Man training, now imagine not having those traps and restraints. How is your life different? How are your relationships different? How is the world different?

- As you have observed the men in your life and their interactions, what changes would you like to see in the way they relate to you or others?

- If you have been a part of male bashing, either by participating or by not stopping it, how can you imagine doing things differently? What future actions can you take to release all men from their stereotypes?
- If you have been hurt or degraded by men in any way, imagine all the ways in which you could have acted and reacted differently in those situations. Is there something you wish you said or did? Is there a different outcome you wish had transpired? Rewrite the story and find ways to behave that make you feel proud of you.
- Of the men in your life you feel close to and supported by, list all of their qualities for which you are grateful.

Act

- If you are a boy or a man, make a list of things you love about being male. If you are a woman, make a list of some things you love about men. In either case be sure to share your list with someone you trust will celebrate with you.
- Approach one man whom you love and ask him if you can share your observations of him. Tell him what you admire about him and also make one suggestion of what you would like to see more of from him. Be gentle and loving in your comments.
- Write a letter to a man you love and admire, and express all your appreciation for having him in your life.
- If you have been a part of male bashing in the past, take a step toward making amends. Either tell someone thar you would like to talk about men differently, or apologize for having been demeaning.

- If you have been hurt by a man, take one step toward healing. Write a letter of forgiveness, ask that man for insight into his emotional world, release any pent-up feelings you may have, get counseling, or otherwise move toward compassion and understanding.
- If you are a father, big brother, or role model to a younger boy or man, the challenge is to make yourself available as a mentor. Offer yourself as a resource to discuss anything about life and relationships.
- If you are a male, consciously look for ways to be an ally to women. Interrupt sexist comments, intentionally acknowledge and include women's voices in groups, ask women to share what life is like for them being female.
- Attend a workshop or participate in a personal growth experience to help break through the box. Our Next Step to Being the Change workshop offers huge healing regardless of your gender. The Hoffman Institute, which played a significant role in my personal journey, is also a great resource.

Celebrate!

Share your experiences and triumphs. Log on to the *Be the Change* website and blog about your success: www.challengeday. org/bethechange.

Everyday Hero ~ Kekoa Won

His name means "courageous one," and Kekoa has courageously transformed his life to bring powerful role modeling and healing to the lives of others. Raised in violence, pain and confusion, Kekoa became trapped in the Be a Man Box early. He realized a dream by receiving a full-ride football scholarship to college, and then started on a path of healing and service. Working with the Boys and Girls Clubs of America, he set out to give the encouragement and support he'd so dearly missed himself.

Today, Kekoa is a master facilitator, speaker, and Senior Challenge Day leader who continues to be driven by his desire to leave a lasting, positive impact on the lives of others. As a father of three boys, he's committed his life to being a role model of love, compassion and vulnerability. His rough exterior and heartfelt expression create an unparalleled opening for connection and healing. Kekoa is a natural leader and now models what a real man can be. He serves as an invaluable part of Challenge Day's leader training team, and he is also instrumental in the growth of the Assembly Program. His life stories and inspirational speaking continue to encourage positive change and transformation for thousands of youth and adults each year.

Kekoa

If you really knew me, you would know that although we call it the Be a Man Box, for me it felt like a prison, a place where I could never be who I really wanted to be. I know my father did the best that he could do, but his own Be a Man training created a lot of dysfunction, destruction and suffering. I was raised in constant fear and anger. Because my father loved me, he taught me to survive, but there is a huge difference between surviving and living at peace.

If you really knew me, you would know that getting out of the Be a Man Box is a constant practice of feeling, forgiving and healing. It is a choice that I have to make every day, moment to moment. I forgive my father. I made a promise to give my three sons a life outside of the box: to accept them for their individuality, to protect their spirits, to never hit them, and to create a home where they feel safe, loved and celebrated. My commitment is to not allow the cycles of my past conditions and habits to dictate how I show up as a man, a father and a friend. My hope is that I am an example that it's possible to break the cycles of whatever keeps you from living at peace or fully alive.

The Be a Lady Flower

15

The woman's mission is not to enhance the masculine spirit, but to express the feminine; hers is not to preserve a man-made world, but to create a human world by the infusion of the feminine element into all of its activities.

~ Margaret Thatcher

Yvonne

If you really knew me, you would know that after my grandpa died, my grandma moved from Minnesota to California to be closer to our family. This was a momentous event in my life since my grandma contributed significantly to my becoming the woman I am today. Her love for me, her caring attention, helped soothed the aches that threatened to swallow me. I was special in her eyes and I have always felt so seen by her.

When I was in junior high school feeling fat and ugly, my grandma often handmade my clothes so they would fit my chubby body better. I would stand in front of a full-length mirror with her standing right behind me and evaluate the new outfit she'd created just for me.

As if reading my mind, she would whisper in my ear, "Don't stop looking until you see how beautiful and perfect you are."

To this day, when I look in the mirror, I hear the echoes of her encouragement. In fact, looking at myself, meeting my own eyes and seeing myself with love, has become a vital part of my life. For this alone, my grandma would be a hero, but there are so many more of her gifts weaved into the fabric of my life for which she deserves credit.

Amazingly, Grandma recently turned one hundred years old. Our family threw her a party, complete with a hundred years of pictures, stories, memories, and songs to celebrate our remarkable matriarch. It was a divine opportunity to see all the astonishing, almost unbelievable changes she has witnessed in her lifetime. My daughters, privileged to hear the stories first-hand rather than merely as lessons in books, have received an all-too-rare peek into the dramatic transformations that have occurred for women. Grandma's century of living has blessed us with a personal window into history – or, in this case, "her-story."

When my grandma was born, women and children were legally considered to be the chattel, or property, of men. Women of my grandmother's generation were commonly told how to walk, talk, and act, and even what to wear. Many women lived as unpaid servants. Those seen as strong or outspoken were routinely subject to ridicule, ostracism, violence, and even death, just for being themselves.

In 1920, when my grandmother was 12 years old, the U.S. government passed the 19th Amendment to the Constitution, allowing women the right to vote. Despite the fact that the Declaration of Independence had been signed 144 years earlier proclaiming, "that all men are created equal," women had been overlooked. It's almost impossible to overstate the enormity of the gap between the privileges, opportunities, and freedoms of men and women. We've certainly come a long way since then, and even since "Women's Liberation" became part of the national conversation in the early 1970s. My grandmother's stories pay homage to just how much.

We've made such significant gains in equality that the stories from our relatively recent past seem outrageous or even unreal to many young people. It's hard to fathom that the women of my grandmother's generation lived through what we would now consider to be criminal acts of mistreatment and violence that at the time had little or no legal consequences. So, when looking through the eyes of my hundred-year-old grandmother, we clearly have much to celebrate. However, even though we are no longer considered chattel, women born today will still be subjected to conditioning that is limiting at best, and in the extreme, utterly dehumanizing.

I call this conditioning the "Be a Lady Flower."

Live It!

I feel that as women, we've allowed ourselves to be diluted by certain ideas that hold us back, such as the overglorification of masculine consciousness. To me, liberation does not mean that I can think just like a man. Real liberation means that I can think, act, and be like a woman and receive equal respect, honor, and compensation.

~ Marianne Williamson

The "Be's", "Do's" and "Don'ts" For Women

Be polite! Be thin! Be gentle! Be a mom! Be with a man! Be ready for guys when they want you! Be a homemaker! Be neat and clean and smell good at all time! Be smart, but not too smart! Be the nurturer! Be the listener! Be sexy! Be responsible for birth control! **Be, Be, Be!**

Do wear makeup! Do keep your legs crossed! Do have long hair! Do shave your legs and armpits, and pluck your eyebrows! Do have dinner ready! Do keep the house clean! Do make men look good! Do put other woman down behind their backs! **Do** raise the children! **Do** get paid less for the same jobs as men! **Do** look like the women in the media! **Do** remain silent when men whistle, call you names, or disrespect you! **Do** question if you did something to deserve getting raped or molested! **Do, Do, Do!**

Don't be single! **Don't** be easy! **Don't** be fat! **Don't** be loud! **Don't** be stronger or smarter than a man! **Don't** say no! **Don't** be "masculine!" **Don't** think other women are pretty! **Don't** put yourself first! **Don't** do "men's" jobs! **Don't** *ever* burp, fart, sweat, or be angry! **Don't** eat too much! **Don't** talk back! **Don't** tell anyone when you have been raped, molested, or physically hurt! **Don't** talk about your period! **Don't** grow old! **Don't, Don't, Don't!**

These "Be," "Do" and "Don't" rules form the basis of what we call the Be a Lady Flower training. When we talk about this at our Next Step workshops, we use the visual of a flower with many petals. I like to use the color pink for this exercise to exaggerate the point, because in our culture pink is the ultimate "girl" color. We label the five petals as:

1. The Unattainable Dream
2. Internalized Oppression
3. Disrespect and Violence
4. Emotional Caretaking
5. Rights, Privileges and Power

Each of the petals on the Be a Lady Flower comes with their own set of "rules" for being female. What makes it particularly difficult is that many of the messages are contradictory. For instance, we should be assertive in our business dealings, but we shouldn't be like a man. We need to know how to please a man, but we shouldn't be "easy."

If we want validation or attention from men, we should dress like a porn star; but when we do, we're considered to be whores. We are the primary caretakers of the children, and we must also do the cooking and cleaning; if we need to have a job outside of the home, we should always seem happy and rested.

Women live with these contradictory messages every day.

Girls Will Be Girls?

Before we look at the five petals of the Be a Lady Flower, let's first look at where the training begins. The conditioning of both the Be a Man Box and the Be a Lady Flower starts from the moment we know the gender of a child. Many conscious parents say it does not matter to them if their child is a boy or a girl. While they do their very best to avoid falling into gender role stereotyping, pink and blue distinctions are everywhere.

Clearly, there are some structural differences between boys and girls, but as the relatively new science of epigenetics suggests, gene expression is strongly affected by the environment. In *every* culture, children receive different treatment based solely on whether they are a boy or a girl[1].

Studies have shown that for even the most aware parents, once they find out their child's gender, their energy, tone of voice, and behavior changes accordingly. For example, on average, baby boys receive less kissing, comforting when hurt, cuddling, and nurturing than baby girls. Parents are more likely to hold boy babies facing out and girl babies facing in. It is not because they don't love them as much, it is simply that they have unconsciously adopted our cultural training[2].

Differences between the way boys and girls are raised are vast and obvious, from the clothes in which we dress them, the colors we choose,

---

1 http://findarticles.com/p/articles/mi_qn4179/is_20010304/ai_n11763335
2 http://www.menshealth.com/cda/article.do?site=MensHealth&channel=health &category=other.diseases.ailments&conitem=03a9b1774a5e0110VgnVCM200 00012281eac____&page=1

the toys we buy, the tone of our voices, and the expectations we have. Just as with boys in the Be a Man Box, much of the Be a Lady Flower training happens in early childhood under the loving care of parents who are completely unaware of the powerful lessons they are teaching their baby girls. Parents are supported in this training by schools, counselors, churches, and other social institutions. In school, girls are considered to be more feminine if they are cheerleaders than if they participate in strenuous sports. Helpful guidance counselors tell us to be smart, but not too smart, as they encourage us to consider careers with more opportunities for women. And in some churches, only men can give the sermons and offer communion while the women are seen as adjunct supporters.

It is frightening how hypnotized most of us have become by the time we are teenagers, especially as we navigate through our materialistic, low touch, image driven society. For many, we are so deeply into the Lady Flower role that we become obsessed with weight, hair, makeup, clothing, dieting, breast enlargements, liposuction and other forms of plastic surgery, and having a litany of material possessions. In fact, some of us our are so dominated by our image that maintaining it has become more important than our love for our families, our gratitude for life, our respect for the planet, and our desire to help others.

The Lady Flower messages are so pervasive in our society that my own daughters have spent a big part of their lives thinking they are fat, ugly, or can't achieve their goals. This is devastating to me! We need to stop sleepwalking through life and *wake up*! Only when we recognize how we have all been programmed can we begin to re-write the script.

Petal One - The Unattainable Dream

Be attractive! **Be** the most beautiful woman in the room! **Be** thin! **Do** dye your hair! **Do** shave your legs! **Do** get a tan! **Don't** wear unfashionable clothes! **Don't** leave the house without makeup! **Don't** eat more than he does! **Be, Do, Don't!**

The Be a Lady Flower programming teaches us that we should be beautiful. But who decides what beauty is? What has been considered beautiful changes over time and from one culture to another. Tall, short, big, small, curvaceous, thin, tan, pale, dark, blonde, brunette, pierced, tattooed, or otherwise decorated, have all been considered to be beautiful at one time.

The common thread seems to be that for women, beauty does not come naturally. From the invention of makeup and perfume in ancient times, women have needed to change, alter, and "improve" themselves to be considered beautiful. Frequently, this can lead to unhealthy practices or even physical mutilation in order to achieve society's ideal. In Victorian England, women wore constrictive corsets to achieve the fashionable wasp waist. Up until the 20th century in China, young women of the upper classes had their feet broken and bound with bandages so they would not grow to be more then four to six inches long.

In the U.S. and many other countries, standards of beauty are set and perpetuated through the mass media. We are so bombarded with information that television shows, movies, commercial advertisements, magazines, and billboards begin to dictate our opinions. Our unconscious minds soak up information everywhere we go and if we sleepwalk through life, we end up literally killing ourselves with disease as we try to meet those impossible standards.

Our mainstream media glamorizes women who are young, thin (even anorexic), large breasted, suntanned, small waisted, Caucasian, or having European features. Attempting to emulate the models they see, girls and women, young and old, resort to desperate measures such as fat burning pills, miracle diets, laxatives, diuretics, and starvation. Breast augmentation or other forms of plastic surgery have become a part of everyday life. Hundreds of thousands of such procedures are performed every year, and surgery among teens is frighteningly on the rise.

Playing With Deception

Let's look at one of the most popular toys for girls – Barbie™. Obviously, it is a doll. As a fashion doll, Barbie is considered to be *the* standard for beauty. Just a harmless plaything for girls, right? Perhaps, but consider these stats about this harmless toy[3].

If Barbie were life-size, she would be six feet tall, weigh 101 pounds, wear a size four dress, and have a 39-inch bust. Her head, at 19 inches, would be the same circumference as her waist. Her hips would be 33 inches. She would have room for only half a liver and a few inches of intestines (as opposed to the usual 26 feet). The result: chronic diarrhea and death from mal-absorption and malnutrition. Because Barbie's neck is twice as long as the average human's, it would be impossible for her to hold up her head. Her legs are 50% longer than her arms, while the average woman's legs are only 20% longer. Assuming she could walk, she would wear size five shoes and always walk on her tippy toes. However, since her feet are too small and her chest would pull her forward onto her knees, she would have to crawl on all fours instead.

This may sound funny, but as a mother of four daughters, I find *nothing* funny about it. Barbie may be just a "toy" but she is the image millions of girls are looking at and playing with from the earliest years of their lives. Unconsciously, the seed has been planted.

When my girls were young, I was so passionate about this topic that I insisted they not play with Barbies or other dolls that are unrealistic. I did the righteous, "controlling" thing until I realized that wasn't going to work either. My daughters would end up rebelling because all their friends had these dolls and then Barbie would get even *more* attention.

So, our goal isn't to shelter our kids from Barbie, it is to wake up and teach our kids the facts so they can *notice*, become conscious, and *choose* a different course of *action*.

3 http://www.anred.com/stats.html

Perpetuating the Fraud

The way women are portrayed in the media is not an accident, it is a conscious and intentional choice. We learned this firsthand while making the documentary, *Teen Files: Surviving High School.*

Rich and I, along with the 11 teenagers chosen for the show, were invited to witness a live photo shoot featuring Magali Amadei, a popular fashion model and actress. Awestruck by all the glamour and glitz, the teens watched Magali step out of a black stretch limousine and graciously introduce herself. Her fame and shimmering beauty enchanted them all. The boys by her side playfully flirted as she swept regally into the studio with the rest of us following close behind.

Before the shoot, we all sat with Magali who spent over an hour openly sharing her experience as a well-known super model. To our surprise, she was amazingly real, allowing us to peek into the shadows behind the bright lights of her world. The teens hung on her every word as she vividly described her daily struggles to reach unrealistic weight and beauty goals. She candidly shared painful memories of desperately eating and throwing up in the hopes of losing weight. We all listened in growing dismay while she revealed her history of depression, self-doubt, and even thoughts of suicide.

I wiped tears of compassion and understanding from my cheeks as she described the same feelings I had while I was in the grip of this same disease. Her story highlighted the struggle, shame, and danger that can befall women who try to fit the image of the Lady Flower.

After our conversation, preparations for the photo shoot began. It took hours for Magali's staff to prepare her for the hot lights. Concerned that her nose was too big, she instructed them to darken one side with extra makeup. The teens became uncomfortable but remained silent as photographers, producers, and makeup artists worked on Magali. They inserted fake breasts, tucked in clothing, taped back skin, added hair extensions, and adjusted lighting – all deliberately designed to create the "perfect" female image. Everyone watched, shaken, as their new friend twisted, tilted, and angled herself in ways that hid what she deemed to be her "flaws."

At the conclusion of the shoot, we all said good-bye to Magali and headed to the computer lab for part two of the experience. Our host sat behind his high-powered computer and proudly began demonstrating his photo alteration skills on the large screens that surrounded him. We stared in disbelief as he smugly created the "ideal" fantasy woman by lifting her hairline, adding even more to her breasts, reducing her already thin waist, shrinking her nose, and lengthening her legs. Magali's photos had become almost unrecognizable.

Mike, one of the teens in the group, squirmed uncomfortably and asked, "Do you touch up guy's photos, too?"

The technician chuckled and nodded, "All the time." He went on to explain that the majority of all the photos in magazines have been altered in one way or another.

Christina, another teen, bravely asked the question that was on all of our minds, "Is what we are seeing even real?"

Without hesitation, the technician responded. "Not at all, this is not a person anymore."

Christina crumpled to the floor in tears.

Petal Two - Internalized Oppression: Women Hurting Women

Be passive! **Be** obedient! **Be** submissive! **Be** insecure! **Do** criticize others' physical appearance! **Do** compete for men's attention! **Do** put down other women behind their backs! **Do** be threatened by both working and stay-at-home moms! **Don't** defend other women! **Don't** do "men's" jobs! **Don't** put yourself first! **Don't** celebrate being a woman! **Be, Do, Don't!**

Internalized oppression happens when *any* group of people begins to believe the negative stereotypes so much that they take the very same methods of hurt they've received and turn it on one another. We see this played out time and again in our relationships with our sisters. Rather than supporting each other in our bid to break out of the Be a Lady Flower role, we feel threatened by another's success.

Part of the Lady Flower training convinces us that we *need* to be with a man in order to be complete. Since we believe that men are programmed by the media standard for beauty, we adopt those same standards in an effort to be "desirable" or "chosen." Holding ourselves to these criteria not only perpetuates these ideas, it also leads to competition among women. Then, what do we do if one of our sisters – another woman – actually resembles the media's image of a "perfect" woman? We view her as the enemy. Jealousy and competition fosters mean, rude, distant, or disrespectful behaviors such as sabotaging relationships, spreading negative rumors, or gossiping. In short, we learn to hate each other as the Lady Flower training separates and divides us.

A woman without a man is like a fish without a bicycle.

~ Gloria Steinem

As wonderful as it can be to have fulfilling relationships with men, we as women need to understand that we are complete and whole without them. We don't ever need to be with a man. As long as we believe we are not complete unless we "have" a man, we can become desperate, devalue ourselves, lower our standards in friendships with men, stay in disrespectful or abusive relationships, judge or put pressure on ourselves or others, and fight, hurt, and compete with other women for men's attention.

Competition among women is not limited to our appearance, it extends to the choices we make in our work lives and even to the way we raise our children. For example, women who work outside the home, and especially those who achieve success in business, are often judged and treated poorly by other women for contradicting the rules of the Lady Flower. Successful businesswomen are often accused of being cold or "manlike." Several years ago, the front cover of Time™ magazine highlighted the "Mommy Wars" and reported on instances of women hurting, ridiculing, or even destroying other women for working rather than staying at home with their children. Even in contemporary baby books, mostly written by women, there is a lot of judgment around whether women should work when they have children, and how long they breastfeed. There isn't nearly enough support in making decisions that are best for each woman's unique circumstances or preferences.

Petal Three - Disrespect and Violence

Be Careful! **Be** obedient! **Be** virtuous! **Do** remain silent when men whistle, catcall, or disrespect you! **Do** keep your legs crossed! **Do** have a man with you when you are out! **Don't** spoil the mood! **Don't** act in ways that call attention to yourself! **Don't** tell when you've been violated, raped, molested, or physically hurt! **Be, Do, Don't!**

The sad truth is that because of the of the Be a Man Box training in our society, men often use insults, abuse, control, and even violence against women to keep them stuck in the Lady Flower. Throughout history, violence against women has taken many forms. In the middle ages, for example, women who stepped out of the Lady Flower paradigm as healers or midwifes often were labeled as witches and burned at the stake. Certainly, we have made tremendous strides in our culture since then. Now, more than any time in history, women are free to choose the life that *they* want. However, we still have a long way to go.

Modern Day Oppression of Women

Most people in this country, as well as in many parts of the developed world, don't realize just how prevalent the oppression of women remains. In fact, the Secretary General of the United Nations believes that systematic oppression of women is the biggest crisis of our time.

Here are just a few of the horrific truths that illustrate this point. You may not know that many of our sisters around the world cannot drive vehicles, hold jobs, or own property because of their gender. Some women are considered to be property. Some women cannot legally vote, or if they do, they must have their husband's permission. Some women are burned after their husbands die because they are seen as an additional burden that families must take on. In some countries, it is not against the law for men to rape their wives or the wives of their brothers. Then, once these women are raped, they are often disowned or even stoned to death by their family because the rape is seen as having brought shame to the family.

Women are contracting HIV/AIDS at the fastest rate of any group due to a lack of education and funding for health care, and because of their inability to protect themselves from their husbands and other men. Women are being trafficked for sexual exploitation. Women are being legally sent to other countries as brides to unknown men. Women are being mutilated as a "rite of passage." Women are being murdered because their families can't pay their dowry. Women are being tortured and killed for engaging in premarital sex. Women are being sexually assaulted as a tactic in war. In fact, according to World Bank data, women between the ages of 15 and 44 are at a greater risk of suffering rape and domestic violence, than cancer, motor vehicle accidents, war, and malaria[4].

These stories and statistics merely scratch the surface. It's clear that we need to wake up! If we don't notice what's happening, there is no way we can change it.

Petal Four - Emotional Caretaking

Be gentle! **Be** the nurturer! **Be** a homemaker! **Do** raise the children! **Do** make men look good! **Do** have dinner ready! **Don't** talk back! **Don't** go to bed angry! **Don't** say no! **Be, Do, Don't!**

Throughout history, the traditional role of women has most often been that of nurturer and caretaker. Women were expected to raise the children and take care of the household, while men were expected to put food on the table and a roof over their heads. The duties of women in this role were to keep house, feed and clothe the family, and be a sexual partner and emotional support system for the man.

These expectations are still very much a part of the Lady Flower role. In recent years, however, the "duties" of women have become even more complicated. One of the results of the Women's Liberation movement of the early 70s is that it is now acceptable for a woman to take a job or even have a career. In many cases, because of the economy, taking a job outside of the home is now a necessity.

What this means, though, is that many women now have two jobs – one job being the traditional nurturer and caretaker, and the other working to earn money. This imbalance of responsibility seems to tip the scale in favor of men. Studies have shown that the emotional support women provide is one of the reasons married men tend to live longer than unmarried men[5]. Unfortunately, the same cannot be said about women.

That's why, as women, we need to find sources of emotional support for ourselves. In addition to my relationship with Rich, it has been crucial for me to have a women's support group where I can cry, be angry, be tired, empty my balloon, and receive nurturing. And, as we mentioned in Chapter 11, everyone in our organization also

4 United Nations Development Fund for Women; www.unifem.org/campaigns/vaw/facts_figures.php

220

has accountability buddies who offer ongoing emotional support and hold us accountable for getting what we need and deserve.

As a couple and as parents, Rich and I have worked very hard to unlearn the habits and lessons of the Man Box and the Lady Flower. As two people with full time jobs outside the home, we have had to stay very awake and intentional in making sure we are equally sharing household tasks. These include cooking, cleaning, laundry, listening and loving as well as disciplining and raising our kids. Taking time for our own individual needs, including rest, exercise, friends, hobbies, and time alone, have all helped to keep us in balance. And I can't stress enough how important it has been in our relationship to have a date time *every week* when we love, listen to, and nurture one another.

Given the changing times and the rise in single parent households, it is crucial we come together as communities to give single parents help. Parents attempting to keep a job, run a household, and nurture and spend time with their children often find little or no time to rest, take care of themselves, or empty their emotional balloons. Together, as friends and family, we can make a huge difference by spending time listening to, loving, and nurturing single parents and their kids.

Petal Five - Rights, Privileges and Power

Be Polite! **Be** smart, but not too smart! **Be** responsible for birth control! **Do** move when your man is transferred! **Do** respect authority! **Do** get paid less for the same jobs as your male counterparts! **Don't** ask him out first! **Don't** complain! **Don't** be too athletic! **Be, Do, Don't!**

When a group of people moves from the status of chattel property to equality in the eyes of the law, there will always be resistance from those formerly in control. Since my grandma was born, women in

---

5 Sheehy, Gail, "Why Marriage Is Good Medicine for Men," Parade Magazine, June 12, 2006

the United States have demanded and won the right to vote, equal employment, and sexual freedom. However, there are still many overt and subtle ways in which women are denied full equality or have less power than men.

Because of our pervasive training, when a man and a woman are seen together in public, many people will assume they are a couple and that the man is in charge. If they are in a restaurant, the man will most likely be presented with the check. If they are signing a document, the man will often be asked to sign first. Sometimes the woman won't be asked to sign at all.

In conversation, women typically feel as though they have to push their way to be included, particularly in the business world. During sporting events, fans are much more likely to show up to watch men compete than women. And in the religious arena, many faiths prohibit women from taking leadership roles or even from worshiping in the same room as men.

In the medical world, much of the research in this country was conducted using male subjects as participants. Treatments were approved for use on both men and women assuming women's bodies would respond similarly to men's.

In regard to reproductive health issues, women are often expected to be the responsible ones. Fortunately, women are much more likely to have at least some of these costs covered by insurance than they were only a few years ago.

In business, women generally earn less money for doing the same work. Women are also less likely to be hired or promoted for important jobs out of concern that they will fall in love and leave, they will have a baby and leave, or they will be more concerned about their families than they are about their careers. Many professional women are afraid to use maternity and family leave benefits available to them for fear they will be looked over for a raise or dropped from the fast track. For those women who do succeed in their careers, the Lady Flower training says that they are bitches, while their male counterparts are merely aggressive.

How Do Women Unlearn The Lady Flower Training?

Until my early twenties, I kept myself firmly inside the Flower. I would *never* leave my home unless I was freshly shaved and wearing makeup. My clothes had to be just right. My breath, pits, and other parts always smelled like flowers. The biggest problem was that I wasn't doing it for me; I was doing it because I thought I *had* to. Like so many girls and woman, I lived trapped in the Flower.

When I started to wake up and *notice* the painful, limiting, degrading conditioning I had unconsciously accepted as part of my upbringing, I deliberately practiced stepping out of the Flower. At first, it was hard to distinguish between my choices and the conditioning. So I experimented by shaving one leg but not the other, one armpit, neither, or both. I would go to school, the mall, or other places in public, switching between wearing grubby old clothes or cool, trendy clothes. Some days I wore no makeup and other days I wore a lot. I practiced being strong, loud, and outspoken. Other times I explored being soft and gentle. Some of these choices may sound funny, but I needed to know that I was the one doing the choosing, and to realize that I would not die if I chose differently from what the Lady Flower rules dictated.

My goal was to discover what *I* wanted, what *I* liked, what *my* choice was. To me, this is what it is all about – women free to choose what we want in our lives – and do what we were born to do.

It is a great time to be alive!

Although much of this chapter was written to bring awareness to what is happening, I don't want anyone to get overwhelmed or feel hopeless. In spite of any suppression we may face, I think this is probably one of the best times in the history of the world to be alive and to be female. The world is ready and hungry for us to embrace who we are, step into our power, and proudly bring forth the unique feminine medicine we all carry inside.

It is time for all women to come out of the closet of silence and conformity, and boldly own and celebrate our femininity. I am not talking about perfume or makeup, I am talking about the power and energy that comes through us and is so much bigger than we can imagine. Its flames come from love, nurturing, and deep passion.

We are the mothers, the givers of life, and in our souls we know that that now means more than just giving birth to babies. It means birthing a new world. It means remembering the innate gifts that we are born with as women. It means holding space for something that we all crave to emerge. It's time for us, more than ever before, to honor, love, and nurture each other as we usher in what is needed to heal and transform our world.

The preparations have been made. As a human family, we are now connected by phone and by computer to the global mind. It is time to connect the global heart. The human heart is longing for an end to violence, war, destruction, waste, separation, and hatred. We are ready and praying for the time of the global feminine awakening in both women and in men – a time when we all listen closely and allow our emotions and intuition to guide us inward. When we do that, we will find that we have everything we need.

As women, instead of viewing our natural forces and rhythms such as our menstrual cycles as an unwanted curse, we can learn to use the energy and the receptive power that is heightened at those times to further awaken and propel us. Not long after my breakthrough in the hospital, a wise woman taught me that my period brought special power. Instead of being afraid of my intense feelings and pain,

I learned to track and welcome my period, my "moon," and use it like fuel for an engine. With my circle of women, I would go deep inside, cry, scream, and feel, and like electricity to a light bulb, I would let it ignite me. All of my major life breakthroughs, ahas, and creations, such as Challenge Day, happened while I was having my period.

As women, it is crucial to honor change and to welcome aging as a time of wisdom and the entrance into a new reign. At this time in my life, emerging from the gift of menopause, I am discovering a completely new power. I use the metaphor of the caterpillar often, and so once again I liken my journey through menopause to a caterpillar entering the cocoon. Over and over I have told myself to trust, to have faith in the miracle of creation as I surrendered to the natural process as a woman and let myself completely melt down in my cocoon. Literally hot as fire and dripping with sweat, I allowed my mind, body, heart, and spirit to transform and emerge and soar as a new woman. I hardly recognize myself. In a wonderful way, I am now too wise to care what other people think and I am too determined to take any crap. I say yes to what is next for me in service to all life.

Please don't get me wrong; this is not about separating or excluding men.

In fact, when we truly remember who we are, we will join with men and midwife them as they give birth to the feminine parts of themselves that for many have been dormant. One of the things that attracted me to Rich was the beautiful balance of masculine and feminine in him. He is both powerful and sensitive. To accomplish what we were all born to do, men and women need one another. We need to hold hands in a new way.

We are coming together, sisters with sisters, brothers with brothers, and sisters with our brothers. Together we are birthing a magnified love and internal peace like never before. It is time to honor the expression of spirit that can be experienced through the feminine in each of us – as men and woman – through the arts, music, dance, and all forms of expression.

It is time to tap into the compassion and forgiveness that it will take for us all to heal. It is time to embrace and to celebrate our sacred femininity, and use it to create the life and the world of our dreams.

Thanks to the Women Who Paved the Way

In closing, I thank our mothers, grandmothers, and all of our female ancestors. Today we stand on the shoulders of every woman who courageously stood up and spoke out against daily acts of disrespect, anger, and violence in order to create a new world for all of us. They, with the support of many compassionate men, have dramatically altered the consciousness of our world. Women are heads of state in many countries, have top leadership roles in the United States, and are powerful, compelling candidates for high office.

My work on behalf of my daughters, and all women, will not end until I die or *every* woman around the world is free and safe to be who she is – fully alive and fully expressed. I challenge every woman and man to join me. Start right now by standing in front of the mirror and looking into your own eyes. *Don't stop looking until you see how beautiful and perfect you are!*

Be the Hero

Being a princess isn't all it's cracked up to be.

~ Princess Diana

Notice

- How has your life been affected by the Be a Lady Flower? In what ways have you or the women in your life been limited by its training? In what ways has this training influenced your expectations and relationships with the women around you?

- In what ways have you bought into the Lady Flower training? If you are a woman, what role, if any, does the flower have in your life? If you are a man, how has the training of the flower impacted your relationships or your choice of relationships with women?

- If you had trouble answering the above, we'll explore each of the 5 petals... In what ways, if any, are you or the women in your life trying to live up to some unattainable dream? How often do you or the women in your life judge themselves as fat, ugly, or in some way flawed?

- How often, if ever, do you or the women in your life negatively judge, put down, or gossip about other women? How has internalized oppression affected you or your relationships with the women in your life?

- How often, if ever, have you or the women in your life been expected to be responsible for the emotional wellbeing of those around them? What impact do you think these expectations have had on their lives?

- Have you or any of the women in your life ever been the victims of violence, abuse, or sexual pressuring? If so, how did it feel? What, if anything, did you do or say in response? How do you think these experiences have affected you?

- Consider the women in your life whom you know and admire. What is it that you admire most about them and why? What is their relationship with the Lady Flower?
- In what ways, if any, have you or the women in your life been given less privilege than the men? What impact do you think these limitations have on these women's lives and relationships?
- Consciously notice the ways women have advanced the cause of equality. Take note of the ways women in history – or "herstory" – have spoken out, sacrificed, and faced ridicule or abuse to make things better for women today.

Choose

- Sit quietly in a room alone. Close your eyes. Take each of the petals of the Lady Flower in turn and think of instances in which you or any woman you know has been limited. As you play each scene in your mind, imagine breaking the confines and releasing yourself or someone else from any traps they may have, from themselves or from society. Let your mind be free to dream. Rewrite the ending of the story or envision an entirely new world. This may take a while. Perhaps you will choose to dream a new dream for yourself or for a woman in your life. When you do this, you put energy into the world. Energy has power. Dreams become realities.
- Imagine new relationships for yourself and for others – women with women, and women with men. Notice if your dreams fall into any unconscious traps.
- Imagine having conversations with women you admire, either living or dead. What do they say to you – about you, about women, about men, about the world?

- This is part of allowing the feminine presence into your life more and more. When you can be still and make room for your internal voice – the voice of your dreams and of your wisdom – then you are making space for the divine feminine to arise within you. This is important for everyone, men and women.

Act

- If you have been affected by the Lady Flower training in any way, take one action every day this week to break out. Change your clothes, compliment someone for making a bold choice, love and honor your body, apologize to someone for any gossiping, call someone on their use of any degrading words or actions, or do anything else you can think of to free yourself and others of this training.
- Find an advertisement that portrays women in a manner you are proud of (the recent advertising campaign for Dove soap is an example). Write a letter to the company thanking them for their respect for women.
- Go out of your way to appreciate the women in your life. Acknowledge them for all the ways you see them as powerful, profound, brilliant, or living outside of the Lady Flower.
- Attend a personal growth workshop that deals with empowering women. The Next Step to Being the Change workshop, for example, has a powerful, often life-changing exercise based on the Lady Flower.

Celebrate!

Find a woman in your life who is significant to you – a woman who has either birthed you or has otherwise given you life in some way – and celebrate with her in honor of her gifts.

Everyday Hero ~ Sela Gaglia

Sela is a living example of everything we teach. Alive with passion and knowing, she has a magical way of bringing love and connection to every relationship. Sela is the holder of our legacy. She lives and breathes integrity. After graduating from San Diego State University where she was a gifted student, writer and athlete, Sela joined Challenge Day as part of our first leader training. Since that time, she has consistently brought her rare depth of character and passion to diverse rooms of youth and adults all over the U.S. and Canada.

As a mother of three boys, Sela is a passionate ally for men, and a role model to women everywhere. A brilliant speaker, presenter, and Senior Leader, Sela is part of Challenge Day's leader training team. She has been directly responsible for much of the expansion of Challenge Day's Circle of Change program, and she is a key player in the creation and presentation of its growing assembly program.

Sela

If you really knew me, you would know that I have been extremely outspoken my whole life. I come from a family of strong, educated women. I don't think there has ever been a time where the Be a Lady Flower has truly held me back – there is a voice inside me that naturally fights against all forms of oppression. That voice was nurtured by my mom, and I believed her when she told me I was smart and valuable, and that I could do and be anything I put my mind to.

But the generations before me did not have all the privileges that I take for granted. Like a lot of girls, I got the message that the trick to getting what I want is to let men think they are making the decisions, when really women are running the show. As a mom of sons and an ally for many incredible women and men, I believe we are at a time in history where we need to stop not only the oppression between sexes, but the many sneaky manipulations that we've used to overcome those oppressions.

I also look forward to the day when we, as women, automatically look for the beauty and power in one another. Women, can you imagine what we could accomplish if we took all the time and energy we've used to pull each other down, and use it to lift each other up?

The Power of Appreciation

16

Appreciation is one of the most powerful, yet overlooked aspects of successfully motivating and empowering people and teams. When individuals and organizations put more attention on what IS working, instead of focusing on "problems," they thrive.

~ Mike Robbins

Rich

If you really knew me, you'd know that I don't often enjoy holiday family gatherings. As much as I love my family, getting together with them during the holidays has often left me feeling tense, judgmental, and separate. In the past, there has often been too much food, too much alcohol, and too much television. Yvonne and I have felt the need to retreat when we reached our limit of small talk and bantering.

One Thanksgiving, we decided to do things differently. Yvonne and I invited my entire side of the family to our home for a "different" kind of holiday celebration. After everyone arrived, all fifteen of them, we asked them to sit in a circle. Knowing that we're the "touchy-feely" types, they were all a little nervous. I jokingly acknowledged their discomfort by saying, "We know this may feel a little weird but," I smiled at Yvonne and slipped in her favorite icebreaker, "just humor us."

We explained to them that everyone would get a turn in the "warm seat" while the rest of us expressed all the things that we love and like about that person. Of course, there was a lot of resistance, eye rolling, jokes, and nervous fidgeting, so we went first to set the example. I took my place at the center of attention and Yvonne started in order to show them what it looked like. First, she expressed how much she loved me, and how proud she was to be my partner. She looked lovingly into my eyes and told me that she loves spending her life with me and making a difference in the world together.

We went around the circle giving everyone a turn to express something from the heart before another person took the warm seat.

We knew that as time went on, the discomfort would give way to a deeper level of sharing. What we didn't know was how vulnerable people would get. But slowly, one by one, my entire family began to "drop the waterline."

After Yvonne and my kids had taken their turns in the warm seat, my sister was next. My sister is always up for this kind of stuff but she guards herself from looking for it and being disappointed. As my family showered her with their love, the tension melted from her face as if turning back the hands of time.

It was magical to watch everyone become more and more vulnerable. Slowly but surely the joking stopped as everyone, including the most resistant members of my family – my father, my brother, and my grandfather – shared tears of love and gratitude. It was like having a private Challenge Day with the people I loved most in the world.

I met Yvonne's beautiful eyes, and I smiled big, realizing how proud I was to have our daughters witnessing their grandparents, great grandparents, aunts, uncles, and cousins so vulnerably sharing their appreciations.

My biggest dream was unfolding before my eyes. My family was in complete love and connection.

The biggest gift was yet to come; it was the miracle of my grandfather.

I love my grandfather dearly but he lived his life stuck in the Be a Man Box more than almost anyone I have known. He was never one to express his feelings – in public or in private – and when he did, he'd minimize the impact with joking and banter. But this time, when my grandmother took her seat, my grandfather met her eyes. Caught in the momentum of the night, he finally expressed the words my grandmother had waited a lifetime to hear. With time, care, and the most intentional choice of words, he told her how much he loved her and thanked her for a lifetime of love and patience.

The entire room was gripped by the miracle they had witnessed – my tough-guy grandpa had softened – and there truly wasn't a dry eye in the house. Even though down deep we had all known he loved us, to hear him actually say the words was life changing. I can't remember feeling more proud to be his grandson.

My grandpa died less than a year later, but the memory of the love he shared with all of us that night is a gift we will cherish forever.

 **Live It!**

Appreciation can make a day, even change a life. Your willingness to put it into words is all that is necessary.

~ Margaret Cousins

Words have power. For better or worse our words have a huge impact on the way we feel and on how we live our lives. Unfortunately, all too often, we use our words to focus on the negative – we talk about what is not done, what is not right, what we don't like about others. Rarely do we give as much energy to the positive things that are going on. Even when we finish a major project or task, rather than jumping up and down and celebrating, many of us pick it apart, talk about what we could have done better or, perhaps more commonly, just move on to the next project. Can you imagine Leonardo da Vinci, after completing the *Mona Lisa*, looking at his freshly painted masterpiece and saying, "Do you think the nose is just a little too big?" It is so easy to focus on the little imperfections, that sometimes we don't realize how good things really are.

Yvonne and I believe that it is important to take time to celebrate the blessings in our lives. We have made it our practice to start and end every day by sharing gratitude. The first one of us to open our eyes in the morning starts with the words, I am grateful for... our life, our love, our health, our home, our kids... whatever comes into our minds and hearts. At the end of every day we take the time to share the things we loved about the day – the accomplishments, miracles, people, and experiences that make it great to be alive. As we focus on the positive, we get to notice how much it grows.

A celebration is a conscious, visible expression of positive energy. We recommend that you celebrate every chance you get. Celebrate publicly, don't keep it to yourself. Let the people around you join you in honoring yourself; be a living example of self-love for them to witness.

At our Challenge Day office, anytime someone has something to celebrate, they ring the gong and announce it. That way, everybody can be part of the celebration. The energy in the room becomes electric and sustaining when people are having fun and celebrating, rather than complaining and calling out problems all the time. We certainly have our share of problems, but we make a concerted effort to give as much attention to the good things that happen as we do to the bad.

Yvonne and I have noticed three things that don't get celebrated as much as they should be: completions, mistakes, and people.

Celebrate Completions

Many of us become so goal-oriented that we forget to take our nose off the grindstone. If we do take a moment after completing a task, often that moment is spent on noticing what isn't working. Some of that may come from our training in school. When we finished our homework, we really didn't know how good it was until the teacher corrected it and gave it back. We didn't celebrate being finished, instead we waited until we saw how much of it was wrong. Often, when the grade did come back, even if it was good, the time had passed and we were already buried in the next assignment.

Celebrating completions means acknowledging not just your accomplishments, but also all the milestones along the way. Whenever you finish something, take a moment to honor the fact that you are done. Getting a good grade may seem vitally important, but it should also matter that you did your best and completed it. Then, when you get your grades, you can celebrate the accomplishment as well – celebrate that you got an A, celebrate that you did as well or better than you thought, celebrate that you won't have to do the assignment over again, or even celebrate that you have another chance to master the homework.

Yvonne and I have been working on this book for over three years. There have been many ups and downs in the process. If we had waited until the book was finally published to celebrate anything, it would have been a dreary three years indeed. Instead, we celebrated each meaningful completion along the way. If we set a goal to have a chapter completed by Wednesday and it was completed by Wednesday, it was time for a celebration.

This is the last chapter I am responsible for – and it's done – Woo Hoo!

Celebrate Mistakes

Everybody makes mistakes. Unfortunately, our culture places emphasis on perfection, while making a mistake is cause for punishment. As a result, we become ashamed of our mistakes. We try to hide them, we avoid blame, we try to pin them on someone else, or we pretend that nothing happened. But Yvonne and I believe that mistakes are what make us human and that is cause enough for celebration. At Challenge Day, when someone makes a mistake, we encourage that person to acknowledge it publicly so the group can offer a round of applause for being an example of our humanity.

Mistakes represent powerful opportunities for learning. Isn't it true that some of the most important lessons you learned were around mistakes you've made? If mistakes are something to be ashamed of, and we hide our errors, we lose the chance to learn. On the other hand, if mistakes are celebrated publicly, we have the support of the people around us to help us learn important lessons.

If I ran a school, I'd give the average grade to the ones who gave me all the right answers, for being good parrots. I'd give the top grades to those who made a lot of mistakes and told me about them, and then told me what they learned from them.

~ Buckminster Fuller

Celebrate People

Every day, we have a choice. We can choose to look at the people around us with judgment, noticing what we don't like or even what we hate about them, or, we can look at them with love and acceptance, noticing what we like or even what we love about them.

For many of us, to honestly share the full depth of our love and appreciation for the people in our lives is one of the scariest and most uncomfortable things we can do. It is much more comfortable to criticize others than it is to appreciate them. Every day, we train ourselves how to look, what to notice, what we consider to be most important. When we begin to wake up and *notice* what we are looking at most, we can make new choices, unlearn old habits, and retrain ourselves in powerful new ways.

Whether we admit it or not, we all need to be noticed and appreciated. Some of us are so desperate to be seen, we act out or cause disruptions simply to get attention. Sadly, negative attention is the only attention some of us ever get.

Imagine how different our world would be if all of us were celebrated and appreciated on a regular basis.

Appreciation has the power to transform people's lives. It's not the passing comments about our hair or looks, since flattery is often something people use to manipulate the feelings and responses of others. Instead, true appreciation comes from a deep place in our heart; it is the recognition of goodness in another, often something we see in ourselves that is reflected by someone else.

For me, the examples are many. My third grade teacher Mrs. Engelman was first to tell me how precious I was; it was her guidance that led me to believe that I deserved the best life had to offer. When I was fifteen years old, I was unanimously selected as an all-star by every other player in my Babe Ruth baseball league. In spite of the negative voices in my head, their vote of confidence provided undeniable evidence that I had skill. In college, my teacher, John Dwyer, helped to shape my entire life when he told me I had a gift for helping people. It was his appreciation and guidance that started me on the path to being a teacher, then a counselor, and ultimately, to the creation of the Challenge Day program with Yvonne.

My guess is that you, too, have had an inspiring teacher, a loving parent, a caring friend, an encouraging coach, a thoughtful co-worker, or someone else who saw something in you that helped you become who you are today. Make a list of some of these people and find a way to share your thanks and appreciation with them.

If you have something to say to a loved one, don't wait until tomorrow. Too late comes sooner than later.

~Nick Welton

Be Intentional

Celebrating people has to be intentional – filled with thoughtfulness, purpose, and meaning. Start by noticing the beauty in someone. By focusing on their positive aspects and consciously choosing your words, you begin to shape and re-shape your attitudes. Then decide on the form your communication will take – a card, a letter, an email, a conversation. Giving honest appreciation costs nothing and yet it pays enormous dividends for both the giver and the receiver. Sharing our love and appreciation not only improves our relationships with others, it sets the tone for our lives.

As you begin to admire others, recognize that what you see in them is also in you. Make notes of all the qualities you love about yourself. Notice the times when you step out of your comfort zone, risk vulnerability, and add to the lives of the people around you. Make sure you are also honoring and appreciating yourself in every way possible. The more you learn how to love and appreciate yourself, the more you can share it with others.

Don't Let Reactions Discourage You

Because sharing our feelings is uncomfortable for many of us, the person you appreciate may not respond in the way you expect. It is not uncommon for people to shrug it off, throw away a compliment, or become embarrassed by the positive attention. Although it always feels better when we know another person has taken our appreciation to heart, I urge you to not give up if the person invalidates or laughs off your effort in some way. I assure you that regardless of how your compliment is initially received, the gift has still been given and is taking effect.

Many people find it hard to trust. It's possible that they have been so shamed and humiliated, they find it hard to believe anyone can see them as good or special. Others have had their emotions toyed with by insincere flattery so much that they don't recognize a true compliment when it appears. Still others, like those stuck in the training of the Be a Man Box, are taught not to be emotional or to depend on others to make them feel good. In cases like these, the wall of separation can seem insurmountable. Keep trying. Like my grandfather proved to me, even the most guarded among us will eventually melt and open in the face of honest appreciation.

Challenge Day Appreciation Activity

At Challenge Day, we encourage participants to share the gift of appreciation with the people they love most. We provide them with cards so they can write to people in their lives whom they really love and care about, but for whom they may not have expressed their love lately. Many young people choose to write to their mom, dad, stepparents, grandparents, foster parents, or other family members. On a regular basis, we are blessed to receive calls, cards, and letters of appreciation from ecstatic family members who have been moved to tears by the words they receive in these cards. Here is an excerpt from one such letter.

I am a parent of a 14-year-old boy who took the Challenge Day workshop yesterday. I didn't know a whole lot of what the workshop was about but my son did tell me a bit about it yesterday after it was done. He said that it was quite emotional and that everyone that cried was touched in some way at some point or another, even one of his friends who proclaims to be the "tough guy." I got a few things out of him regarding it but didn't fully understand what it was all about.

Then I went to bed last night and underneath my blanket was a card that he was given by the organizers to be filled out and given to someone he loves. My son has been going through the "teenage" experimental stage this last year and has had some run-ins with not such great situations. It's been a struggle for us all. He also recently found out that me and his father will be separating so he chose to write us a note sharing his love for us and how we have always been there for him and that he didn't want to see us "split in half." He said no matter what he would always love and appreciate us.

You can imagine that my heart sank but also swelled with pride that he chose us to write to. We have always tried to be very close to him but like most teenage boys, he is sometimes a hard nut to crack. I was overwhelmed that he shared his feelings with us like that. That one gesture from the workshop may have just pushed the door open for my son… Thank you for making this possible.

~A grateful parent

Appreciation Reminders

1. Celebrate completions. Big or small, your accomplishments deserve to be noticed. Be generous, and appreciate yourself often.

2. Celebrate mistakes. Everyone makes them; it means you're alive.

3. Celebrate people. Don't wait for tomorrow to let the people you appreciate know how you feel. It may sound cliché but tomorrow may never come.

4. Be intentional. Look for and create regular opportunities to intentionally appreciate the people in your life. Make a game of it. You'll be amazed by how it makes you feel.

5. Don't get discouraged by the reactions of others. Even the most resistant among us can be won over by heartfelt, vulnerable recognition.

Be the Hero

Appreciation is a wonderful thing. It makes what is excellent in others belong to us as well.

~ Voltaire

Notice

- Do you live your life in celebration? Do you take the time to count your blessings? How often do you notice and appreciate the good things in life? Journal about all that is right in your world.

- Consider all the people in your life whom you love and appreciate. Journal about what you admire and notice about them.

- In what ways could you celebrate more or be more generous with your compliments?

- How often do you notice and appreciate those who serve or work for you? Do you take the time to thank them? Do you appreciate them for what they do? When you see or experience something you like, do you take the opportunity to say so? If not, what gets in the way? How often do you notice the good in people and let them know what you see?

- Have you celebrated yourself for making a mistake? If you have, how did it feel? If you haven't, what stopped you? Journal about some of your biggest mistakes and the lessons you learned from them.

- When was the last time you shared an intentional heartfelt appreciation with someone? Who was it with and how did it feel? What impact do you think your appreciation had on your relationship with that person?

- Are there people in your life who would love to hear more appreciations from you? Who are they? What, if anything, is holding you back?

Choose

- When you journaled about what is right in your world, did you get trapped in negativity about what's wrong? If you did, appreciate the reminder that you tend to gravitate toward negative thinking and choose again. If there is anything that came up for you that you wished you had, or that you wished you were, write about that now. Or better yet, create a vision board and appreciate all the things that are coming toward you in your life.

- Look back over your list of what you appreciate about the people around you. Now envision communicating those things. How would you do it? Do you want to have a conversation? Would you write a letter? Would you send someone on a treasure hunt to find all your notes of appreciation? Dream about all the ways you can express yourself to the people you love.

- As you review your mistakes, can you connect them to any gifts you've gotten as a result? Did any of your mistakes lead to a victory in some way? If not, imagine that they will. Take one mistake that feels painful, and imagine a reward you'll receive for having suffered.

- Think for a moment about someone in your life whom you really love and care about but you haven't told lately. Who comes to mind? What about this person makes them so special to you? How has he or she touched your life? Now imagine that you knew somehow that this was that person's last day on earth. What would you want this person to know? What is it you would say if he or she were standing right in front of you right now?

Act

- Write an appreciation note or e-mail to at least one friend, teacher, co-worker, or family member each day for the next seven days.
- Write yourself a letter outlining all the things you love and appreciate about yourself. Share the letter with someone you love and trust, someone who can also tell you what you missed.
- Send a thank you note to someone who would never expect it.
- Set time to look someone in the eyes, drop the waterline, and let them know what you appreciate about them.
- Start an appreciation circle around your family's dinner table.

Share your Celebration!

Log onto challengeday.org/bethechange and tell us how great it feels to express your love and appreciation for the people in your life.

Everyday Heroes ~ The Greenman Family

The Greenman family exemplifies the power and possibility that comes from committing to lives of service.

Initially inspired to make a difference for students in her community's schools, Judy Greenman was the first to bring Challenge Day to the state of Florida. She was able to overcome great initial skepticism and enroll support not only in her small community of Marathon, but up and down the Keys as well.

In addition to her community organizing, Judy has also been responsible for producing personal growth and healing work in communities all over the United States. As a result of Judy's continued commitment and role modeling, the entire family has been involved in Challenge Day programs, Next Step trainings, conferences, and a variety of other personal growth and leadership projects.

Her husband Frank, an attorney by trade, served as a member of Marathon's city council where he was an invaluable part of the community's planning and growth projects. But perhaps Frank's crowning achievement as a parent came when he and Judy decided he would take a leave from his law practice so the entire family could receive the education that can only come from a trip around the world.

The Greenman girls, Kelley, Suzie, and Katie, already passionate leaders in their schools, returned from their trip committed to making a difference for families and communities less fortunate than their own. All three girls have graduated from high school with honors, and are currently perusing their dreams to change the world.

Our hats are off to the entire Greenman family for the passion, commitment, and role modeling they provide as Everyday Heroes and agents of positive change.

The Greenmans

If you really knew us, you would know that Challenge Day has been a huge part of our connection, growth, and success as individuals and as a family.

Judy was first introduced to Challenge Day by a fellow Integrated Awareness® teacher who knew of her interest in the personal empowerment of youth. While her three daughters were still in elementary school, Judy brought Challenge Day to her county. Frank says, "Being the only male in a family of five, exposure to helpful communication styles and the acknowledgement of feelings, helped me be a better father, husband, and person."

Everyday Heroes ~ The Greenman Family

    With a foundation created by the skills and lessons of Challenge Day, Kelley, Suzie, and Katie became their own agents of change by starting a non-profit to help underprivileged children in Kenya, addressing congressmen to protect the Florida Keys environment, and hosting diversity and leadership trainings to promote respect and inclusion in their school and community.

    As Kelley graduates from Washington University in St. Louis, she notes that, "Without a doubt, my early training with the Challenge Day program led to my growth as a leader, eventually guiding my pursuit for, and commitment to, environmental policy change." Suzie, now at MIT, is known for reaching out to those in need of a smile, friend, or hug, in traditional Challenge Day fashion. Katie, at Tufts University, is pursuing a career along the lines of Challenge Day's work: "Because of CD, I know and demonstrate on a personal and social level, that I am a catalyst for change."

The Courage to Say, "I'm Sorry"

An apology is the superglue of life.
It can repair just about anything.

~Lynn Johnston

Yvonne

If you really knew me, you would know that in my eyes, my dad was truly a knight in shining armor; he could do no wrong. Generosity and love were two of his best qualities and his most powerful gifts. He was an adoring husband, a doting father, and one of my most important teachers. My dad taught me what all the many forms of love really look like by repeatedly demonstrating them. He personified what it means to be a gentle-man, and as I watched him on our family farm with seemingly endless patience, he would tell me, "If you know how to love and respect animals, you will know how to love and respect people."

A carpenter and contractor by trade, and an absolute magician with wood, my dad could build almost anything – a house, a jewelry box, a rocking horse, or a baby's cradle. I remember once, while he was working as a building inspector, he discovered that despite obtaining the proper permits, a family had illegally built their new garage too close to their fence. When my father discovered the mistake, the family was devastated. They had no money to rebuild it, and no idea what to do. They mentioned that they had planned to be gone for a few weeks visiting family in Mexico, and now they wondered if they should cancel the trip. My dad told them not to worry; they would figure it out when they got home. But while they were in Mexico, my dad secretly went over to their house every day before and after work, and rebuilt their entire garage for them before they returned.

He was like that with everyone, and yet he was still able to reserve something special for his family. As his children, we always knew how much he loved us. Not afraid to show affection, Dad would tuck us in at night with stories, tickles, and hugs, then he'd wake us in the morning with songs and kisses. Yet, as much as he loved us, we all knew that his greatest love was for our mom; he would do anything for her. I remember how excited he'd become as a holiday neared. For him, each one was another opportunity to surprise Mom with a new, creative gift.

My father was often at work and it was left to my mother to manage the household. Unfortunately, while juggling the needs of four children, she didn't get much time to herself. She had no support system and no outlet in which to release the heaviness of her emotional balloon. She was also battling health problems that left her depleted and overwhelmed. And if that wasn't enough, I was often stubborn and didn't have much compassion for her stress and frustration.

If Mom yelled at me, I yelled louder. The more angry she was, the more hurt and defiant I became.

I'm sure it didn't help that I clearly expressed my adoration for my father and left little room for her. As a result, our relationship was strained for most of my young life.

When Alzheimer's struck our dad six years ago, it happened suddenly and without warning. Though his body was healthy, he started to leave us little by little, and his mind and memories faded away. Our entire family was terrified. As he grew increasingly more childlike, he could not remember much of anything – not even his children or his wife of 50 years. The burden of his illness weighed especially heavy on my mom who knew very little about the disease. "For better or worse" took on a whole new meaning as Mom began watching her husband slowly slip away. Facing head-on the depth of her own pain and grief, as well as the loss of the dream she built with my dad to spend their golden years of retirement at the house on the lake, my mother courageously stepped into an entirely different role with my father. Her love for him and the commitment she had made seemed to guide her every action. With more love and gentleness than I could have imagined, my mother became my father's caretaker.

Early one Saturday morning the phone rang. When I answered it, I immediately recognized the familiar choking sound of my mom attempting to disguise her swallowed tears. "What is it, Mom?" I asked gently, knowing that every day with Alzheimer's can bring more pain and devastation.

She described the scene to which she had just awakened. Apparently, my dad had attempted to make a pot of coffee, but couldn't remember how. Coffee grounds and a flood of water covered the countertop and floor.

I asked her what she did when she found the mess, and she tearfully replied, "I took a breath, gave him a hug, and patiently cleaned it up. Then I made him a new pot of coffee."

My heart ached for both of them. I wanted to reach through the phone and hold her as I listened to her cry. Instead, all I could do was acknowledge her for the enormity of her love and patience.

"I had to call you," she said. "I have something I need to say."

I sat slumped on the floor with the phone pasted to my ear, completely unprepared for what came next.

"I am so sorry I couldn't do that for you." Her voice cracked with emotion as she continued. "When you were little, I always thought you should know how to do things before you really knew how. I was impatient and got so mad at you. It must have been hard to hear me yell so much." And then, quietly, "I'm sorry."

My heart was racing. It's possible I had waited my whole life to hear that. Tears on both ends of the phone filled the silence. I imagined how difficult it must have been for her to say, and I melted knowing there was no greater gift my mom could ever give me.

I felt so moved by my mother's courage and vulnerability that I decided to match her. My face was awash in tears, my nose was a runny mess, and my heart was threatening to leap out of my chest, but I took a big breath and said, "I'm sorry, too, Mom. I'm sorry for all the years of anger and resentment I held against you. I'm sorry for all of the fighting and for all of the pain."

I realized that I'd done the same thing to her that she'd done to me. It's amazing how we are all mirrors for each other, reflecting the places in ourselves that we don't want to see. "Part of me blamed you for all of my trouble because I expected you to know what to do all the time. I expected you to know how to be a parent to an angry daughter, and how to fix me. And although I forgave you a long time ago, I've never apologized. I'm sorry, Mom."

Though the conflict and pain of our relationship was built over decades, the healing was instantaneous. In a moment of grace, our past was forgiven, and we both were eager to start anew.

Today, my mom continues caring for my dad with ceaseless devotion. She has become a role model of true unconditional love. Lost in his new reality, Dad doesn't know who Mom is, but she is there loving, caring, and holding him through this devastating journey with Alzheimer's.

My mom and I talk almost every other day now. I am able to offer my love and support like never before. In many ways, she has become the mother I have always longed for. As crazy as this may sound, a part of me is grateful for my dad's disease because it's given me my mom. My entire family has done an amazing job rising to the challenge of caring for my father. I am especially grateful to my two sisters Rochelle and Kim who live near my parents and selflessly offer their support with daily visits or calls.

Even though I continue to feel sadness and great loss, the gift of my mom's apology will live in my heart forever.

Live It!

Apology is a lovely perfume; it can transform the clumsiest moment into a gracious gift.

~ Margaret Lee Runbeck

Rich and I believe that in every situation, we all do our best. That includes everyone – our parents, family members, friends, kids, teachers, bosses – every single one of us does the best we know how to do with the tools we have and any unhealed hurts we carry from our past. However, we are all human, and part of being human is making mistakes. At times, this can include hurting people. Regardless of whether we cause the pain consciously or unconsciously, we are still responsible for cleaning up the mess.

Why is it that so many of us find it hard to say we're sorry when we realize we've hurt someone? What are we afraid of?

Some people believe that saying, "I'm sorry," is a sign of weakness or a way of admitting guilt. Others feel that when they do acknowledge that they are wrong, they can find it extremely difficult to forgive themselves. At times, we can all be our own worst enemy, and use our guilt as a weapon with which to beat ourselves up.

Some of us have very little experience with people apologizing to *us*, or we've had bad experiences in apologizing to others. Perhaps you've said you were sorry, and your vulnerability was used against you. Maybe you admitted you were wrong only to have another person refuse to forgive you or, worse yet, turn it into an opportunity to attack you. For many of us, it wasn't safe to make mistakes, let alone admit to having made them. Regardless of the reasons, many of us remain silent, hoping people will just forget what happened or that somehow the hurt and painful memories will just go away.

As I observe our world today, it sometimes seems as though many of us would rather go to war and kill people than get vulnerable.

Whether the hurt happens between nations, families, or individuals, our reluctance to admit we are wrong and to apologize can have a devastating and destructive effect on our ability to peacefully co-exist.

Rich and I believe that saying, "I am sorry," and *meaning* it, is one of the most humble and liberating things any of us can do. We believe that the act of apologizing is not just for the other person; it's for *you*. Even though it may not feel good in the moment, and regardless of whether or not your apology is graciously received, saying, "I'm sorry" can be a powerful way to unburden yourself of your own sense of guilt and shame.

We all know people who, like my mother, have lived for years with balloons filled with shame for hurts they have caused. Even if they don't think about it on a daily basis, the unresolved regret and remorse still festers inside them like poison. At the very least, not apologizing or making amends creates distance, and at most, it creates dis-ease. Is it just a coincidence that heart disease is the number one killer in our country? My mother's courage in expressing her sorrow to me, not only healed our relationship and brought us closer, but it also set *her* free.

Part of our Challenge Day leader training process is modeled after a 12–Step program in that we encourage our leaders to take a truthful, vulnerable review of their lives and see what has been left undone. Who have we wronged? Does anyone deserve an apology from us? It might mean looking into our past and evaluating any hurts we have caused to a friend or to someone we've teased in school. For parents, it can mean admitting our mistakes and apologizing to our children. As adults, we might want to apologize to our own parents or other relatives for the emotional distance we've created, or the grudges and resentments we've held while wishing they were perfect.

It is important to note that an apology is different from making amends. Saying we are sorry simply means we apologize for what we did. Making amends means that we not only apologize, but we also take steps to make the situation right. It is like the analogy of a nail in a fence; even after you take the nail out – in our case, apologize – the hole is still there. Making amends is like patching and painting the hole.

When I first had the courage to review my past, it was quite a vulnerable process. One of the things I knew I had to face was a time in college when I was throwing a party for a friend and I was totally broke. Too ashamed to ask for money from friends, I took food and beer from the restaurant where I worked. Although I was mortified to face my own history, I knew what I needed to do. I needed to contact the owners.

Humbly, and with more than a little embarrassment, I apologized to them for my dishonesty and for breaking their trust. Then I offered to pay for everything I had stolen, plus interest. They were so shocked by my desire to make amends that I had trouble convincing them to take the money. I wanted them to understand that although it may have seemed like a small thing, it was *huge* to me. Afterward, I felt liberated and proud. Finally, I was able to forgive myself and move on.

One of the most common regrets people carry with them is the hurt their teasing or unconsciousness has caused other kids in school. At every Challenge Day, we give participants a chance to apologize to the people they have hurt. Whether it happened in first grade or the week before, they get an opportunity most of us never have – to clean things up and start brand new. Over the years, we have watched thousands of young people heal hurts and take down walls of separation that otherwise may have been there for years. At every Challenge Day, courageous young people step up to our challenge, drop the waterline, and vulnerably apologize to one another. And inevitably, the resulting tears of humility, compassion, love, and forgiveness, shower the floors of school gyms, and create a new foundation of love and understanding.

Is there anyone from your school or your life whom you have hurt, someone who might feel healed by receiving an apology from you?

During my ten-year class reunion, I realized I was intentionally staying on the opposite side of the hall to avoid the embarrassment of looking into the eyes of my classmate, Scott. Scott was one of the few people I had teased and humiliated back in junior high school. I had stuffed my guilt away for years, but when I saw him, all the memories of my degrading comments and jokes now raced through my head. I wondered if he would ever forgive me. Pushing through my fear, I found the courage to walk over and tell him that I was sorry. His face lit up with gratitude and he gave me a loving hug. I don't know who felt better – me or him. He told me it meant so much to him to finally have me acknowledge what I had done. As it turns out, I had been keeping myself imprisoned by my own guilt. One simple conversation, and a sincere apology, was all it took to set us both free.

How would our families, schools, communities, and workplaces be different if we all had the courage to say, "I'm sorry," and to make amends when we hurt people? How might that simple act change our world? Can you imagine if all the leaders of the world got together and, on behalf of all of our ancestors, had the courage to apologize to one another?

It starts with us. How is your heart doing right now? Are you ready to take up our challenge to apologize and make amends?

Steps for Apologizing and Making Amends

1. Make a list of everyone you've hurt or wronged in some way.

2. Choose the form your apology will take – verbal or written.

3. Start by being humble and vulnerable enough to acknowledge that you made a mistake.

4. Be willing to make things as right as possible.

5. Express yourself from your heart. Demonstrate remorse.

6. Regardless of what you said or did, be defenseless and open to hearing the other person's hurt, frustration, and possibly even anger.

7. After the other person has finished responding to your apology, ask if there is anything you can do to make it right.

8. If the answer is yes, do what you can to make amends. If the answer is no, thank the person for his or her truth, and do your best to let go.

9. Celebrate yourself for having the courage to apologize.

10. Trust that you have done all that you can do.

Be the Hero

Never ruin an apology with an excuse.

~ Kimberly Johnson

Notice

- Is there anyone in your life who would love an apology from you? Perhaps something you have said or done, or even something you didn't do (consciously or unconsciously) has caused someone pain. If so, is there anything in the way of your apology?
- Is there anyone whom you believe owes you an apology? If so, what is it for? Are you willing to accept an apology, forgive, and let go?
- Are there people in your life whom you avoid because you have wronged them in some way? If so, do you ever try to block the situation from your memory? How do you feel when you see or think about these people? Do you think they avoid you as well?
- Is there anyone in your life who has ever refused to forgive you? If so, how does it feel?
- Think of the times someone has apologized to you. Were you able to forgive the person, or did you find the need to keep the hurt alive? Did the person try to make amends? If so, how did their actions affect your relationship?
- Admitting we were wrong can be a vulnerable act. Have you ever gone to someone and taken 100% responsibility for your actions only to have that person blast you or use your vulnerability against you in some way? If so, what if any affect

did their actions have on your willingness to be vulnerable enough to apologize to others?

- Do you have trouble being humble or admitting your mistakes? What, if anything, keeps you from offering an apology to other people when one is in order? Do you ever find yourself trying to blame or put the responsibility on another person?

Choose

- Imagine that giving an apology is like spreading magical healing lotion on the person to whom you are apologizing. Imagine that your words soak into their heart and begin to heal the scars. Imagine that regardless of the person's reaction to your words, the healing lotion still takes effect. To whom would you apologize? What would you say? What would be the result?

- If there is someone from whom you would like an apology, under what circumstances can you imagine receiving one? Do you need to ask for one? Do you need to apologize for anything yourself first? Imagine the perfect scenario, imagine the words that you receive, and then feel the feelings.

- Create an imaginary healing circle – perhaps it's a special room or it's on a beach or in the forest – any place that feels magical to you. Invite the people with whom you'd like to forge a better relationship. What do you say to each other? How does your relationship change?

- List all the things you think get in the way of you admitting your mistakes and taking full responsibility. Do any of the things on your list relate to any wounds you might have? If so, how can you imagine healing those wounds? What would it take to step fully into complete integrity?

- What do you think would happen if you apologized for every hurt you've caused in the past? How might your life be different?

Act

- Make appointments to call, meet with, write to, or otherwise apologize to people for past hurts and mistakes. Choose one person per week, and offer your magical healing lotion. Be sure to own 100% responsibility for your actions. Notice how it makes you feel.
- The next time you make a mistake, don't hide it – shine a light on it! Freely admit that you were wrong and claim membership in the human race. Notice how those around you react to your vulnerability.
- If there's someone from whom you need an apology, take steps to create the conditions that might bring one. Be patient. Humbly ask for what you need. Be clear about why you need it.
- Take a step toward removing any blocks you may have to apologizing. If there's anything on your list of wounds that inhibits you from living in full integrity, take action on healing that wound.

Celebrate!

Share your experiences and triumphs. Log on to the *Be the Change* website and blog about your success: www.challengeday. org/bethechange.

Everyday Hero ~ Roxana Marachi, Ph.D.

Roxana was a participant of one of our earliest Challenge Day programs. She went on to complete her undergraduate work, and earned her Masters and Ph.D. in Education & Psychology. Roxana is an educator and researcher, and she has been selected to share her research at numerous national and international conferences. Roxana joined Challenge Day's Board of Directors in 2007, and is currently assisting the organization's research and evaluation team in an effort to bridge the academic educational research community with the work of Challenge Day.

Roxana

If you really knew me, you would know that I appreciate Challenge Day for the fact that they so openly address the most "difficult dialogues" that youth are craving in schools. When Rich and Yvonne first facilitated a Challenge Day in my middle school, I remember being deeply moved by their openness in sharing about their own experiences. I also remember experiencing a great sense of relief that finally someone was bringing up issues that occupied our minds and hearts, but that often went unspoken. Having studied school climate and youth development over the past 10 years, I believe these conversations are critical to creating schools where students can thrive. We must address issues of interpersonal respect, care, and emotional health if we expect our students to be their best and to succeed in school and life.

I am inspired by the leaders of Challenge Day for their unrelenting passion for making positive changes in school environments, and for encouraging students to treat one another with respect (especially when social habits and trends may pressure otherwise). I believe in Challenge Day's work because they focus on what students need in a learning experience: "Relationships, Relevance, and Rigor." I teach about these three R's to Teacher Credential Candidates in my Educational Psychology courses, and see the R's echoed as well in the focus of Challenge Days. Challenge Day encourages the development of healthy relationships, inspires conversations that are truly relevant to students' lives, and upholds rigor by "challenging" youth to take action.

Forgiveness - Patrick's Story

We must develop and maintain the capacity to forgive. He who is devoid of the power to forgive is devoid of the power to love. There is some good in the worst of us and some evil in the best of us. When we discover this, we are less prone to hate our enemies.

~ Martin Luther King, Jr.

Rich

The room buzzed with anticipation. Word had spread that Global News Canada would be filming a portion of the first ever Challenge Day program at a local school for broadcast on the evening edition. If you really knew me, you would know that as excited as I was to showcase our work in Canada, I wondered how participants might be affected by the cameras. Committed to maintaining the emotional safety in the room, Yvonne and I negotiated boundaries with the anchor and her camera crews. Although everyone had given permission for the filming, most participants had little or no idea of what the day's events might bring. Once we had ensured that anyone could stop the filming at any time, we agreed to proceed with the program.

The doors opened and more than a hundred students began trickling in along with parents, teachers, and community members. Some were wide-eyed with anticipation, some frowned with apprehension, while others hammed it up for the cameras. One friendly young man with an easy smile bounded up to us and introduced himself. His name was Patrick. He told us that both his mom and his sister were here, too, as he looked over our sound equipment and touched the box of supplies.

Patrick had big eyes and an open face full of innocence. And he seemed hungry to connect.

As the participants took their seats, Yvonne and I scanned the circle of faces and immediately identified the obvious leaders and their various groups. It was clear that Patrick was not part of a group.

As with most Challenge Days, the program came together beautifully. We began with icebreakers to loosen up the energy in the room. We played games and activities designed to get the participants talking and opening up. We had them divide into pairs, and then into small sharing groups. Over the next several hours, early morning fears and judgments gave way to connection and understanding. As the day unfolded, I found myself surprised by how quickly most people seemed to ignore the cameras completely, as though forgetting they were even in the room.

Eventually we reached the "Speak Out" part of the day when the students have a chance to stand up and share what they've learned. One by one, students from every clique stood and talked about how sick and tired they were of the bullying and separation on campus. They generously thanked their friends, family, and teachers, they expressed their appreciation for the support they had received over the years, and many of them took the opportunity to apologize to those whom they had hurt.

My heart broke open as student after student stood up and apologized to Patrick. Clearly, he was one of those kids who had been the target of relentless bullying and teasing, like I was in junior high. My eyes filled with tears as I imagined what life must be like in his world, and I found myself feeling increasingly protective of him. Their apologies were heartfelt but they weren't enough for me; something else had to be done.

As I walked in Patrick's direction, I saw his mother squirming in her seat as if she wanted to scream out, "Please don't hurt my son! Please don't humiliate him anymore."

When I arrived at Patrick's side, I asked him to stand with me. Then, as I often do, I used the microphone to point out the obvious.

"For whatever reason," I said, "Patrick, more than anyone else in this room, has somehow become the brunt of other people's jokes."

I paused for a moment and let that sink in. One by one young people raised their hands, flashing the international sign for "I love you." Then, I challenged them to stand in front of their chairs if they had personally hurt Patrick, or had stood by in silence when he was being teased or humiliated by others. Nearly every student, and even some of the teachers, quietly stood up. A collective gasp filled the room, and a palpable, awkward silence descended. My heart ached as I watched Patrick, his mom, and his older sister absorb the devastating truth that Patrick had routinely been hurt by almost every person in the room.

Because most of the group was standing, I wanted to make sure everyone could see Patrick. I invited him to stand on his chair. As all eyes turned to him, I began to cry. Finally, I thought, he would get the respect and attention he's always deserved.

Inspired by the group's support, Patrick decided that he wanted to speak. I handed him the microphone. He stood for a moment and scanned the room. And then, quietly, he said,

"I forgive you. Today, I understand that you hurt me because you were hurt. And now I forgive you."

I listened in disbelief. In spite of all the bullying and harassment he'd suffered at the hands of his peers, his first impulse was to forgive. "Wow, Patrick, you're my hero!" I said. Then, turning back to the group, I asked, "Who will have Patrick's back when we leave? Who will stop the disrespect?"

Nearly every hand in the room shot up.

Patrick beamed as tears of joy rolled down his face.

My voice was husky with tears. "If, in this moment, you see him as perfect just the way he is, and you want to celebrate him, give him a huge round of applause!"

The entire group simultaneously leaped to their feet and erupted into a thunderous ovation. There he stood, the one-time brunt of harassment and humiliation, now wildly celebrated as a hero by more than 120 teachers, parents, and peers. Stunned by the response and the power of his forgiveness, Patrick stood on his chair simultaneously grinning, crying, and laughing. What better gift could we give to someone who wants only acceptance and love?

In the rush of emotion, lines of students surrounded him to apologize personally. They promised that things would be very different for Patrick, and all the other "Patrick's" who so desperately want to be accepted. As they spoke, this proud young man stood tall as tears of ecstasy and healing continued streaming down his cheeks.

The day turned out to be special in many ways. As a result of that Challenge Day, Global News Program anchor Jill Croteau decided to create a documentary on the effects of bullying. The 23-minute award-winning documentary entitled *The Bully Solution* highlights Patrick and his family. The program aired all across Canada and won the Gold Ribbon Award from the Canadian Association of Broadcasters.

We heard from Patrick and his mom more than a year later. They both thanked us profusely, saying that the situation at Patrick's school had changed dramatically. Their heartfelt thanks, and the memory of the miracles we witnessed that day, is just one of the ways in which we are all changing the world, together.

To find out more about what happened with Patrick, you can log on to www.challengeday.org and watch *The Bully Solution*.

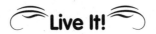

Live It!

Forgiveness entails the authentic acceptance of our own worthiness as human beings, the understanding that mistakes are opportunities for growth, awareness and the cultivation of compassion, and the realization that the extension of love to ourselves and others is the glue that holds the universe together. Forgiveness... is not a set of behaviors, but an attitude.

~ Joan Borysenko

It has been said that holding onto resentment and anger is like feeding yourself poison while hoping the other person will die. I'm sure all of us have family members or other people in our lives who hold grudges for years. They stay angry, avoiding the person with whom they are in conflict or not speaking to them at all. In my experience, some of these same people don't even remember what happened or what they were angry about, and yet they still maintain their distance.

Holding onto hurt and blame binds us to the past and taints our hope for the future. It takes a lot of energy to maintain our anger, and doing so comes at a great cost. For some people, it may feel as though holding onto resentments gives us power over another. But what if true power and freedom lies in our ability to forgive? As Gandhi taught, it actually takes great strength to forgive. He said, "The weak can never forgive. Forgiveness is the attribute of the strong."

Since 1987, Challenge Day has worked with hundreds of thousands of teenagers in almost every possible setting, from typical urban and suburban high schools, to private prep schools and juvenile detention centers. In *every* situation, we have been blessed to witness the incredible healing power of love and forgiveness.

In a world where teenagers are often misunderstood, underestimated, and even feared, we have the honor and the privilege of watching them shine. What we have experienced over and over is that teens everywhere want and need the same thing. Like all of us, young people want to be included and accepted; they want to feel safe, loved, and celebrated for being exactly who they are. We have found that by providing a safe and compassionate environment, the overwhelming majority of teens (and adults as well) will inevitably rise to their highest selves. Having now witnessed countless miracles of forgiveness and healing all across the United States and Canada, we have come to believe that it truly has the power to transform the *entire world*.

Forgiveness is the way to break the cycle of blame and pain.

Are you or people you know holding onto anger and resentment? Perhaps you have waited years for people to make things up to you. If you fail to forgive, you will remain imprisoned in the past – as though you handed over the reins of your life to someone who hurt you. By understanding that you are completely powerless to change the past, you can reclaim your life and move on. Your real power lies in changing your perspective, not in changing the people who hurt you. We call this creating peace from the inside out. It takes courage. In order to truly forgive, we must first be willing to remember (notice), and confront our pain. Only then can we authentically choose to release the pain of the past and move into the freedom of forgiveness.

In his book *The Art of Forgiving: When You Need To Forgive and Don't Know How*, Lewis B. Smedes says, "It takes one person to forgive, it takes two people to be reunited." He cautions us against needing a particular outcome from another person in order to heal by adding that we are "powerless over other people. Spoken forgiving, no matter how heartfelt, works best when we do not demand the response we want. I mean that when we tell people we forgive them, we must leave them free to respond to our good news however they are inclined. If the response is not what we hoped for, we can go home and enjoy our own healing in private."

Though none of us can go back in time, we can all create a new future. The gentler you are with yourself, the easier it will be to forgive others. The gift of forgiveness is a gift we give ourselves; it is the birth of new hope, *regardless* of how the other person responds.

Patrick:
Hero of The Bully Solution

Be the Hero

The practice of forgiveness is our most important contribution to the healing of the world.

~ Marianne Williamson

Notice

- Is there anyone in your life with whom you are carrying any hurt or resentment? If so, how do your resentments affect your heart? When you think about forgiving the people who hurt you, how does it make you feel? What, if anything, holds you back?

- Do you have any hurts or resentments that keep you trapped in the past? Are you waiting for someone to make up or apologize to you before you can forgive?

- Gandhi said that forgiveness is an attribute of the strong. How often, if ever, have you been "strong" enough to truly forgive someone? Has there been an instance in which it was hard to forgive but you did it anyway? If so, how did it make you feel?

- Has anyone ever forgiven you when you were clearly in the wrong? If so, what difference did it make?

- How has the courage to forgive changed the way you live your life or the way you relate with others?

- When you consider all the people and situations in your life where you have felt mistreated or wronged in some way, which of these situations can you find compassion for the other person's point of view?

- Is there anything in your life for which you still haven't forgiven yourself? If so, what are you gaining from holding yourself hostage? What will it take to let go and forgive yourself?

- Are there any people in your life now who are holding you emotionally hostage by withholding their forgiveness of you? If so, how does it feel and how do you react to them? Do you punish them in return? Do you distance yourself or otherwise withhold your love?

Choose

- If you have ever given an apology but did not feel as though it was received and that you have been forgiven, imagine a scenario in which you feel complete forgiveness. Imagine the words you exchange with someone, and especially take note of the feeling inside your body. Then, every time you see that person, remember the feeling of being completely forgiven. Hold it in your heart.
- If there is someone to whom you feel that you owe an apology but you just can't seem to summon the courage to do it, dream about what you need in order to complete this act. Envision the roadblocks that separate you from healing your relationship. And imagine dissolving those blocks.
- Make a list of all the apologies you've received that made you feel better. Is there anything on your list that you could use in apologizing to someone else?
- As in the last chapter, create an imaginary healing circle. Invite yourself into it. Invite anyone else whom you consider to be a role model, either living or dead. Have that person or those people stand with you as you have the courage to forgive yourself for anything you still consider to be blocking you or holding you back from your full, magnificent self. Forgive yourself, release yourself, set yourself free.
- If there are people who are holding you emotionally hostage, what might you do to set yourself free? Do you need something from

them? If so, can you imagine creating that opportunity? Or can you release yourself from their hold without their participation? What would that look like?

Act

- Review your lists and options from above. Take action on one thing. Perhaps you approach someone you'd like an apology from, and you are able to tell that person how much you'd like to heal your relationship.
- Write a letter to someone who has hurt you. Whether that person is dead or alive, and even if you don't intend to deliver it, give yourself the time and space to capture your feelings. Be sure to include how the hurt has affected your life, include any lessons you have learned, and then, by all means, be sure to let the person know that either you forgive them or that you would like to forgive them. Then, of course, we challenge you to deliver your letter or message directly.
- If you have created a healing circle and forgiven yourself, take the next step. Find a mirror and practice completing the sentence, "I forgive myself for…" – filling in the blank as many times as possible or until you experience yourself as guilt free.
- Once you have done that, take the next step. Share your experience with someone you trust. Ask that person to support you in fully receiving the gift of forgiveness.

Celebrate!

If you've created a healing between you and another person, that's cause for real celebration. Congratulations! Be sure to honor your success with someone you trust will appreciate your breakthrough – maybe even someone who was involved.

Everyday Hero ~ Vinny Ferraro

Vinny is a unique character – a bridge between many worlds. His leadership, compassion, and commitment, have literally helped to transform the face of our entire organization. A deeply compassionate and inspiring speaker, teacher and leader, Vinny has parlayed an upbringing filled with poverty, violence, abandonment, and drugs, into a lifetime calling and passion for healing. Committed to giving others that which he rarely received, Vinny uses his past as a springboard into a magnificent present.

Recognized in many circles as a master mediation teacher, he brings his unique blend of a streetwise survivor, Buddhist teacher, and comedian into everything he does. Currently, Vinny works as a senior Challenge Day leader and co-director of training, and he is also realizing his lifelong dream to bring Dharma and meditation into the prison systems.

Vinny

If you really knew me, you'd know that I grew up in a world where I thought I had to hide my heart. There was no place I could just be myself that was caring, compassionate, and full of wonder about life. Kindness was considered a sign of weakness. I was a little boy who never knew freedom. At my house, I constantly walked on eggshells, not knowing when my father would go off. So I tried to escape to the streets, my neighborhood. There I found more violence as I just tried to survive. I was a teenage crack head with so much to forget – my family, my neighborhood, and most of all, that little kid inside me that just wanted to be himself.

If you really knew me, you'd know that I'm grateful for this unlikely path to freedom. Through it, I found service and the ability to help people who are in the same situation as I am. How do we muster up enough courage to be who we really are? Together, of course. No longer will I stay locked up in a box settling for comfort. That's not why I was put on this planet. When I came to Challenge Day, they told me that everything that I was ashamed of, I should talk about – that all my habits and conditioning helped me survive, but I get to be in choice about how I do this life. Finally, there was the promise of freedom I always knew was possible, even for me.

The Different Game

How wonderful it is that nobody need wait a single moment before starting to improve the world.

~ Anne Frank

Yvonne

If you really knew me, you'd know that on the day I die, I want to feel proud knowing my life made a difference. If you really, really knew me, you'd know that I think we can completely change the world through human connection, one person at a time.

I sat on the family room floor enamored with my new grandson – all five months of his giggles, beaming smile, soft belly, and electric eyes. The front door of our daughter's newly rented house was wide open to allow the spring breeze to blow through. Basking in grandparenthood and precious moments with our daughters is one of my most treasured ways to spend time.

I glanced out the door and noticed a man working in the yard across the street. My daughter was standing behind me watching me adore her son. "Do you know your neighbors?" I asked her.

She wrinkled her face, "No, I don't think they like us."

I was surprised by her response. "Why would you think that?"

"They never even look at us when we're in the yard," she insisted with a hint of hurt and perhaps a little judgment.

I am so often taken aback by the fact that even though our kids have been raised in the "Challenge Day way" – taught to be open and non-judgmental, and encouraged to embrace everyone – they can still slip into easy habits and unconscious insecurity. I sometimes forget how human we all are and how great the potential is to create separation out of fear.

"I'll watch the baby," I urged. "Why don't you go over and say hi."

She lowered her voice, "I am not sure if they speak English."

I recognized the excuse for what it was – the fear of possible rejection. "A simple hello, a handshake, and a smile, they're universal," I suggested. Then, more firmly, "GO SAY HI!"

Just as I'd finished my commandment, a dark-skinned woman in a brightly colored dress emerged from the house with a small girl in tow. The girl's smile beamed pure delight – the same delight I'd seen in my grandson.

My daughter watched them cross the yard. "Okay, Mom," she sighed, "I will go say hi." She rolled her eyes as she exited.

I smiled, hopeful, as she approached her new neighbors. They looked up at her, surprised. I was too far away to hear the interaction, yet I could feel the pleasantries of their exchange.

Several minutes passed before my daughter returned. By then, I was blowing kisses on my grandson's belly and cooing. I looked up as she entered the room, and noticed tears in her eyes.

"You will never believe what happened!" she said with a mixture of embarrassment and excitement. "I walked up to them and said hi. The woman turned around without even a pause to see who I was and said, 'Wow, our neighbors are talking to us.'" Tears streamed down her cheeks as she continued, "Mom, she was so shocked that I came over."

Emphatically, she described what the woman had told her. "She said they've lived in the neighborhood for over a year and no one has ever said a word to any of them. The woman, her husband, their kids, and some extended family. They all moved here from Hawaii and have felt very lonely ever since."

I could feel the sadness and empathy in my daughter, as if her heart had opened to a new understanding.

"On the island, they had many friends and family members nearby. Here, people ignore them, no one is friendly." Touched by the woman's story, my daughter obviously felt embarrassed by her initial resistance to reach out. "You know," she said, "I'm going to bake them some cookies and go back tomorrow."

Live It!

**If we cannot now end our differences at least
we can help make the world safe for diversity.**

~ John F. Kennedy

Everywhere we look, we see differences. We make up stories about who people are and what they are like based solely upon appearances – skin color, gender, class, culture, religion, or politics; where someone lives, what they wear or drive, their hair color, their abilities, and even the job they hold. We continually compare, compete, judge, and often stay away from, separate from, and even hurt others because of our perceived differences. We learn to distance ourselves out of fear, ignorance, bigotry, or habit. We learn to judge from our families, our social relationships, and, increasingly, through mass media. Many popular films and television shows use banter and sarcasm to humiliate people who are different, just to get a laugh.

When we focus on our differences, we rob ourselves of the opportunity to meet a potential friend and learn about other people, including their styles, cultures, beliefs, and ways of being. It's like building a wall with bricks fashioned out of judgment. Brick by brick, the wall gets higher and higher. After a while, we find ourselves all alone behind the wall – or in my daughter's case, on the other side of the street. Whatever the reason for our negative judgments, the costs are always separation, loneliness, and, all too often, violence.

At Challenge Day, we do an activity called the Different Game to break through the walls of judgment. Each participant is asked to find someone in the room they don't know, someone who appears to be different from them. Once everyone finds a partner, we ask each of them to answer a personal question that will help them get to know each other for who they *really* are on the inside. "Take turns completing this sentence, 'If you really knew me....' What is your relationship like with each member of your family? What are some of the things you are most grateful for in your life? Complete this sentence, 'Something I might be afraid for you to know about me is....'"

During the Different Game, each person has time to answer the question before finding another partner, so everyone has several opportunities to meet new people. By the time we finish, people who wouldn't even have talked to one another before, have, in some cases, become lifelong friends. Often they will find they share many things in common. At the very least, they have learned that their initial judgments about one another were often way off base. The game demonstrates how easy it is to bring groups of people together and find common ground between them.

Differences are wonderful. Our differences are not the problem. It's the divisions we create based on those differences that hurt us all.

Why don't we choose to see people through the eyes of love, compassion, and acceptance? Why aren't we looking for opportunities for connection in every new person we meet? Why in the world would anyone ever choose to look at others through the eyes of judgment or hate?

Because that's what we've been taught to do.

Fortunately, we believe that anything we have learned can be unlearned. We believe that what you see has nothing to do with the person you are looking at and everything to do with the eyes you are looking through – your own. Therefore, celebrating diversity in the people around us is a matter of choice.

We challenge you to *notice* what you do out of habit. And we challenge you to create connections with others. Whether it's a simple hello, a what's up, or a more in-depth and intimate conversation filled with truth and vulnerability, whatever the case, you always have opportunities to connect.

Sometimes we live across the street from people we don't know or don't acknowledge. We stand in line at the grocery store, we walk down the halls at school, we ride on a bus or take other public transportation, we stand in a crowded elevator, or someone waits on us in a restaurant – regardless of the situation, how often do "others" go unseen, unacknowledged, or ignored by us? Are we afraid of being rejected, or are we just rude? Are we really too busy, or just too shy to interact?

Our greatest wounds are caused by separation, isolation, and loneliness. But there is not a lack of love on our planet; there is simply a lack of courage to show it.

How can we feel separate and lonely when we have a problem with over-population?

We believe that it's because we do not allow ourselves to love and be loved by those who are often right next to us.

What if separation, isolation, and the fear of "others" is a choice? What if the person right next to us came into our lives directly to help us grow? Perhaps they bring love, friendship, joy, or better yet, offer an opportunity for us to step out of the comfort zone of our fear and be in relation with another human being. Perhaps, just like my daughter, they are just as afraid as we are, hoping and waiting for someone else to have the courage to say, "Hi."

Steps For Crossing the Difference Line

1. Notice your reactions to people who seem different from you. Make a special note of the stories you tell yourself about people you see on a regular basis.
2. Once you notice your reactions and monitor your thoughts, take

an honest look at where your feelings might be coming from. Are your reactions based on personal experience with that person, or are they based on stereotypes and beliefs you have built up over the years? Are your beliefs based on fact, or on guesses or passed-on ideas from other people?

3. If you notice that your beliefs and judgments about others are creating distance, see if you can discover the truth about them.

4. Risk reaching out. Introduce yourself and get to know people around you. While it's always great to say hello and to greet people you pass on the streets, it is especially important to make an effort to reach out to the people you see on a regular basis. People in your classroom, at work, at church, or in your neighborhood might just end up being some of your closest friends. You'll never know until you meet them and get to know who they really are.

5. Once you take the step of reaching out, the next choice is yours. What kinds of relationships, if any, do you want to have with these people? Perhaps you'd like to spend more time together, offer them a hand with something, reach out for support, acknowledge some of the great things you notice and appreciate about them, or simply choose to relate in friendly and respectful ways. Whatever you choose, your decision now comes from your first-hand experience.

6. Whatever your experience may be with one person, be sure not to lump them into a category of people who look, act, or dress like they do. Avoid stereotypes as much as possible. Remember that every one of us is unique and deserves to be seen for who we truly are.

7. Spread only good news. If you have a negative experience in meeting someone, keep your thoughts and opinions to yourself unless the person is a danger to others. Do your best to avoid fueling the negative stereotypes and judgments of others. If, however, you have a good experience with someone, by all means spread the news and let others know some of the things you like about the person. This is where "Positive Rumors" come in handy. A little good news can go a long way toward helping others to connect.

Be the Hero

People will forget what you said, people will forget what you did, but people will never forget how you made them feel.

~ Maya Angelou

Notice

- How often do your thoughts, beliefs, and stereotypes about people who seem different from you affect the way you relate with these people? Do you find yourself treating others differently because of actual differences or perceived differences?

- Are there ways you avoid making eye contact or connecting with people around you? What blocks you from connecting with people you don't know?

- Are you someone who regularly laughs at or perpetuates jokes that make fun of differences? If you are, how do you think it affects your ability to reach out to certain people?

- People often unconsciously pass on the lies and stereotypes they have learned. What lies, stereotypes, and differences have you been taught that you might be passing on? If you can't answer this question, or even if you can, spend a week *noticing* your friends, your parents, your colleagues, and the judgments they might have. Be conscious while you're watching television or a movie about the stereotypes and labels assigned to people that set them apart.

- How have other people's judgments and stereotypes affected you? In what ways, if any, have you been hurt, judged, or left out because of differences? How did it feel and how did you deal with it? What, if any, of those labels do you like?

- In what ways do you think you are different from others? Your appearance, your thoughts, your feelings, your actions? And how do you feel about those differences? Are you proud of some, ashamed of others, appreciative, disapproving?

- Have other people made up stories about you, told lies, spread rumors, or gossiped in ways that either made you feel different and separate, or in ways that were intended to set you apart? What were they? Who did them? How did they make you feel? Did you resist or take action to express yourself or to stop it, either in the moment or later? If not, why not?

- We also unconsciously take the stereotypes and labels that others have assigned to us and use them to demean ourselves. *Notice* your thoughts about yourself – your self-talk. Are you planting seeds of self-hate within you and allowing them to grow by leaving them unchecked? Can you take an entire day to monitor your self-talk and witness the ways in which you annihilate yourself? Make a list of what you tell yourself about who you are.

- Do you feel safe in your neighborhood? Have you met and do you acknowledge your neighbors? Do you know their names? Can you depend on them? Can they depend on you?

- How often do you stop and take the time to reach out to people you pass by on a regular basis? Are there people you see every day whom you have never met? Maybe these people are in a grocery store, in your class, at work, on an elevator, taking public transportation, or waiting on you in a restaurant or on an airplane. What keeps you from introducing yourself?

- Have you ever been *sure* you didn't like someone before you ever really knew that person? What made you so sure? Has there ever been a time where you somehow discovered you were wrong about someone? Perhaps you even became friends. What changed?

Choose

- Look at what you've noticed about your differences from above. Which of those things would you like to change about yourself, and why? Think about aspects of yourself that you can change, like behavior, and also think about things that you *can't* change, like eye color.

- Of the things you'd like to change about yourself, do you want to actually change those things or can you simply change your mind about them? Can you choose to feel differently about yourself?

- If there are people in your life who are unconsciously perpetuating stereotypes and differences, how might you make them more conscious of what they're doing and how it affects people? Can you do it without judging them, labeling them "bad" or "wrong," stereotyping them as bigots, or making them feel ashamed? It's very important that you imagine and plan first before you take any action. And it's okay to merely notice, and choose to conduct yourself differently.

- Make a list of the people you see on a regular basis with whom you have not connected. Then list what keeps you from reaching out to that person. Once you identify specific people and particular blocks, you can choose whether or not you wish to bridge the divide.

- If you have made jokes about or laughed at certain groups of people, make a silent, imaginary apology to that person or group. Identify if there are any types of people you tend to single out. Choose whether or not you want to continue your behavior.

- If you have been hurt or left out because of being stereotyped, create an imaginary healing circle as we've discussed in the last two chapters. First imagine speaking your mind to the people who have hurt you. Then ask for an apology. What happens? How do you feel?

- If you've monitored the labels that have been given to you and the self-talk you feed yourself, did you notice only what was "wrong" or did you also notice what was "right?" Are there any changes you'd like to make? Are there any thoughts you tell yourself that you'd like to change?

- Make a list of all the things that make you different, and write one benefit to having that difference.

Act

- Look in the mirror and tell yourself how proud you are of the things that make you special and different.

- Reach out to the people who live closest to you. If you already know them, use this as an opportunity to reconnect, see how they are, and nurture your relationship. If you have never met, take the time to introduce yourself, perhaps even bring them a gift. Do your best to find out who they are, and what matters most to them. Ask them what you would know *if you really knew them.*

- Go out of your way to meet and learn the names of the people you see on a regular basis, perhaps those you still have not met in your school, workplace, community, or place of worship. Choose at least one new person each day, and ask them to tell you about their life.

- Create a habit of smiling at and acknowledging everyone you pass. Find out the names of people who serve you or wait on you. If someone asks you for directions or for the time of day, ask them what their name is first before responding to their question. Whenever possible, make a point to share something you specifically like or appreciate about these people.

- Experience different cultural activities, concerts, and events. Educate yourself on differences by traveling to other communities or countries. Search the web, read books, and try eating at restaurants from other cultures. Spend time (including meals) at the homes of friends who are different from you.

- Get a diverse group of people together and watch a movie that deals with differences and diversity issues. We recommend movies such as *Crash, Freedom Writers,* and *Mississippi Burning*. Be sure to leave time after the movie for people to share their thoughts and impressions.

Celebrate!

If you take the risk of reaching out and then have a successful experience, consciously celebrate your success. Then spread the good news about the great things you've learned about people who are different from you. Taking this step will make you feel good and will also serve as an inspiration for others to take similar risks!

Everyday Hero ~ Nola Boyd

Few people live more full out than Nola. Humor, generosity and love lead the way as she dances her way into the lives and hearts of everyone she meets. An outrageous, fearless survivor and descendant of Hawaiian royalty, "Auntie Nola" has transformed the hardships of homelessness, and family alcoholism and abuse, into an undeniable example of survival and Christianity.

A model of compassion, Nola brings a depth of life experience and childlike appreciation to everything she does. Unabashed and fully expressed, she effortlessly enrolls everyone she meets into the Be the Change Movement. As a Challenge Day Leader, mother, grandmother, hula dancer, church volunteer, and interpreter for the deaf, Nola is a walking example of what it means to live and love in service to others.

Nola

If you really knew me, you'd know that…

- *I always wanted to be a motivational speaker, but never thought I had a message important enough to share.*
- *Family alcoholism, childhood abuse, sexual assaults, neglect, shame, and my own victimization was my only story.*
- *I'm proud that my parents grasped sobriety and became my chief mentors.*
- *From them, I learned that Whining and Prayer are not the same. Actions do speak louder than words and I will always find what I'm looking for, negative or positive.*
- *I am responsible for what I feel, and how long I feel that way.*
- *I learned that "God's got me," so, now that I'm not worried about me, I am free to serve others, heal others, and thus, heal myself.*
- *I saw humility and service to others "lived out loud" in my home.*
- *As a Challenge Day leader, I joyfully share a message of hope to the "babies" I get to hug and serve.*
- *There is no Shame and no Blame big enough to keep us from being who we were born to be, and who we want to be. We all get to write how our story ends! It's not how you start, but how you finish that is important.*

Everyday Hero ~ Nola Boyd

- *I love to laugh, cry, hug, smile, share, dance, pray, sing, worship and play. I LOVE the story I'm now writing. It will have a beautiful ending.*
- *I am a "Thriver." I'm not merely a Survivor of the harsh realities of my childhood, but a person who thrived and grew in spite of it. Yeah ME! ;o)*

I want to share a story from a recent Challenge Day I led. Tanisha is a bright, beautiful, shining freshman. Laughing, wearing a sassy little hat with her short blond hair just bouncing. She was so bubbly. It wasn't until several hours into the day that I noticed how she held her right hand cupped in her left, and kept pulling the sleeve down. She protected her right hand, which I noticed hadn't grown normally, and kept it tucked away, but she was always smiling and open. She had a beautiful spirit about her.

During the Power Shuffle, she crossed over the line for having a physical disability and shed tears about being teased. During the Speak Out she enthusiastically raised her good left hand when challenged to get on the microphone to speak her truth. I motioned to her to join me, and as we waited, I asked if I could hold her hand. Smiling, she quickly held her left hand out to me. I paused as I said, "Can I hold your other hand?" She looked into my eyes, paused, and gently nodded as she placed her sleeved right hand into mine. There was a huge sigh of relief and she leaned into me as I stroked the back of her sleeved hand with my fingers. I said, "I got you, baby girl. You can do this." Then, I handed her the microphone.

She said, "If you really knew me, you'd know that I get teased a lot, by a lot of you, and it used to make me really angry, but now I know it is because you have a big balloon, and so now, I just want to tell you all that I forgive you all for hurting me. I know that you didn't know how much it hurt my feelings, and I just wanted you all to know that I forgive you anyway." She handed me the microphone and was turning to sit down.

I said, "And what else?"

Everyday Hero ~ Nola Boyd

Tanisha's brow furrowed. "What do you mean?"

I whispered, "If we really knew you, what else would we know about you? Now might be a good time to teach people. There may be people who may be curious about your hand. You want to tell them what happened?"

Her face just lit up. "Yeah!" She grabbed the microphone. "If you really knew me, you'd know that I get teased a lot about my hand."

I whispered, "Do you want to show them your hand?"

"Really? I can do that?"

"You can do whatever you want to, baby girl. I got your back!"

She raised her hand, pushed her sleeve back, and amid cheers from the 130+ people in the room, she raised her hand high and shared.

"This is my hand. I was born like this." Soon tears were flowing and a huge smile crossed her face as students and teaches alike gave her a standing ovation for the courage she was showing. I was so amazed at the strength of this young one.

I wasn't ready for the miracle to end, so I asked her for one more, "If you really knew me."

"Like what?"

I whispered in her ear, and she just started giggling and laughing.

"Really?"

"Why not? Go for it, girl!"

She took the microphone, took a deep breath and said, "If you really knew me, you'd know that my name is Tanisha." And, looking at her raised hand, she wiggled her fingers and with a sheepish grin said, " And if you REALLY, REALLY knew me, you'd know that I wear a size 6 ring on my finger." She smiled.

Pandemonium, applause, tears and joy filled the room for little Tanisha, who found her voice and victoriously raised her hand.

Hugs and Safe Touch

Hugging has no unpleasant side effects and is all natural. There are no batteries to replace; it's inflation-proof and non-fattening with no monthly payments. It's non-taxable, non-polluting, and is, of course, fully refundable.

~ Anonymous

Rich

If you really knew me, you'd know that one of my most difficult challenges became one of my greatest gifts.

It happened when I was in grad school. One night as I walked into my group psychotherapy class, I found one of my classmates outside the lecture hall in tears. When I asked him what was wrong he said, "My dad just died." I tried to comfort him but he was inconsolable. Not sure what else to do, I encouraged him to keep crying. I placed my hand in the middle of his back, and sat silently as the teacher and others in the class turned their attention in our direction.

"I hated my father," he continued. "There were even times I wanted to kill him. And I feel so guilty."

I nodded with compassion.

"You don't understand," he continued. "You don't understand."

But I did understand. I was harboring anger for my father, too.

"I just wanted him to hold me. I wanted him to love me. I wanted to tell him that I loved him. And now I'll never get the chance."

My heart broke into a thousand pieces. His pain suddenly became my pain. In that moment, I realized that I, too, had never had the courage to look my father in the eyes and tell him that I loved him; I, too, just wanted my dad to hold me. And as I watched my classmate sink to his knees, debilitated by the loss, I decided I would not let this happen to me.

I always loved my father, and I tried on many occasions to tell him. But my fear was so big and my emotions were so raw that I'd start to cry. Since my father was uncomfortable with tears, he would often cut me off and, embarrassed and humiliated, I would swallow back my love and just walk away.

My dad had trained me well. Growing up, he'd always made it clear that the words "I love you" meant little to him. He didn't say them, and he didn't want to hear them. I remember him saying, "In my house, people would tell me they loved me all the time and it was bullshit." And so "love" became a meaningless word.

Now, however, with a newfound sense of determination, I phoned my parents and told them I wanted to come over because I had something important to tell them. I knew that if I told them I was coming, then I couldn't chicken out or talk myself out of it.

In the 40-minute drive to their house, I vacillated between fear and resolve. For my entire life I had only felt like I'd succeeded if I'd won my dad's approval. This time I was determined to feel proud of myself on my own.

I wasn't going to let my father's pain, his fear, or his beliefs, interrupt me and keep me from expressing my love for him.

I fantasized about the magical connection I was about to create with my parents. We were going to step into another world together, and it would be the most incredible real life love story, made complete by a happy ending. I envisioned the three of us expressing our feelings with depth and tenderness, and then embracing and holding each other. I bounced back and forth between feeling confident and hopeful, and feeling crazy. *What's the point?* I asked myself. But it was the memory of my classmate's pain that kept me driving toward their house and away from my own insecurities and doubt.

When I arrived, my childhood home was just as I had left it years ago. Dad was sprawled out on the couch in front of the television, a drink in one hand and smoke curling up from his cigar in the other. Mom was tucked away in the kitchen washing dishes. They didn't greet me at the door; they didn't sense the grandiosity of this impending event.

I asked my mom to come in from the kitchen, and I had my dad turn off the TV. I did my best to set myself up for success. I said that I had something to tell them and I wanted them to listen, without interrupting me, until I was finished. They stared at me politely as I summoned every ounce of courage.

"I'm really sorry for all the hard times we've had and for the trouble I've gotten into in the past. I know it wasn't always easy and that we've had our challenges but I want you to know that it was perfect. I've always been afraid to tell you that I love you but I really want to tell you now. I really want you to know that I love you both. A lot."

Without missing a beat my mom jumped in, "We love you, too." My dad just sat there. "Thanks," he said.

My heart sank. I waited for more, but the silence was crushing. *What's wrong with me?* I thought. *Why won't my father tell me he loves me, too?*

Despite my reluctance, I continued. "There's something else," I gripped my hands, nervous. "I've always wanted you to hug me, Dad. There have been times when a coach or a teacher of mine has hugged me and it felt really good. But I've always wanted a hug from you."

My dad crossed his arms and legs uncomfortably. "I wasn't brought up that way."

It became clear to me that I wasn't going to get my happy ending. I swallowed my heart and any sense of hope I ever had.

I felt stupid for ever thinking that it would be magical, and I left before they could see my tears.

As soon as the door had closed behind me, the tears were flowing freely. And as I walked across the lawn I felt relief with every step. *I asked for what I wanted. I did my part,* I told myself. *And that's all I can do.* It's not my problem, it's his. And then, from a place of compassion, I realized that my father couldn't give me a hug because no one ever gave one to him. The realization was only a band-aid for my pain. The truth was much harder to grapple with. The truth was that I don't have the kind of dad or the kind of family who can communicate with me in the way my heart desires.

I cried off and on all the way home, and by the time I arrived, I'd made a decision to never do that again. I was not going to risk investing my heart and opening myself up to more pain.

The following day, my parents arrived unexpectedly for a visit. I was standing in the front yard about to change the sprinkler when my dad came up behind me. He put his arm around my shoulder, and pointed to the top of the house casually. "What's that up on your roof?" he said.

I glanced over at him, confused, and then my eyes suddenly welled with tears as I realized that he had just initiated his first hug.

Since that day, every time my dad reaches out to shake my hand, I just pull him close and embrace him. Honestly, I think he's starting to like hugs as much as I do.

As I think about it now, I know it all started because I had the courage to do my part. I asked for what I wanted, and then I released my expectations. Despite how disastrous I thought it had all been, the truth is, from the moment I told my father I loved him, our relationship has never been the same.

Live It!

You can't wrap love in a box, but you can wrap a person in a hug.

~Author Unknown

Therapeutic touch has long been recognized as an essential tool for healing. Experiments have repeatedly shown that touch can make us feel better about ourselves and our surroundings. When I was in college, one of my professors showed us a film about some researchers who had worked with a librarian to demonstrate the power of touch.

They gave the librarian a simple script. First, she was to look each person in the eye and smile as she collected their library cards. Next, when checkout was complete, she was to again look them in the eye and say, "Thank you." Step three was to touch the tips of every other person's fingers as she handed back their library cards. As people left the library, researchers asked them about their experience in the library. The responses of people who had not been touched varied, ranging from great to indifferent. However, for those who had been touched, the responses were remarkably similar. The people who had been touched *all* had glowing remarks about the library as well as about the librarian. Some even went so far as to say the librarian was exceptionally friendly even though the only thing she did differently was touch the tips of their fingers.

I can't help but wonder how they would have responded if she had offered them a hug.

Safe, conscious, intentional touch is a powerful tool for deepening our connections with loved ones and friends. Hugs are a natural expression of care. They can serve as a warm way to say hello, goodbye, or thank you, or to show support to others. Studies have shown that without touch, newborn babies can actually die[1]. It's clear that whenever two people share in a hug, they both benefit.

That's not to say that any of us will literally die if we don't get hugged or touched, but perhaps in some way a part of us actually does die.

At Challenge Day, we teach that everyone needs at least three hugs *every* day, just to get by. Without at least three hugs, we start to decline. If we all got six hugs a day, we would probably feel pretty good about ourselves and not notice any lack of connection with the people around us. But if we really want to thrive, the magic number is more like twelve hugs. If we get at least twelve hugs every day, we might feel the love and support we need to do whatever we came to this planet to do.

Safe Hugs

We can certainly understand that hugs and touch might be uncomfortable for some people. Some of us were raised in families where there wasn't much hugging or touching. In that case, giving and receiving hugs can often feel awkward. Others may have been touched inappropriately; perhaps they were hit, slapped, beaten up, molested, or even raped. For people raised in these kinds of environments or

---

1 http://www.toddlertime.com/mh/terms/healing-touch.htm

having these experiences (without counseling and/or healing), hugs and touch can even be frightening.

There's also the problem of homophobia, which can make people afraid to reach out and hug someone of the same sex because somebody else might think they're gay, whether they are or not. Many people fear being put-down, teased, maybe beaten up or even killed for having that label.

The idea that one person won't touch another out of fear is heartbreaking to me, whether it's a woman hugging a woman, a woman hugging a man, a man hugging a man, a brother hugging a brother, or a father holding onto his son of any age. A hug says nothing about a person's sexual orientation. It simply means they have the courage to reach out and share affection.

In a Challenge Day program, we teach people how to hug appropriately. Over the years, we've worked with young people, adults, camps, churches, corporations, and obviously high schools and junior highs. And when we talk about hugging it's pretty common for someone to raise a hand and say, "Didn't you know, we can't hug in our school?"

Believe it or not, at many schools, hugs are banned. Young people can get in trouble, *even suspended,* for hugging! The same is true in many of the corporations with which we work.

A hug is only therapeutic if it is a safe hug – safe for the person giving it, and safe for the person receiving it. If hugs have been banned there is usually a really good reason – *people have hugged or touched inappropriately.* Unwanted touching can be a way for people with power to target others for oppression. If that's the case, we work closely with administrators and supervisors to change those bans because we believe the way our world is today, we *need* to be able to support each other with hugs.

Instead of banning hugs and other forms of safe touch, we encourage people to learn how to hug or touch appropriately.

First, *always ask for permission.* A real hug takes two or more people; make sure all parties are willing to participate. After you have had some practice with this, sometimes all you need to do to ask permission is to open your arms to offer a hug, and make eye contact with the other person. Be sure the other person says *yes* – they will tell you with their eyes. If a person does not want to participate, respect that person's *no.* If a person chooses not to participate, it doesn't mean they don't like you or they are rejecting you. Consider a thought such as, *Wow, they trusted and respected me, and themselves, enough to tell me their truth.*

Second, *hug appropriately.* Share your love and affection for the person in honoring and respectful ways. Be compassionate, not passionate. Be sure to honor other peoples' boundaries. Although we know not everyone wants to be hugged, a great many people live their lives hungry for the support and connection hugs and other forms of safe touch can bring. If hugging is not appropriate, try finding alternative forms of safe touch that can work for you. Some organizations prefer handshakes or even high-fives. On the other extreme, at Challenge Day, we have a lot of fun with group hugs – the more the merrier. The point is, that physical touch is a way to acknowledge our connection to each other as human beings who are sharing our journey on this planet together.

Finally, *if you need a hug, ask for one!* It takes at least two people to hug and one of them has to initiate it. Take responsibility for communicating what you need around giving and receiving hugs. And be sure to honor your own boundaries.

Can you imagine how different our schools and workplaces would be if everyone felt secure enough to ask for or offer hugs and safe touch? How might our interactions and relationships be changed? How much more productive might we become? What if everyone had the courage to freely share their support, affection, and appreciation, in safe and meaningful ways? How much more connected might we all feel?

A few years ago, Yvonne threw a surprise party for me. The first surprise was that she invited my parents. The second surprise was that she had everyone fill out validation cards in which they wrote out all the things they loved and appreciated about me. My mom and dad handed me cards in which they had written on both sides. Then, with tears in his eyes, my dad pulled me close, and gave me a hug and a kiss. He told me that he loved me, and that he was proud that I was his son. It was one of the best moments of my life.

Right Here, Right Now

Today hugs are an important part of the way Yvonne and I share our love and affection with one another and with others we care for. Because Yvonne and I spend a great deal of time together – working, playing, parenting, etc. – we have many opportunities to share love and hugs with one another. Even though we hug often, there was a point not too long ago that we realized at times when we hugged, our bodies were there but our minds were on things like our to-do lists or where we were going next. Neither of us was getting the full benefit of our connection.

As a result, we've come up with a practice that instantly brings us into our hearts so that we can be completely present with one another. Now whenever we hug, we pause, take a breath, and one or the other of us simply whispers the words, "Right here, right now." This simple practice reminds us there is nowhere to go, and nothing more important than sharing the present moment together. I strongly recommend you consider adapting a similar practice with those you love.

The Challenge Day Office

I am incredibly proud that the Challenge Day office has become a model of what's possible. We reach out to one another, to visitors, clients, people on the phone, and just about anyone with whom we interact. This may or may not come as a surprise, but we have a *very* diverse staff. This diversity takes many forms – different cultures, beliefs, and yes, even different desires. Not everyone in our office is comfortable with all the "touchy-feely" sharing and interactions that take place, so for us, the key is in asking permission and making sure that every person gets to *choose* for him or herself.

Our goal is not just to tolerate the differences between us, but to celebrate them. Over time, when people experience that they really do have choice, we have found many eventually choose connection. The result is that Challenge Day people love coming to work. Many of them have left higher paying jobs to work longer hours and volunteer time on after-hours service projects, all because they feel connected and recognized as an important part of our team.

Our commitment in the workplace is the same as our vision for the world – *that everyone feels safe, loved, and celebrated.*

Challenge Day Guidelines for Safe Hugging

1. *Always* ask permission.
2. Hug appropriately.
3. If you want or need a hug, ask for one!

Be the Hero

**Hugs can do great amounts of good -
especially for children.**

~ Princess Diana

Notice

- What is your history with hugs and touch? Growing up, was your family affectionate? How has your upbringing affected your relationships or the amount of hugs and contact you have with those around you?

- When someone offers you a hug, do you say your true yes's and no's? If not, why not?

- Is there anyone in your life with whom you would like to share more hugs or support? If so, what gets in the way? Have you offered or requested the connection you'd like?

- Who in your life hugs or holds you? Are you getting all the safe hugs and touch that you want? If not, why not?

- How often do you offer to hug or support the people in your life? How comfortable are you with offering hugs or physical support to the people around you?

- Have you or others in your life experienced inappropriate touching? If so, how has that affected your life or relationships? If you were hurt in some way, do the people closest to you know what happened? If not, what stops you from telling them?

- How do you feel about hugging? Do you enjoy hugging, or do you prefer other forms of touch and affection? Are the people you connect with on a regular basis clear about your desires? If not, why not?

- Think of all the groups you are a part of. Are some of them huggers and others not? Notice which groups you like to spend more time with and why?
- When you want or need a hug, how likely are you to ask for one? What, if anything, stops you from asking for what you want?

Choose

- If you are someone who is comfortable with hugs and touch, imagine your ideal relationships with the people closest to you in your life. If you would like to share more hugs and safe touch, ask yourself what gets in the way, and make a plan for how you might change things.
- Only you can decide what feels comfortable and safe for you. Noticing your resistance, fear, and bad feelings for people and situations may well be a heightened intuitive response. There are good reasons for you to feel fear. If your fear comes from wounds, honestly look at how to heal those wounds. If your fear and resistance is something you can't explain, explore your thoughts and feelings with a friend, a professional, or through journaling.
- Imagine who you ultimately want to be and what your goal is in receiving hugs and affection. If you are not where you want to be, plan a course of action to understand and heal your fears. But always listen internally and never ignore your boundaries.

Act

- If you have realized you don't have the relationship with hugs and touch that you would like, take steps to achieve your goals.
- Challenge yourself to give and get at least 12 hugs every day for at least the next week.

- Try offering hugs to at least five people a day who would never expect them from you. Be sure to ask permission. Notice what happens and how it makes you feel.
- Visit a retirement home, elderly relatives, a children's ward, or someone who may be missing out on hugs and safe touch. Go out of your way to touch, listen to, and connect to them in ways that bring joy to both of you.

Celebrate!

Let the people who love you, hold you, and hug you, know how much it means to you! If you have great success stories or make special connections with people, be sure to blog about it on our website at www.challengeday.org/bethechange.

Everyday Hero ~ Amani Carey Simms

We have known Amani since he was a young boy, and it is an honor to watch him share his unique gifts, and fully stand in his power as a man. His name means "peace," and Amani brings with him a profound sense of peace and connection everywhere he goes. A multitalented and visionary young leader, Amani has committed his life to the liberation of all people. He proudly carries on the legacy of his father, Harrison Sims, who was our friend and mentor.

Amani is not only a professional musician, rap artist, and poet, but he is also a powerfully magnetic and inspirational speaker who has helped to transform the lives of countless youth as a both Challenge Day leader, and the director of the Mosaic Project, which provides diversity education and alliance-building for elementary students. A loving son and brother, Amani is a living example of what it means to live life outside the confines of the Be A Man Box.

Amani

If you really knew me, you would know that, like you, I am the child of my parents' training. We are all trying our best to squeeze our limitless selves into the promise of acceptance, through the needle's eye of expectation, sewn by the hands of fear. Like you, I know we deserve more.

My father was a spirit daddy most of my life, and the hearth of his smile, the strength in his tears, the fullness of his love, and the forgiveness in his arms remain forever tangible. He grew up a Black man in a world filled with so much fear and hatred toward him, with so many messages telling him he would never be enough. He fought to stop fighting; he loved to offer us a better world.

Still, I work hard every day so that the judgments in my mind don't scare me away from myself. Most of my life I aspired to have his intellect, his heart, his strength, his power. I reached out for power, confused about how it works. I thought I needed to get more to be the man my father was, to be a man my father would be proud of, and to be a man with power in this world. After crying with hundreds of boys, young men, and men;

Everyday Hero ~ Amani Carey Simms

after loving thousands, dancing with them and singing joyously, laughing ourselves silly and speaking our fears, dreams, and realities – I know better. I am no longer striving to be a man, I am learning to be myself.

Amani's music can be found on memusic.com

Dorian & Chris from Oprah's
High School Challenge

Teen Files: Surviving High School Heroes

Why Aren't You Normal? - Lena's Story

People concern themselves with being normal, rather than natural.

~ Robert Anthony

Yvonne

If you really knew me, you would know that although I would very much like to change the world, I know I can't do it single-handedly. And so when Sharon Ramirez, a continuation-school teacher, called and recommended that I meet her student Lena, I was resistant. At the time, I had four young kids of my own, I was leading three to five Challenge Days a week, and I was running two women's support groups. I didn't need or want any more responsibilities.

As I spoke with Sharon, I could tell that she was one of those special teachers who led with her heart. I knew that she was probably the first educator who had shown Lena any real respect and caring. She told me about the fifteen-year-old student whose life was filled with truancy, drugs, alcohol, homelessness, and violence. As a result, the girl's options were limited: she would be kicked out of school – again – or worse, end up in juvenile hall. Despite all the trouble, Sharon was able to see through Lena's pain into the magic underneath.

The concerned teacher described a desperate girl who would not make it without support, and then she poignantly added, "I know you will see what I love about her."

The faces of all the people who had found time for me when I had needed help and support paraded through my mind. I'm sure their lives had been just as full as mine was now, yet they chose to make time for me. Some of them had saved my life. And so I agreed to meet Lena.

The minute she walked into my office, my heart opened for her. Without exchanging any words, I could see and feel her wounds. If I hadn't known better, I might have thought she was a boy. She was dressed in stereotypically male clothing: oversized baggy shorts and T-shirt, tennis shoes, and a hat covering her short, cropped hair. My years of experience working in schools helped me understand why she'd gotten into so much trouble with the "system." I shuddered to imagine how the world treated her. By appearances alone I knew that Lena had simply been acting out and making choices from the pain of being a *constant* target.

As with every person who comes into my office, I greeted her with a warm hug. I didn't know until later that it was the first hug she'd received in months. We sat across from each other and chatted about the directions to my office. I commented on how much her teacher loved her and believed in her. Once the ice was broken, I gently asked, "Lena, if I really knew you, what would I know?"

She was surprised by the depth of my question, and met my eyes as if testing my authenticity. I could see the softness in her, a tenderness that she protected from all the betrayal she must have endured to be in so much trouble at such a young age. I was surprised but deeply honored when, seemingly without effort, she opened up and gave me a window into her world.

She began unpacking the vulnerable details of her life. Her family, like many, lived with hurt and struggle. She shared about her parent's divorce as well as living with violence, alcohol, and drug abuse at home. Her parents had few parenting tools and struggled with full emotional balloons. Lena's greatest pain, though, did not come from her family; it had been inflicted by the world. Tears fell from her sparkling green eyes as she unraveled a story filled with heartache, humiliation, and shame.

Lena told me that from a young age most people could not tell if she was a boy or a girl. And for some, that gave them permission to humiliate her. She described time after time in which she had been laughed at by insensitive teachers, suspended for fighting after being called a "f-ing dyke," even beaten by law enforcement.

Simply by walking into a mall, by going to a convenience store, or by just sitting in class, Lena was a target of stares, whispers, shouted aggression, humiliation, or threats of harm. By fifteen, she had already survived episodes of cruelty most of us will never experience in our entire lives. No wonder Lena was angry. Our world and our schools had betrayed her.

My stomach clenched as she spoke. I knew that much of her "bad kid" stigma had been earned out of Lena's best attempts to defend herself and to survive. Shocked by society's seemingly willful ignorance, I experienced new compassion for those who endure the constant torment of derogatory shouts like, "What *are* you, a boy or a girl?"

Every part of me wanted to reach out and pull her onto my lap, rock her, and attempt to make up for the multitude of people who had betrayed her.

I began spending time with her on a weekly basis. I listened, cheered her on while she beat up pillows instead of people, and simply held her while she processed her pain. Over time, she learned how to take the excruciating agony of her past, transform it and release it, in order to heal herself and to help others. It was easy to see who she really was beneath her hurt, but Lena clearly needed much more than just a compassionate ear. It didn't take long before the mama in me fell in love with her. Her teacher was right, she was loving, funny, daring, courageous, and packed with enough inspiration and spirit to light up the world. I had no idea when I first met her that Rich and I would soon open our home to her as a "foster" daughter.

As the days turned into weeks and months and then years, Lena became part of our family. She blessed us with many gifts. More than being a big sister for our four young daughters, every day she demonstrated how to turn hate and judgment from the world into the passion to live 100% alive.

The greatest gift Lena bestowed on us, however, was an opportunity to see the world through her eyes. She represents the millions of kids who are labeled, mistreated, misunderstood, kicked out of school, stuck in juvenile hall, discarded onto the streets, and sometimes, sadly, even killed. The miracle of Lena is the reminder that safety, love, acceptance, connection, and celebration are the transformational forces that literally move mountains.

Live It!

The possibility of stepping into a higher plane is quite real for everyone. It requires no force or effort or sacrifice. It involves little more than changing our ideas about what is normal.

~ Deepak Chopra

We all want our kids to grow up in safety and comfort; we want their childhoods to be spent playing and dreaming. But by the time our kids attend school, their sense of freedom is often limited. For many, their biggest concerns have nothing to do with eating healthy or passing tests; they stop imagining a way to end pollution, halt global warming, or even feed the hungry. Instead, our kids spend their energy in fear of being labeled weird or thought of as not normal.

Why are so many of us afraid of being different? Why is being normal the goal we seek? While the answer may be straightforward, it is also frightening. We are desperately afraid of being teased, humiliated, rejected, threatened, beaten up or even killed.

Far too many people like Lena, Albert, Victor, Patrick – even Rich and I – were teased and humiliated regularly because we did not meet the standards of what others considered to be normal. Like many others, perhaps even you, we were on the "too" list. Too fat, too thin, too short, too tall, too weird, too gay, too stupid, too dark, too light, too poor, too rich, too angry, too popular, too old, too young, too different.

What is normal and who defines it? The dictionary says that it means standard, common, regular, usual, or conforming. However, because our standards change from day to day, era to era, and community to community, none of us can ever be sure of getting it right. If we look for society to tell us who we should be, what we should look like, and how we should act, we will never get to relax into who we are.

Our uniqueness is the price we pay for acceptance and inclusion.

For some, avoiding ridicule or isolation can be as simple as changing clothes. For others, being normal means keeping our values and opinions to ourselves by remaining quiet or just going along with the group. It means selling ourselves out in order to please someone else. The danger is that we stop choosing for ourselves. In fact, we may not even know or remember what we want because we are so caught up in the world of trying and pleasing.

If the definition of normal is always changing, how can any of us can ever really measure up? We can't, and so we continue to fear, judge, condemn, and even attack others.

No one is immune. Everyone experiences teasing at one time or another. But then there are those who are tortured.

Some of us cannot fit the norm no matter what. Maybe we were born looking very different from those around us, or perhaps we have things about ourselves that cannot be easily changed or hidden. For Lena, and the countless others who are born with qualities they can't change, their appearance, skin color, size, abilities, or sexual preference seem to make them targets for endless oppression and ridicule no matter what they do.

Working for over 25 years with school systems all over the U.S. and Canada, I know just how cruel many kids have learned to be. Even when they think they're just kidding around, "That's gay!" or "Don't be a faggot!" are all-too-commonly heard on most every school campus, along with other labels that demean groups of people in both subtle and overt ways. Similar to how sexism and racism have been condoned, these expressions, and others like them, are still often ignored or even tolerated by many students, teachers, and administrators. This is how insidious oppression can be. We make it okay if we pass it off as humor. What may seem harmless can lead to oppression in its most brutal forms.

Regardless of our values or beliefs, can we at least agree that no human being deserves to be disrespected and humiliated? Because today, and every day, our children are suffering in ways that are both tragic and completely unnecessary.

- In an average elementary school classroom, two to three students spend their day afraid and in need of help.[1]
- In U.S. schools, over 800,000 students every year are harassed because of their race.[2]
- Every day 160,000 students miss school because of bullying.[2]
- 61% of students who are bullied do not tell their parents.[2]
- Gay kids are six times more likely to commit suicide.[2]
- 50% of boys and 75% of girls are unhappy with their appearance.[3]
- One out of every eight teenagers suffers from depression.[3]
- Suicide has become the third leading cause of death for high school youth.[3]
- 79 % percent of students represent the silent majority watching as others are being teased.[1]
- More than three-quarters of teens (78 percent) report that kids who are gay or thought to be gay are teased or bullied in their schools and communities. Nine out of ten teens (93 percent) hear other kids at school or in their neighborhood use words like "fag," "homo," "dyke," "queer," or "gay" at least once in a while, with 51 percent hearing them every day. Four out of five teen respondents said they disapprove of the taunting.
- According to a study by the Safe Schools Coalition, three out of four kids targeted by anti-gay bullies are heterosexual. Although all children suffer from anti-gay prejudice, gay youth tend to suffer the worst consequences. According to various studies, one third of gay students are physically harassed due to their sexual orientation and one in six is beaten badly enough to need medical attention. Compared to straight kids, gay teens are four times more likely to be threatened with a weapon at school, and three to seven times more likely to attempt suicide.

1 Global News, *The Bully Solution*; 2 *Oprah's High School Challenge*; 3 *Teen Files: Surviving High School*

Cruelty Is not Innate

Cruelty is *learned* behavior. Kids aren't mean to others unless someone has been mean to them. While virtually every child has been harassed from time to time, there seems to be unwritten permission to systematically hurt certain kids, not only by other students but all too frequently by the adults who are supposed to keep them safe.

What if being exactly who we are was considered normal?

Since we are all beautifully different, we must redefine our sense of normal, and we must change the way we treat one another. If our hearts are open, and love is what we most value, the game of separating from one another, including teasing, humiliating, and even killing one another, will not be possible.

We are at a time on the planet when none of us can afford to stay stuck in petty judgment, prejudice, and separation. It is a critical time of choice. It will require each of us to rise above our hate, fear, and circumstances, and come together as one. Compassion, understanding, acceptance, forgiveness, and vulnerability are the qualities needed in full force on the planet now. The old system is crashing down.

Change starts from the inside out.

Change starts inside of each of us, and in our corner of the world – in our family, school, workplace, community, and place of worship. What if, all at once, each of us committed ourselves to creating a new paradigm for how to be together? What if, in every school, community, and workplace, normal meant seeing how loving we could be? What if we looked out for everyone, especially those who are different or could be potential targets of teasing or isolation? What if, instead of joining in the rumors, jokes, and negativity, we stood up for and included everyone? How might that change the way people feel toward or relate with one another? How might that change the world?

What if changing the world was up to you? What if the time was now? Are you ready to join us in making that commitment?

The Illusion of Normalcy

1. "Normal" is an illusion – we are all born beautifully different.

2. Differences are wonderful; it's the divisions that hurt us all.

3. Our uniqueness is a gift to be celebrated, not to be judged.

4. Negative judgment is a learned behavior.

5. Anything we learn, we can unlearn if we choose.

6. Positive change starts from the inside out.

Lena Celebrates

Be the Hero

To be normal is the ideal aim of the unsuccessful.

~ Carl Jung

Notice

- Have you or anyone close to you ever been negatively labeled or judged as weird, different, or not normal? If so, how did it feel? How did you or they respond?

- How often, if ever, do you feel pressure to change yourself in order to fit in or appear normal? Have you ever changed your style, the way you acted, or reversed or withheld your opinion in order to fit in with a group or clique? If so, what did you do and how did it feel? How does it feel to think about it now?

- Have you ever compromised your values or done something you knew wasn't right for you because you were afraid of what other people might say or do, or because you didn't want to be labeled as weird and then rejected? If so, how did it feel?

- Who, if anyone, do you negatively judge as weird, odd, or not normal? How do your judgments affect the way you relate to these people?

- As a student, have you ever heard or experienced people around you being teased, hurt, or humiliated for not fitting in with the norm? Maybe they looked different in some way, their skin was a different color, their bodies had different abilities than others, they spoke different languages, or maybe they were gay or perceived as having "gay" qualities. What, if anything, did you say or do to stand up for them?

- How often in your life do you now or have you ever experienced or heard rude and judgmental comments based on people's perceptions of what is normal and acceptable? How do these comments and experiences affect you?

- Have you ever taken dangerous risks, been hurt, or been tempted to hurt yourself or someone else because of the pressure to be normal or fit in? If so, what did you do and how did it feel?

Choose

- Do you need to apologize to anyone for judging them, belittling them, making jokes about them, or otherwise hurting them?
- Do you need to ask for forgiveness for causing someone else pain?
- Do you need to create a healing circle in order to forgive yourself for causing someone else pain in any way?
- Do you need to look yourself in the eyes, and remind yourself that you are proud of who you are?
- Do you need to gently confront someone for perpetuating stereotypes, for making jokes about a person or a group of people, or for being unconscious of any pain that person may be causing?
- Do you need to get the support of someone you trust – a friend or a professional – for any actions you may be taking that cause harm to yourself or anyone else?

Act

- If you've answered yes to any of the questions above, take action!
- Find time to get to know some of the people you have been avoiding, people whom you feel are different from you in some way. Ask them to complete the sentence, "If you really knew me, you'd know…."
- Find someone you know who is openly gay, lesbian, or transgender. Ask that person to share how their sexual identity has affected the way people deal with him or her.
- The next time you notice someone else being teased because of his or her perceived sexual orientation, skin color, physical or mental ability, cultural background, or some other difference, offer to be an ally.

Celebrate!

Consider a new way to celebrate. Take one thing about yourself that you most judge or dislike, something you can't change, and honor it with a ritual. "Act as if" it is the most beautiful and special thing about you. Celebrate as if you are a Super Hero, and it is your special power.

Everyday Hero ~ Pam Dunn

 Deep, funny and fully alive, Pam lives her life 100%. A profound diversity educator and facilitator, Pam spins an undeniable web of compassion and connection in every group she leads. As an African American woman raised in a primarily Caucasian military community, Pam has committed her life to building bridges between people of all races and backgrounds.

As a senior Challenge Day leader and a Be Present facilitator, she literally and figuratively laughs and dances her way into people's hearts. An expert with words, Pam utilizes her quick wit and deep seated sense of understanding to challenge people to step up to Being the Change, while helping to put an end to negative judgment and separation based on differences.

Pam

When I was a child, I felt different and alone. I wanted to be like the people I saw around me. But there were very few reflections of myself in the media, and in my friends and community. I learned, like most little girls, that the best thing you can be is thin and have long legs, long blonde hair and blue eyes. Comparing myself to this standard instilled a sense of unworthiness, self-criticism and doubt that one day I trust I can tell you I have completely overcome.

I was lucky there was an adult in my life who saw the impact my environment was having on my self-esteem. She made space for me to talk honestly about my life. I had her support when I began the exploration all teenagers experience when they begin to differentiate between their own voice of truth, and that of other's expectations. And while I had the benefit of being able to hear my own voice, nothing could have prepared me at 17 for the dawning realization that I was gay. If I felt alone and different before, I was unimaginably isolated then.

Now I walk into rooms all over the country to tell young people my story and give them permission to tell their truth. We give them the chance that I got — to be who they really are and to get to know one another past their assumptions and common judgments. I want to be for young women and men what that adult was in my life: an honest adult who will say, "You are beautiful just as you are. You deserve the freedom to be yourself and trust yourself." And, most importantly, "You are not alone."

Be the Change: A Call to Action

Live your life so that your children can tell their children that you not only stood for something wonderful – you acted on it!

~ Dan Zadra

Unaware of the journey to come, or the perfection of the destiny about to unfold, eleven wide-eyed, fidgeting teenagers waited in the library of Yuba City High School in Northern California. In their vast diversity and style differences, they not only represented every group on their school campus, but many schools in America and other parts the world. They also resembled those on the grown-up campuses of *life* and *work* where teenagers in adult bodies still act out the painful habits and lies carried over from their past.

Under bright lights, and with sound and camera crews all around, the filming of *Teen Files: Surviving High School* began. Vice Principal Joan Zappettini introduced us to the group of students selected to participate in the documentary of which they had unknowingly just become the stars.

We began our relationship by sharing our truth. "We do not believe that there are any accidents!" We watched their faces light up with hopeful, excited smiles as we continued. "What if every one of you is here today for reasons far beyond your ability to understand at this time?"

The infectious sparkle of possibility in their young eyes brought tears to ours. We invoked our personal heroes and "sheroes" who were all once teenagers themselves including Mahatma Gandhi, Mother Teresa, Martin Luther King, Jr., Eleanor Roosevelt, César Chávez, and Rosa Parks. We dared awaken them to their highest potential as their faces strained with skepticism. "Even Jesus and the Buddha were your age once." They bit back their snickers as we continued. "Something all these great leaders had in common was that they lived their lives as examples to others, and taught that anything *they* could do, *we too* could do, and much, much more."

With a curious mixture of sarcasm and hope shining in his dark eyes, Ernie, a handsome, bi-racial teenager, blurted out, "Yeah, maybe some day one of us will change the world!"

Although the rest of the group giggled at what seemed to them like an impossible dream, chills ran up our spines as we contemplated the possibility that he was right.

The cameras were rolling as our journey began.

Over the course of the next thirty days, we had the honor of watching as, one by one, each of our would-be heroes stepped up to our challenge to Be the Change. Little did they know that the documentary would offer them the possibility of a lifetime. By plumbing the depths of their own emotions, stepping outside their comfort zones, and courageously confronting issues common to teenagers everywhere, these eleven heroic teens would ultimately shine as leaders and role models for people all over the world.

Perhaps you have already watched the segment of the Emmy Award-winning documentary *Teen Files: Surviving High School* on the DVD that came with this book. (It is also available on the Challenge Day website at www.challengeday.org). Maybe you've had the opportunity to see the full length show. In either case, you've joined the millions of people all over the world who have seen the example these teens have set. Unbeknownst to them, their honesty and vulnerability, as well as their courage to learn and to grow in front of the cameras, has touched and changed many lives, including their own.

Now we offer you the same challenge. What if the choices you make each day, big and small, actually do make a difference? What if, by having the courage to listen to the guidance in your own heart, you could change or save a life, alter history, or even change the world? Do you have the courage to step up and be the hero in your own life?

Live It!

Don't ask yourself what the world needs. Ask yourself what makes you come alive, and go do it. Because what the world needs is people who have come alive.

~ Howard Thurman

For years we have asked young people the question, "What is your greatest dream?" To our horror, the most immediate and common answer has been, "To make lots of money!" Many of our children have bought into the illusion that money will automatically bring happiness. As adults, many of us waste our lives and talents chasing this fantasy only to find ourselves wealthy and disillusioned. Money is not a bad thing, but when making money or having lots of things becomes more important than loving big, feeling proud, or making a positive difference, something is definitely wrong.

So, we decided to change the question and instead ask young people, "If you could make lots of money doing exactly what you want to do, what would it be?" What is it you love to do? What brings you your greatest joy? What sparks your passion? And what if the very thing that ignites you, is what you were born to do?

Many young people, programmed by our low touch, low feeling, materialistic society, seem to have temporarily forgotten who they are.

In our souls, we all know that what is most important in life cannot be purchased. As we watch the planet's financial house of cards collapse around us, it is becoming increasingly clear that if we passively *wait* for a Super Hero to fly in with a cape, ride gallantly in on a horse, or be elected president, it could literally be too late.

What if, instead of looking outside ourselves and blaming others, or waiting for them to change things, each of us looked into our own hearts and found the courage to step into our power? That's been one of the primary goals of our work – to remind people of their own magnificence. In many cases, it only takes a spark to reignite the flame of an individual's fire and purpose.

Challenge Day had its twentieth birthday in 2008. Years before Senator Obama elevated the notion of change to the political forefront, teenagers in schools all over the United States and Canada began rising to the challenge to Be the Change. Inspired by the words and the life of Gandhi, and ready to step into a movement that is changing the world – one kid and one school at a time – young people are role modeling what it looks like to "Be the change they wish to see in the world."

Please Read This Carefully

You are here for a reason! Whether you know it yet or not, you have a special purpose. You have gifts that no one else has. Sparkling with your own light, you bring your individual talents, magic, medicine, and love. Our world needs these gifts and lessons *now*.

It's not what you do but who you *be* that ultimately makes the difference.

Regardless of the circumstances you find yourself in, the job you do, or the career you settle into, you can Be the Change. Every moment we live, each of us has the opportunity to make choices that can profoundly affect those around us. Whether you are a student, teacher, doctor, lawyer, chef, server, dancer, athlete, politician, parent, or custodian, or even if you are retired or unemployed, you have the power to change lives. The world needs people in every profession who commit themselves to living lives of love and service. Who will you be? How will you relate to the people and the world around you?

Passion = Pass – I – On

Every one of us has a still place within that is calling us to greatness. Each of us knows when we are living in line with this call. Whether in a fleeting moment of perfect peace, or in being inspired to a higher place by some external experience or situation, we have all glimpsed our own greatness, and felt our connection with something much greater than we could otherwise imagine.

When we face our fears, heal our hurts, and let go of self-limiting beliefs and habits, we open the door more and more to that greatness, power, and magnificence. When we remember who we are, and why we are here, we take the first step toward becoming the heroes we were born to be.

Now is the time to slow down and listen for the gentle guiding voices of your own heart. Now is the time to answer the call to *Be The Hero You've Been Waiting For*. It starts by having love and compassion for yourself, which grows in relationship with others, and takes form in the example you set in the world. It comes from *noticing* what's happening, *choosing* how you'd like things to be, and then taking whatever *actions* you believe it will take to bring your piece of the puzzle forward.

321

Why Be the Change?

The current state of our world family, with violence, pollution, poverty, addiction, social oppression, isolation, war, and threats of war, has left many people feeling fearful, victimized, or alone. When you commit to Be The Change, you become part of the ever growing Be the Change Movement that provides individuals with clear and powerful ways to become what we call "agents of positive change."

By joining with the ever-growing Be the Change Movement, you not only commit yourself to *being the change* you want to see, you also immediately serve as an inspiration and support to others.

By maintaining a commitment to perform at least one intentional positive Act of Change per day, you not only experience the immediate satisfaction and pride associated with making a difference, you also set the bar for others.

What is Possible?

With millions committed to *being the change*, there are no limits to the possibilities.

Imagine families where every member is consciously looking for ways to contribute. Imagine schools where every student is given time to log, share, and celebrate their positive impacts. Imagine corporations where contribution and service are the basis of the company culture. Imagine a world where the people of every country commit themselves to becoming a positive influence; where international competition and gamesmanship focus not on winning or losing but on generating the most powerful positive change; and where our daily news is no longer dominated by violence, poverty, and destruction, but instead celebrates and recognizes positive acts of change. Imagine young people and adults all over our country and all over the world who are being honored and appreciated daily, weekly, monthly, and annually for their significant contributions.

What does it mean to "Be the Change?"

- It means to liberate ourselves from self-imposed limitations.
- It means to create peace and connection from the inside out.
- It means to move away from hopelessness and fear, and take powerful positive steps toward creating the life – and world – of our dreams.
- It means to notice what's happening in the world around us, choose to make a difference, and take positive action to change things.
- It means committing to perform at least one intentional act of positive change each day.

Daily Acts of Change

Every positive action makes a difference. Every time you notice that something could be better in your life or in the world around you, *and* you take the step of doing something to contribute, you have completed an Act of Change.

Acts of Change can be as small as picking up a piece of trash, standing up so someone else can have a seat, helping someone with a chore, or giving a simple compliment. Every Act of Change counts. Even if others never find out what you have done, your decision to act is all it takes for *you* to benefit. Remember, service is a gift we give ourselves that always comes back. When you serve, everyone wins – especially you! By committing to complete at least one intentional, positive Act of Change each day, you not only become part of the Be the Change Movement, you also become part of the solution on the planet.

What would you need to do with your life to give yourself goosebumps? What acts of love, kindness, or change would you need to perform so that at the end of each day, you could look in the mirror and say, "I am so proud of you!" What would it take for you to blow yourself away?

Don't Think You Can Make A Difference?

If you ever question if your actions can make a positive difference, consider *The Starfish Story* written by Loren Eisley.

One day a man was walking along the beach when he noticed a boy picking something up and gently throwing it into the ocean.

Approaching the boy, he asked, "What are you doing?"

The youth replied, "Throwing starfish back into the ocean. The surf is up and the tide is going out. If I don't throw them back, they'll die."

"Son," the man said, "don't you realize there are miles and miles of beach and hundreds of starfish? You can't make a difference!"

After listening politely, the boy bent down, picked up another starfish, and threw it back into the surf. Then, smiling at the man, he said, "I made a difference for that one."

Imagine that you attend a school or work in a company with 2,000 other people. Even if only half of them committed to perform a daily Act of Change, that would be 1,000 acts of positive change a day, 5,000 a week, and at least 20,000 Acts of Change in a single month.

Together we make a difference, but remember, even if no one else joins you, you can be the change!

Think You've Got To Make A Big Splash?
Think Again.

The following quiz appeared on the web and has traveled around the world. Try taking it.

1. Name the five wealthiest people in the world.
2. Name the last five Heisman Trophy winners.
3. Name the last five winners of the Miss America Pageant.
4. Name ten people who have won the Nobel or Pulitzer Prize.
5. Name the last half-dozen Academy Award winners for best actor or actress.
6. Name the last decade's worth of World Series winners.

How'd you do? If you're like most people, you don't remember the headliners of yesterday. Applause eventually dies. Awards tarnish. Achievements are eventually forgotten. Now try this quiz.

1. Name five teachers who positively aided your journey through school.
2. Name three friends who have helped you through a difficult time.
3. Name three people who taught you something worthwhile.
4. Name ten people who have made you feel appreciated and special.
5. Name five people you enjoy spending time with.
6. Name a half-dozen heroes whose stories have inspired you.

Much easier, right? The people who make a difference in your life may not be the ones with the most credentials, the most money, or the most awards. They will be the ones who care – the people who stepped into action and served. Are you that kind of person, too? Is there anyone who would put you on their list? When you reach the end of your life, will you be one of the people who is glad you did something, or one of the people who wished you had?

Ask For Help When You Need It

At some point in each of our lives, every one of us will find ourselves with our backs against the wall facing a challenge that we believe is somehow bigger than we can handle. For better or worse, the way we respond to these challenges has a direct affect on the way we feel about ourselves as well as the way we relate to others. The question becomes, do we really believe we have what it takes, or will we live our lives waiting for someone to rescue us? Do we trust ourselves, or do we simply put all our faith in the experts outside us?

We have come to believe that the most powerful response lies somewhere in between. It means stepping up to the challenge of loving and caring for ourselves, and actually knowing when it's time to reach out and ask for help. From time to time, we all need and deserve outside support to get us through certain challenges.

While none of us are experts in every possible area of our lives, each of us knows what we need inside. All it takes is having the courage to listen to our hearts and act on what we find there. When you find that you have hit a wall, come to a crossroad, or even simply need a new perspective, *ask for help*. Every hero has a mentor who helped light the way. And every hero was once a hero-in-training – a beginner.

You can learn new things at any time in your life if you are willing to be a beginner. If you actually learn to like being a beginner, the whole world opens up to you.

~ Barbara Sher

Falling On Your Diaper

Nothing we have suggested in this book is particularly difficult. But it's also not always easy. Living 100% fully alive brings moments of great joy and ecstasy. It can also come with great disappointment and pain. The contrast may be striking. Once you move out of living a mundane, numbed out, unconscious life, you may find that getting a taste of real joy, love, growth, consciousness, and authentic passion is delicious but fleeting. You may feel that waking up only means that the fall down is now farther, harder, and more painful. You may question whether or not it's worth the effort to live big, if it also comes with bigger heartache. If you do, you will not be alone. We are all experiencing this. We are all fumbling and stumbling.

For many people, this way of living is brand new and, like most things in life, often takes considerable practice to master. Allow yourself the time it takes to integrate what you learn. Expect to fall from time to time. Give yourself permission to be a beginner.

We like to call this part of the process, "falling on your diaper." The idea comes from our friend Chip who reached out to us during a challenging time, and offered these words…

The changes you are making in your life are new and dramatic. It is as if you are learning to walk for the first time. You see, when you were a baby, one day you became aware of an internal knowing that it was time to learn how to walk. You had the vision – you watched those "big people" do it, and you wanted to do the same. Your first goal was to get yourself upright, to just stand on your feet. Even that would be a huge success. So you reached for something higher than you. You struggled to pull yourself up, building the muscles needed to create the strength for what would naturally come next. You held onto a table, a chair, a leg, or someone's hand as they cheered you on. They believed in you. They had no doubt that you could learn how to walk.

Even when someone was not there cheering you on, you knew inside that this was your destiny and that, when the time was right, nothing would get in your way. You wobbled and finally found your balance. Then, in the exact right moment, you let go of the very thing that had been your only hope of safety. Standing on your own in your new upright world, you gained enough confidence to take your very first step. Bang! You fell on your diaper.

Unlike how you are probably living your life today, you did not criticize yourself. You had no thoughts of being a loser, no yearning for the blissful ignorance of life before the drive to walk had manifested itself. You were utterly focused on making this happen! As you heard the voices cheering you on, you grabbed onto something higher than you. You struggled and wobbled to find your balance. You saw the vision of where you were going, allowed your courage full rein, took a step, maybe two, and then once again, you fell flat on your diaper. This cycle continued for days or weeks until, one fine day, you walked.

At no point when you had fallen, did you ever look up and say, "That's it! I quit! I will never be a walker!" You kept trying, and yes, you undoubtedly picked up a bump or two on the path. You probably stopped and cried with frustration on more than one occasion, but you never gave up. Eventually, you took your first step and stayed firmly on your feet. Before long, you not only walked, you *ran* across the room.

How to be part of the Be the Change Movement

Be the Change is a call to action, a blueprint for life. It's a commitment to a way of being that not only feeds and nurtures your soul, but it also serves the planet. When you choose to practice the lessons in this book, you are part of the Movement. We invite you to join us.

Dare to dream. Stop and *notice* who you are *being* and how you are treating the people around you. Look in the mirror and celebrate what you see. Get vulnerable, drop the waterline and let people know who you *really* are. Step out of your comfort zone and dare to live life 100% alive. Have the courage to interrupt rude or offensive jokes. Have the courage to speak, vote or take action against oppression.

Refuse to pass on rumors. Encourage someone to go directly to the person with whom they are angry. Spread positive rumors. Have the courage to reach out, meet and befriend people who are different from you. Smile, say hi, and ask people their names. Strike up a conversation with the people around you.

Have the courage to say, "I'm sorry" when you need to. Forgive yourself. Forgive others. Look someone in the eyes and *really* listen. Allow yourself to fully feel and empty your balloon in positive ways. Listen to or hold someone who is having feelings without trying to fix, coach, or stifle their emotions. Ask, "What Else?" when someone finishes speaking.

Practice healthy communication. Step out of the Be a Man Box or Be a Lady Flower. Celebrate others who are out of the "Box" or the "Flower." Vulnerably let people know how much you care for, appreciate and love them. Reach out and give someone a hug. Become an ally for those who are being discriminated against, different or not "normal." Allow yourself time to be still and listen to the voice inside that is there to guide you.

Sing, dance, draw, and express your passion, joy and love. Take time to appreciate the people closest to you in your life. Make it your practice to Notice, Choose and Act in every area of your life. Join a cause, step into service, work for change, make a difference in someone's life.

Sometimes it falls upon a generation to be great. You can be that great generation.

~ Nelson Mandela

If you really knew us, you would know that every word in this book has been struggled over – pulled from the belly, held in our hands, evaluated, polished, changed, read, reread, talked about, worried over and eventually agreed upon. It has been, quite honestly, agonizing and exhausting. While it is easy for us to talk, it has been humbling to try to write.

If you really knew us, you would know that the entire struggle has been undertaken in the hope that we might somehow ignite you. And ourselves. The goal, while simple, is also daunting: we want to reach a wider audience.

It's a goal we seek not in an effort to pump ourselves up with our own accomplishments, but rather in a deep and genuine desire to connect with you – more of you – who are just like us.

There is a collective consciousness. It has great power. This is not speculation; this is scientific fact. You can read about the "Hundredth Monkey Phenomenon" as proof, or you can merely witness the miracle that is unfolding right now in our history.

If you really knew us, you would know that on the day Barack Obama was inaugurated as the 44th President of the United States, we were deciding whether or not each of the words we had chosen to be a part of this book were, in fact, complete. Despite the fear we have had that we are not writers, and that we cannot be writers who inspire scores of people, we were pouring through more than 300 pages of our words, an enormous sum, and deciding if we were going to print them or instead halt the presses.

As Mr. Obama was taking the reins of our country and ushering in the most exciting, uplifting, optimistic and world-stopping era of change in our political history, we were wrestling with the idea that we did not yet have an end to our book. In more than 300 pages we had clearly said a lot, but what we did not know how to say was some version of an inspiring send-off.

Part of our problem may be that at the end of a Challenge Day program or a Next Step to Being the Change workshop, we open it up to the people who have come, to "Speak Out" and tell us about their experience. We don't actually do endings without great help. It's the people we meet who provide the inspiring send-off.

Lacking the big ta-dah, maybe all we can do now is come full circle and leave you in the same place in which we started... There is nothing more powerful than sharing our truth.

Thank you so much for listening to ours.

- Yvonne and Rich

Be the Hero you've been waiting for!

Appendix

Most people don't aim too high and miss.
They aim too low and hit.

~ Bob Moawad

The Be the Change Movement

Vision

- To create a world where everyone feels safe, loved, and celebrated.
- To inspire people everywhere to live their lives in service to humanity, and to be a positive part of the solution on our planet by being the change they wish to see in the world.
- To inspire people everywhere to become the heroes they have been waiting for.

Mission

- To create a worldwide network of individuals and organizations committed to service and positive contributions to the world around them.

What It Is

- The Be the Change Movement is inspired by the words and actions of Mahatma Gandhi, and fueled by the vision of Challenge Day.
- It is a non-denominational, non-political, non-violent network committed to inspiring service and positive contribution.
- It is a lifestyle and paradigm shift for the planet, which everyone can live in every moment.

- Its membership consists of like-minded individuals linked by a common desire to make a positive change, and is open to anyone who shares in its vision and principles.
- It is designed to inspire peace from the inside out, to create hope, and to challenge all people everywhere to find their passion.
- It is fueled by people who *notice* what's happening in the world around them, *choose* to create positive change, and *act* as a living example of the power of contribution and compassion.
- It is a challenge to stop waiting for others to change things, and instead be the heroes they have been waiting for.
- It is a commitment to do at least one intentional, positive Act of Change each day for the benefit of others.

For more information about the Be the Change Movement, go to www.challengeday.org and click on the Be the Change link.

Steps For Success

1. **Create a Personal Growth Plan**

   Set goals for yourself and create a plan for how to achieve them. We like to take a holistic approach by identifying goals for our Body, Mind, Heart, and Spirit. First, we *notice* the areas in our life where we want to grow, enrich or change; then we *choose* what we want from our highest vision; finally, we *act* by putting those goals into practice.

   When we create personal growth plans with our staff, we also ask people to identify three major areas they would like to focus on and get support with over the next three months. We call this the person's SOS (Support Our Stuff) list. By deliberately pointing out key areas of growth for ourselves, we open the door to on-going support. With Challenge Day leaders we take this process one step further. Once we have chosen our own SOS's, we invite the group to give us feedback on any blind spots or things we are not seeing. We encourage you to do the same. (For an example of a personal growth plan, visit the Be the Change website: www.challengeday.org/downloads/Personal_Growth_Form.pdf.)

2. **Choose an Accountability Buddy**

You don't have to do it alone. At Challenge Day, we all have accountability buddies who cheerlead and offer support to us on a regular basis. We lovingly hold each other accountable for achieving our own personal goals.

An accountability buddy is someone whom you trust will support you in staying true to yourself and your goals, and who can offer you support when things get challenging. Accountability buddies can be especially helpful in keeping you focused on your SOS list. Find someone who will help you in becoming your most magnificent self and creating the life of your dreams. Create vision boards together. Share your dreams with one another. Get real, drop the waterline, and exchange "emptying balloon sessions." Hold one another accountable. Celebrate your accomplishments.

You and your buddy can agree to meet in person weekly, bi-weekly, or monthly, or you can just commit to leaving one another regular messages of support, such as: *How are you doing at exercising every day? Did you step outside of your comfort zone today? Did you get a session this week? Did you have date night this week with your partner? Did you do your homework every day this week? Did your call your mother and tell her that you love her?*

3. **Create Reminders**

Create and post your vision board, your personal growth plan, or other visual reminders in your home, school locker, or workspace. Keep yourself motivated and inspired.

We use water base color markers to write love notes, reminders, goals, and inspirations for ourselves, and to one another, on our mirrors in the Challenge Day office and all over our home. We wear "Be the Change – Notice, Choose, and Act" bracelets to help us remember to do our daily Acts of Change, and to stay conscious of who we want to be in order to be the heroes in our own lives.

We keep Act of Change Cards handy as a way of enrolling others in the Movement, and of challenging them to "pay-it-forward." We also love to wear Be the Change clothing not only to remind ourselves, but also to inspire others. (Acts of Change Cards and other Be the Change products are available on the Challenge Day website at www.challengeday.org.)

4. **Calendar Your Priorities**

Things won't happen if you don't make time to do them. Our recommendation is that before you finish reading this book, write in your calendar what you plan to do, and by when. Be as specific as possible. Your calendar can be a great tool for keeping balance in your life. If you notice something is out of balance, it is time to choose when and how you will take the actions necessary to change things. You may find you have to schedule time just to figure out what you want to do. Perhaps you have lists of dreams or to-do's that you never get to. Putting them in the calendar can be the first step.

At the beginning of every year, and then again at the beginning of every month, we take out our calendars and write in what is most important in our lives. For us, taking care of ourselves by maintaining our spiritual practice, weekly date nights, exercise, special time with family and friends, service opportunities, vacations, workshops, and things other than work, must go in first. Then we plan the details regarding how we will finish or start the new project, get to the plane, or whatever else it is we need to handle.

Be the Change: Some Powerful Reminders

- **Experience Emotional Freedom** – Since creating peace begins as an inside job, taking these three important steps can help usher in a new era of personal freedom:
   Step 1 – Love and Accept Yourself from Head to Toe
   Step 2 – Love and Accept Others
   Step 3 – Live in Service

- **Practice the Art of Giving from your Heart** – Consciously shift any "what about me?" thoughts to "how can I give, how can I serve, how can I step out of my comfort zone and make a difference?" Not sure how to start? Join others. Get involved in Challenge Day or similar programs. Create a project that moves you. Work with kids, say hello to everyone you see, visit a retirement home, babysit for a friend, volunteer to hold babies in a children's ward, improve the environment, and look for ways big and small to make a difference in the lives of others.

- **Perform Daily Acts of Change** – Dedicate yourself to doing at least one intentional Act of Change every day to feed your soul and nourish the planet. When we know our life makes a difference, it is hard to be sad or depressed.

- **Heal Your Hurt** – To change the course of history, we must start with our own. Ending family cycles of hurt and abuse, and learning how to connect and more deeply love those around us, leads us to becoming more of who we were born to be. Use this book, get counseling, join a support group, or investigate other resources to get the help you need and deserve.

- **Give and Receive Emptying Balloon Sessions** – Schedule regular times in your calendar with someone you trust and support each other in fully expressing your feelings by emptying your balloons. We recommend once a week. Like taking care of your body by exercising and eating healthy, it is just as important that you have time to take care of your emotions and empty your balloon.

- **Start an "If You Really Knew Me" Support Group** – Invite friends, family, and others to empty their balloons, drop the waterline, and get real. Create a place to clear the weeds in your hearts, and watch the seeds of passion and service grow. See chapter 5 for suggestions.

- **Notice, Choose, and Act in Every Area of Your Life** – Make it your intention and your commitment to wake up. Remember that what you focus on makes it grow. Create a vision for yourself, your life, and the world.

- **Join or Start a Be the Change Team or Circle of Change** – Make it your goal to ensure that people around you feel safe, loved, and celebrated. We are each other's cheerleaders and midwives as we continue to birth ourselves into our greatest potential. Creating the lives of our dreams takes commitment and dedication to our own personal growth, healing, and willingness to learn new tools, in order to change passed down cycles and habits that no longer serve us. Teams and circles can include family, friends, co-workers, people from school or places of worship, or anyone who is willing and ready to learn, grow, and be in service. Choose projects that bring you passion and make a difference. (To learn how to create a Team or to get hundreds of ideas of ways to Be the Change, go to Challenge Day's website at www.challengeday.org, or www.dosomething.org. Also see Starting a Circle of Change: The Basics included later in this Appendix.)

- **Create a Be the Hero Book Study Group** – Get together with a friend, Team, Circle, or group to discuss and practice some of the tools and techniques in this book. Take the time to *notice* how the lessons apply to your life, *choose* your highest vision for yourself and your life, and support one another in stepping into *action*.

- **Practice Gratitude** – Sharing gratitudes awakens our souls, and helps to keep the mental critters at bay. Establish regular times to share your gratitudes every day. Let the first words from your mouth each morning be, "I am grateful for…." Creating a gratitude journal can also be a powerful tool. When we focus on what we are grateful for, not only does it fill our hearts, it also creates more of what we are grateful for.

- **Don't Move Until You Are Moved** – Several times a day we intentionally stop and tell ourselves, "I won't move until I am emotionally touched or moved." Then we bring our awareness to the present moment and notice where our attention lands. For example, noticing the squirrel out the window, the light shining on a plant, a guitar riff in the background, the aroma of a peeled grapefruit, a child's squeal of excitement, or the warmth of your own hand – whatever captures your senses can move you, if you allow it to. This practice most often brings us to tears. Before we started doing this, ordinary things in life were just that – ordinary. Now, taking a moment to pause and experience the ordinary becomes an opportunity for a breathtaking taste of life. It is a way of completely celebrating and deepening the aliveness of the moment.

- **Keep Yourself Inspired** – Keep your internal flame lit. You know what inspires you, so do it! Your plug must be in the circuit to keep your energy flowing. Live your life as if you *know* you are part of something greater than yourself. The question is not, will we make a difference, it is *how* will we make a difference? The time is now, and the world is ready. Live your passion and *pass-I-on*!

- **Be Gentle With Yourself** – No matter how committed you are to making a positive difference, there will inevitably be times when your vision and actions don't match. There will be times when you let yourself and others down. The question then becomes, when you notice that you are missing the mark, what will you do about it? Will you stay committed, will you give up, or will you adapt and respond to the situation by stepping up to the challenge of being the change? Perhaps knowing that you will "fall on your diaper" will help you be gentle with yourself when you do.

Starting A Circle of Change: The Basics

- **Invite a group of people.** Make sure they are committed and ready to grow and make a difference. Many people name their circle for fun and networking purposes.
- **Establish a place and time.** Have an ongoing place and time to gather. People can bring snacks to share.

- **Start with purpose.** Start every meeting by inviting someone to share the purpose and reason for the gathering of your Circle of Change. This is to hold the higher vision.

- **Set a timer.** Allow everyone time to drop the waterline, get real and share "If you really knew me's." This is a must! This is how we connect, support each other and end loneliness. The sharing could include personal successes and challenges, putting into practice the tools and skills the group is working on over the designated period, or any other topics you wish to share.

- **Acts of Change and service.** The next part of the meeting is sharing personal Acts of Change and spending necessary time to plan, update, or celebrate larger community Acts of Change.

- **Use this book.** Practice living the Be the Change principles. Choose one chapter each meeting to study and implement into your life. Each chapter ends with challenges that can be used between meetings. The group serves to support each person in creating new habits for living the life of your dreams.

- **Validations and compliments.** End every meeting with time for true vulnerable appreciations and compliments. This is an important step that is never skipped.

- **Challenge Day will help!** We have manuals and support material to help you in each step of creating and being part of a Circle of Change. For more information, visit www. challengeday.org.

Acts of Change Cards

You can dowload and print out Acts of Change cards, each of which includes two "pay it forward" tokens, by going to http://www. challengeday.org/bethechange/. We encourage you to give out lots of tokens for others to use as well as leaving one for every person who is a recipient of your Acts of Change. It is our hope that by doing so, you will encourage others to keep the love going.

Never think your Acts of Change are insignificant. Here is an example of the effect your kindness my have. This letter came to us from a participant at one of our Next Step to Being the Change workshops.

My friend Amy and I decided to pay the toll for the person behind us as we were going over the San Francisco Bay Bridge as our Act of Change. This we did and the man in the car stayed behind us for quite awhile. When he passed us, he waved and smiled. The end, right? I received a thank you letter in the mail today.

Ms. Yates,

Imagine my surprise and pleasure when coming up to the toll booth, preparing to pay the $4 toll, and then being told my toll was paid by the driver in front of me. Police officers deal with horrendous situations weekly and become hardened and cynical over time. I am no exception to this. I wanted to take the time to tell you that your one seemingly random Act of Change had a distinct mental and emotional impact on me. It is heartening to know that there are people out there like you who do things out of the kindness of their heart just to make someone's life easier and happier. THANK YOU!

If you ever drive through my town, please give me a call so I can take you to coffee. In the meanwhile, please accept the Starbucks card as a token of my appreciation for your thoughtful and caring gesture. The world needs more people like you.

Enclosed were his business card, showing he was lieutenant for a Bay Area police department, and a Starbucks gift card. Wow, huh? You should have seen how excited I was as I read the note to my husband and son.

Keep sharing the love, it works!

~ Cheryl

We believe that together we can change the world, one Act of Change at a time. Enjoy spreading the love.

If our book had unlimited pages, every single one of our Staff, Leaders and Board Members (past and present) would have their own Everyday Hero page. Our hearts are filled with love and gratitude for their commitment to living and practicing the tools we've shared in this book.